PART TWO

(SOLSTICE)

Dreaming of Harvestar

THE DRAGONSLAYER

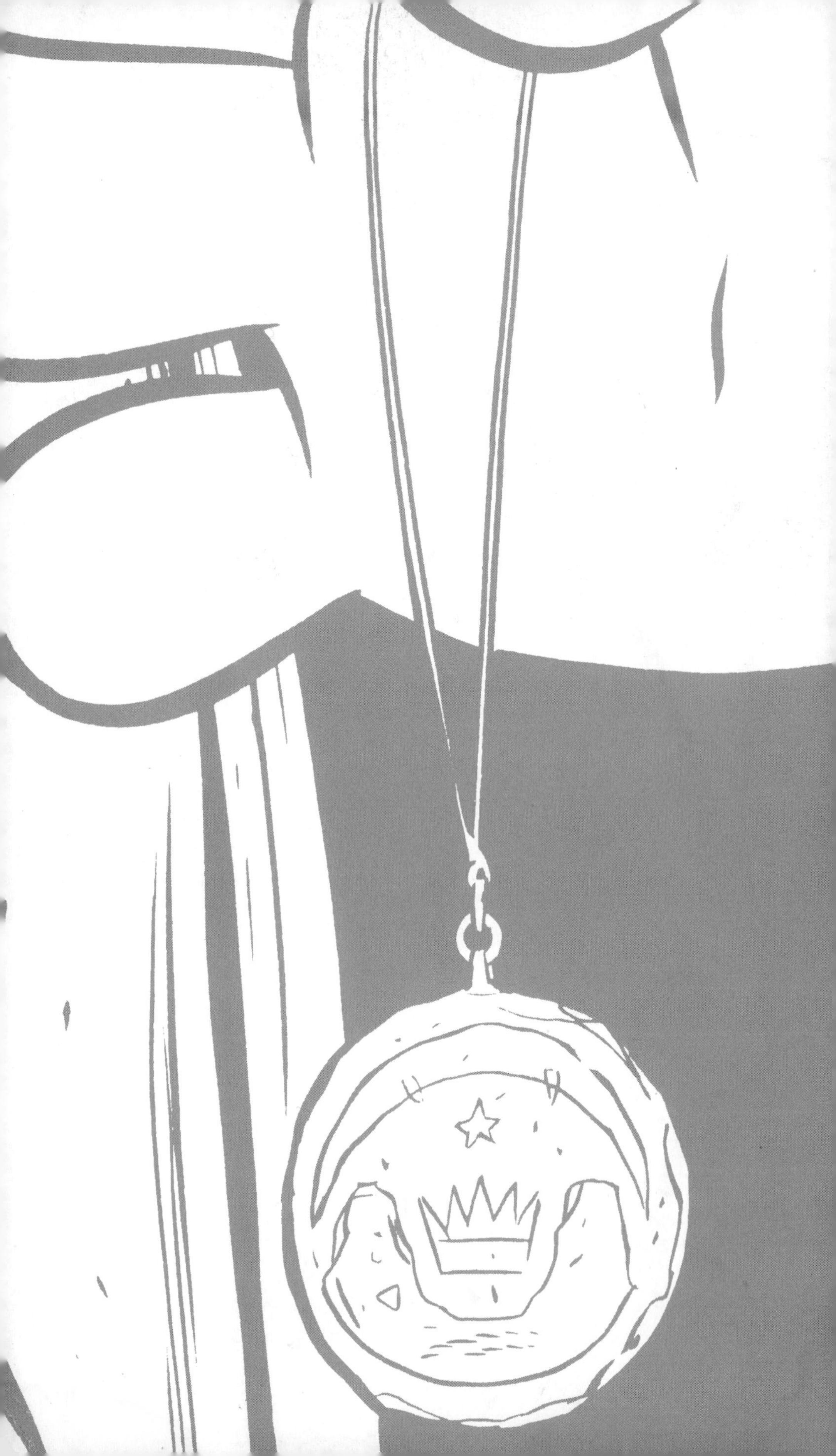

AFTER BEING RUN OUT OF BONEVILLE, THE THREE BONE COUSINS, FONE BONE, PHONEY BONE, AND SMILEY BONE, ARE SEPARATED AND LOST IN A VAST UNCHARTED DESERT.

ONE BY ONE, THEY FIND THEIR WAY INTO A DEEP, FORESTED VALLEY FILLED WITH WONDERFUL AND TERRIFYING CREATURES. . .

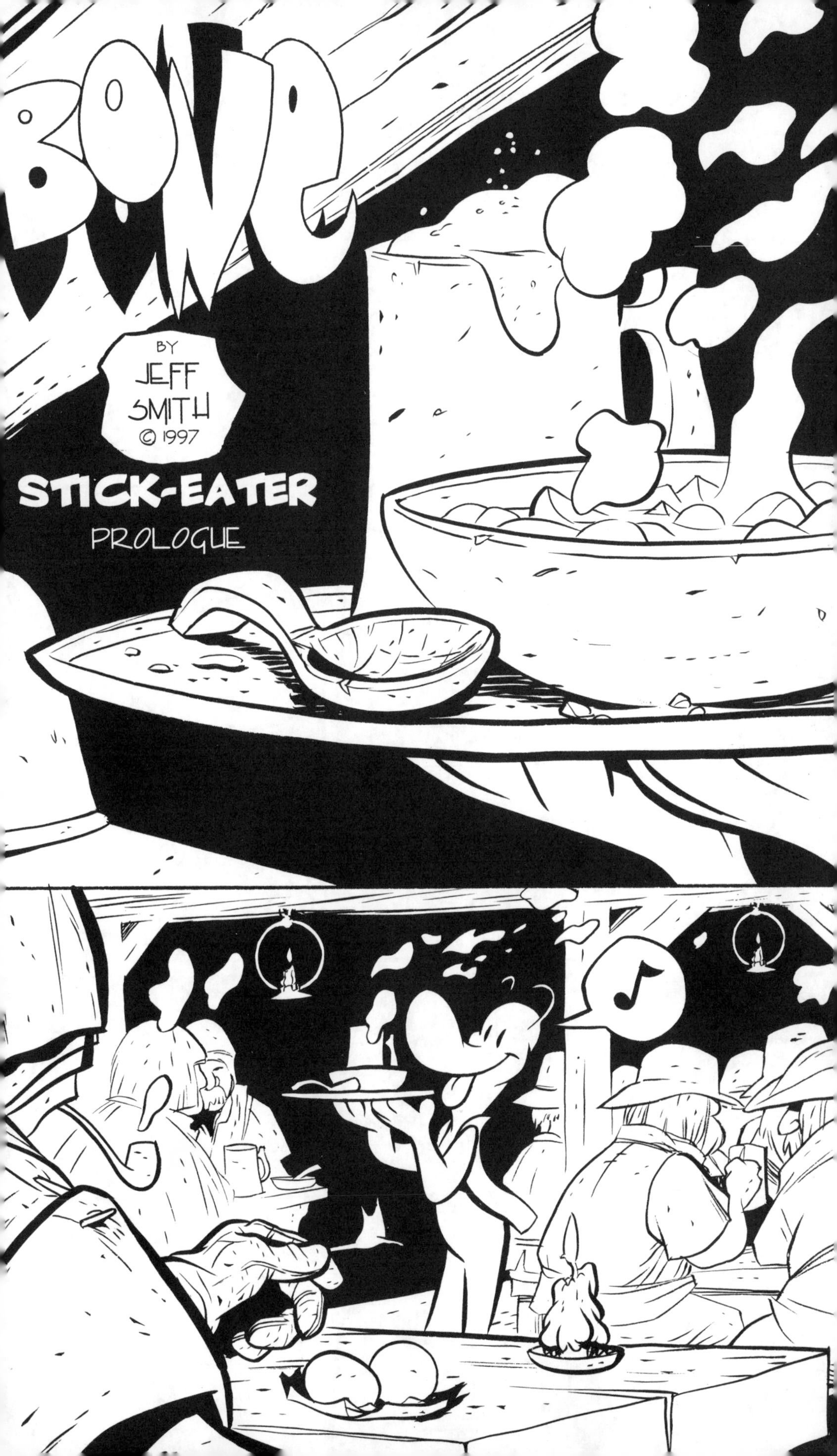
BONE
BY JEFF SMITH © 1997
STICK-EATER
PROLOGUE

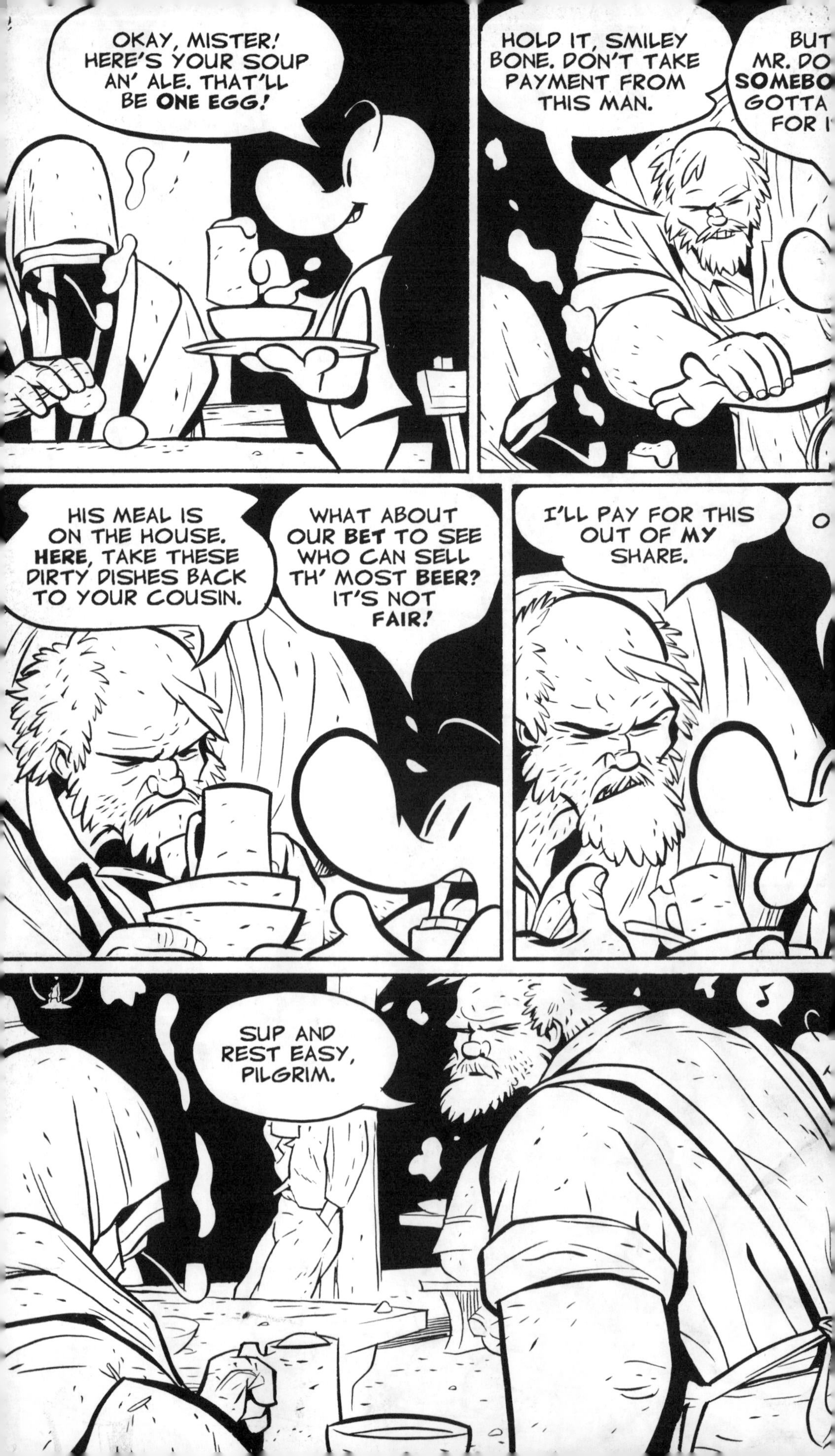
OKAY, MISTER! HERE'S YOUR SOUP AN' ALE. THAT'LL BE **ONE EGG**!
HOLD IT, SMILEY BONE. DON'T TAKE PAYMENT FROM THIS MAN.
BUT MR. DO **SOMEBO** GOTTA FOR I
HIS MEAL IS ON THE HOUSE. **HERE**, TAKE THESE DIRTY DISHES BACK TO YOUR COUSIN.
WHAT ABOUT OUR **BET** TO SEE WHO CAN SELL TH' MOST **BEER**? IT'S NOT **FAIR**!
I'LL PAY FOR THIS OUT OF **MY** SHARE.
SUP AND REST EASY, PILGRIM.

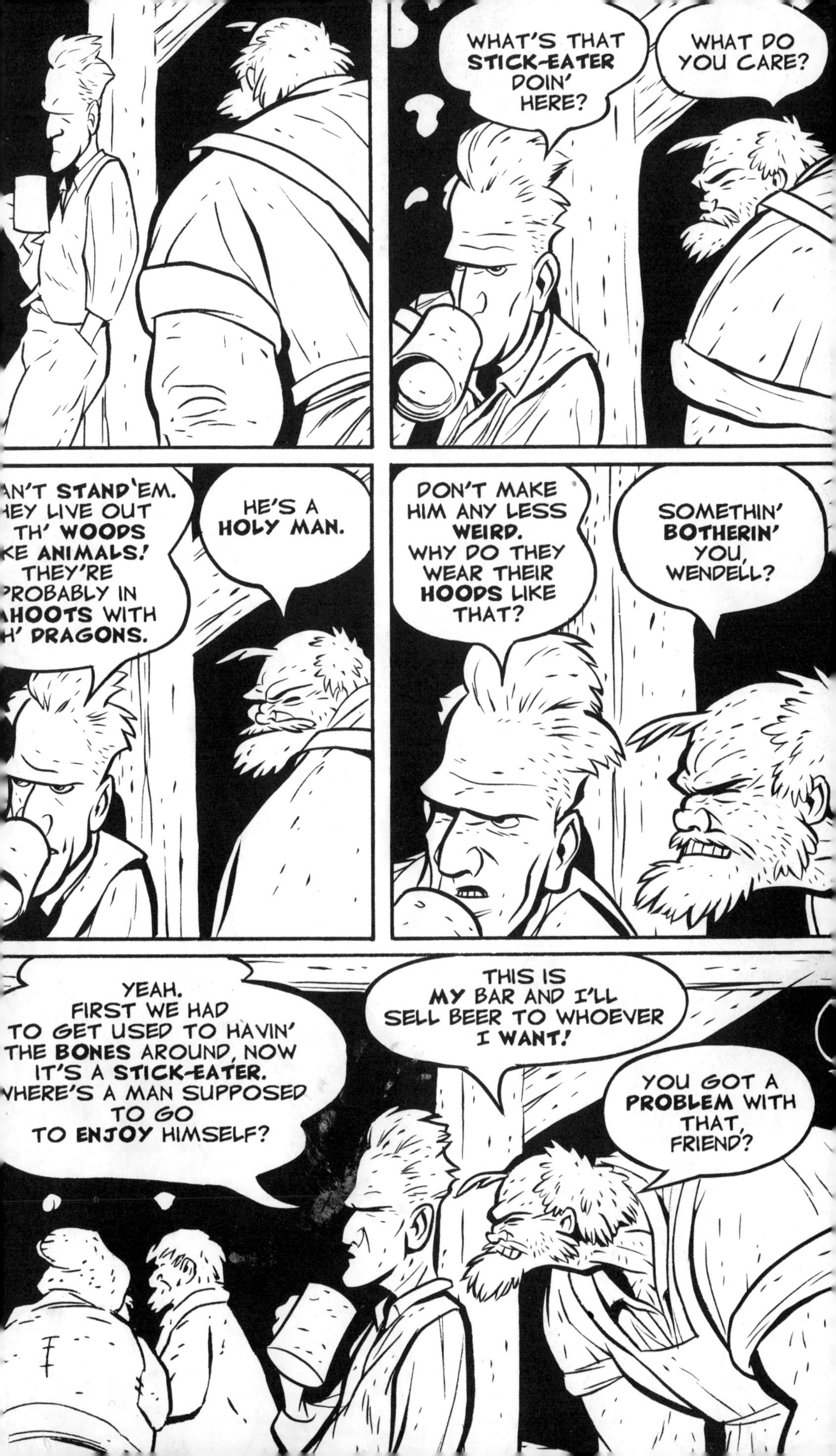
WHAT'S THAT STICK-EATER DOIN' HERE?
WHAT DO YOU CARE?
AN'T STAND 'EM. HEY LIVE OUT TH' WOODS KE ANIMALS! THEY'RE PROBABLY IN HOOTS WITH H' DRAGONS.
HE'S A HOLY MAN.
DON'T MAKE HIM ANY LESS WEIRD. WHY DO THEY WEAR THEIR HOODS LIKE THAT?
SOMETHIN' BOTHERIN' YOU, WENDELL?
YEAH. FIRST WE HAD TO GET USED TO HAVIN' THE BONES AROUND, NOW IT'S A STICK-EATER. WHERE'S A MAN SUPPOSED TO GO TO ENJOY HIMSELF?
THIS IS MY BAR AND I'LL SELL BEER TO WHOEVER I WANT!
YOU GOT A PROBLEM WITH THAT, FRIEND?

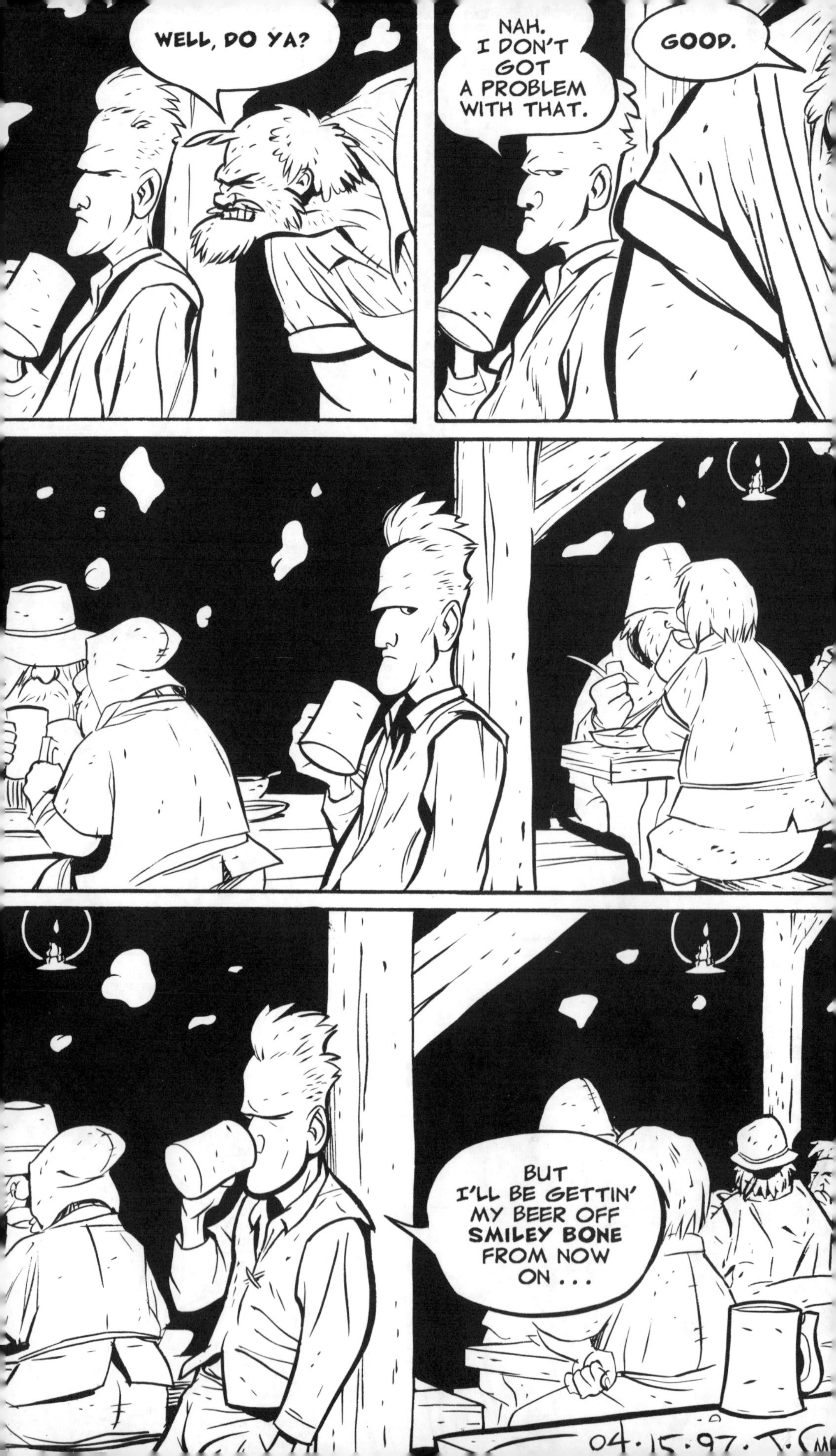
WELL, DO YA?
NAH. I DON'T GOT A PROBLEM WITH THAT.
GOOD.
BUT I'LL BE GETTIN' MY BEER OFF SMILEY BONE FROM NOW ON . . .
04.15.97.

THE DRAGONSLAYER

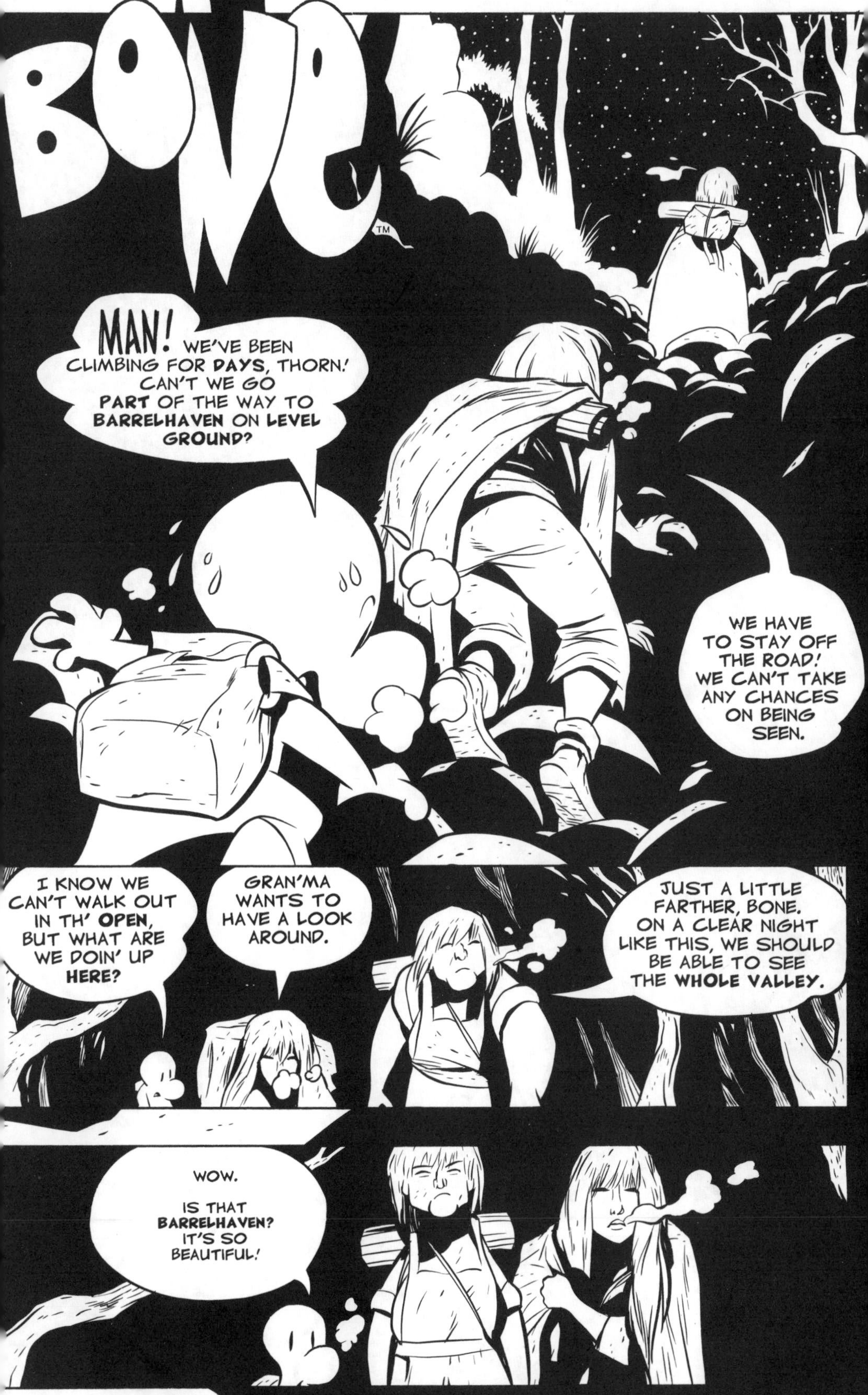
BONE™
MAN! WE'VE BEEN CLIMBING FOR DAYS, THORN! CAN'T WE GO PART OF THE WAY TO BARRELHAVEN ON LEVEL GROUND?
WE HAVE TO STAY OFF THE ROAD! WE CAN'T TAKE ANY CHANCES ON BEING SEEN.
I KNOW WE CAN'T WALK OUT IN TH' OPEN, BUT WHAT ARE WE DOIN' UP HERE?
GRAN'MA WANTS TO HAVE A LOOK AROUND.
JUST A LITTLE FARTHER, BONE. ON A CLEAR NIGHT LIKE THIS, WE SHOULD BE ABLE TO SEE THE WHOLE VALLEY.
WOW.
IS THAT BARRELHAVEN? IT'S SO BEAUTIFUL!

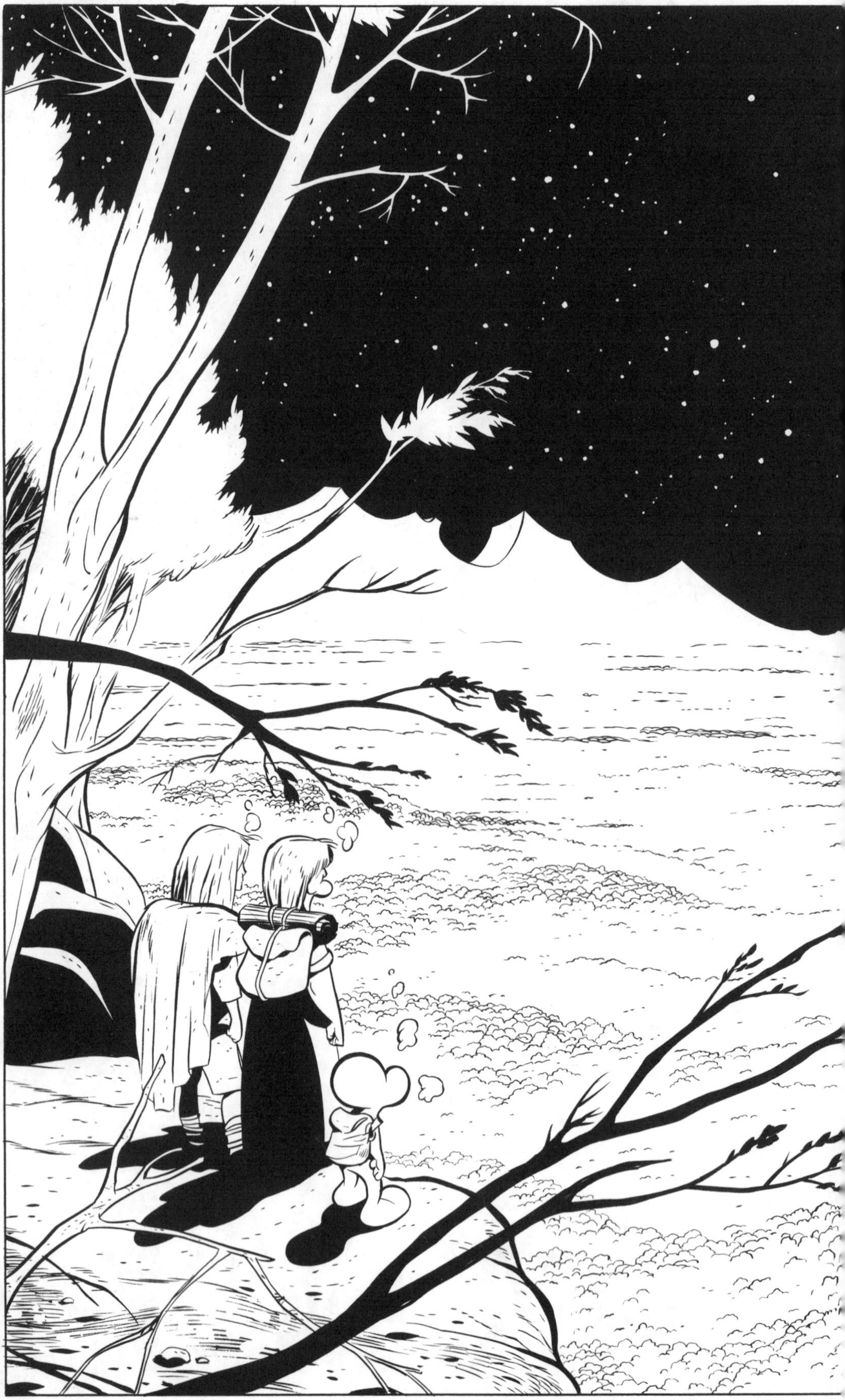

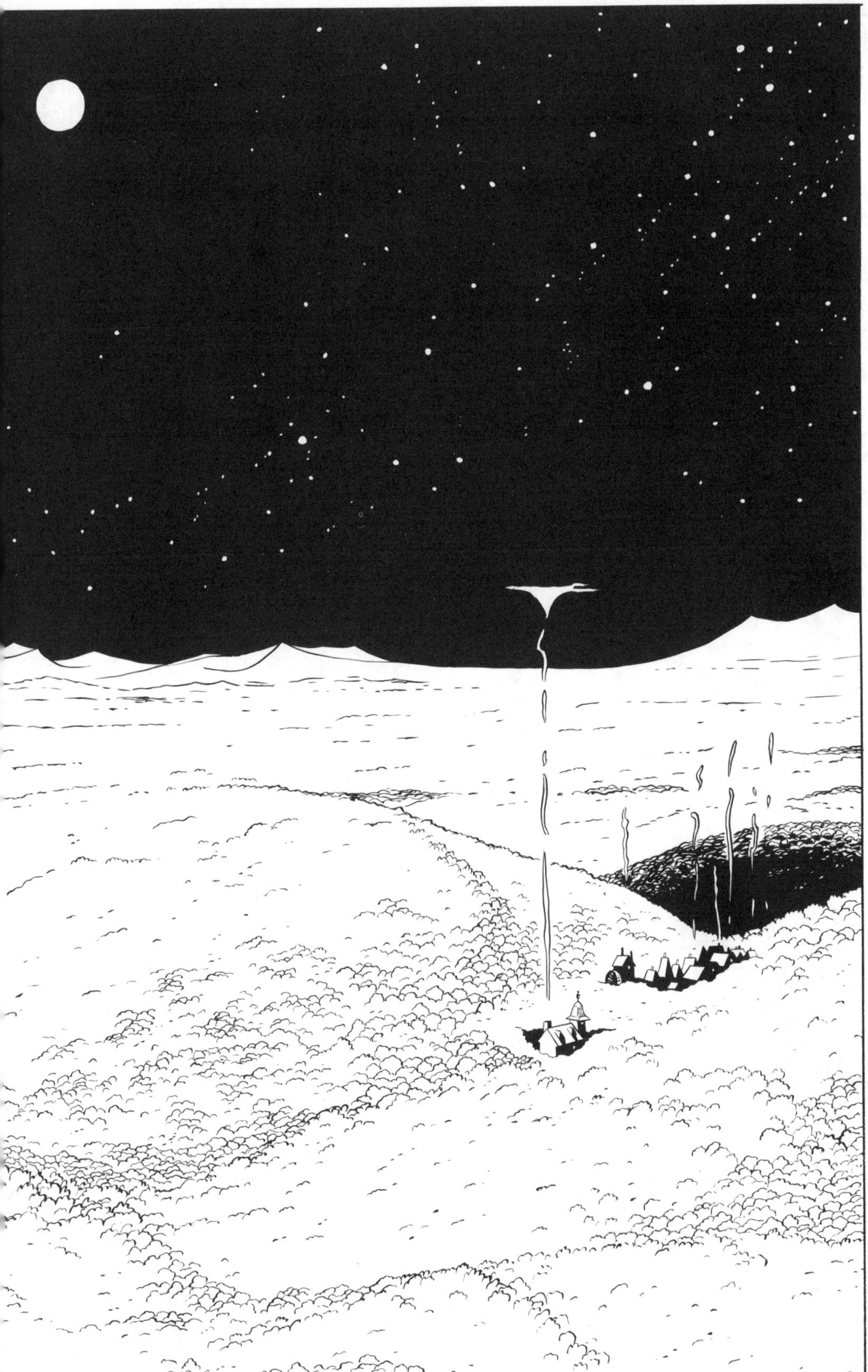

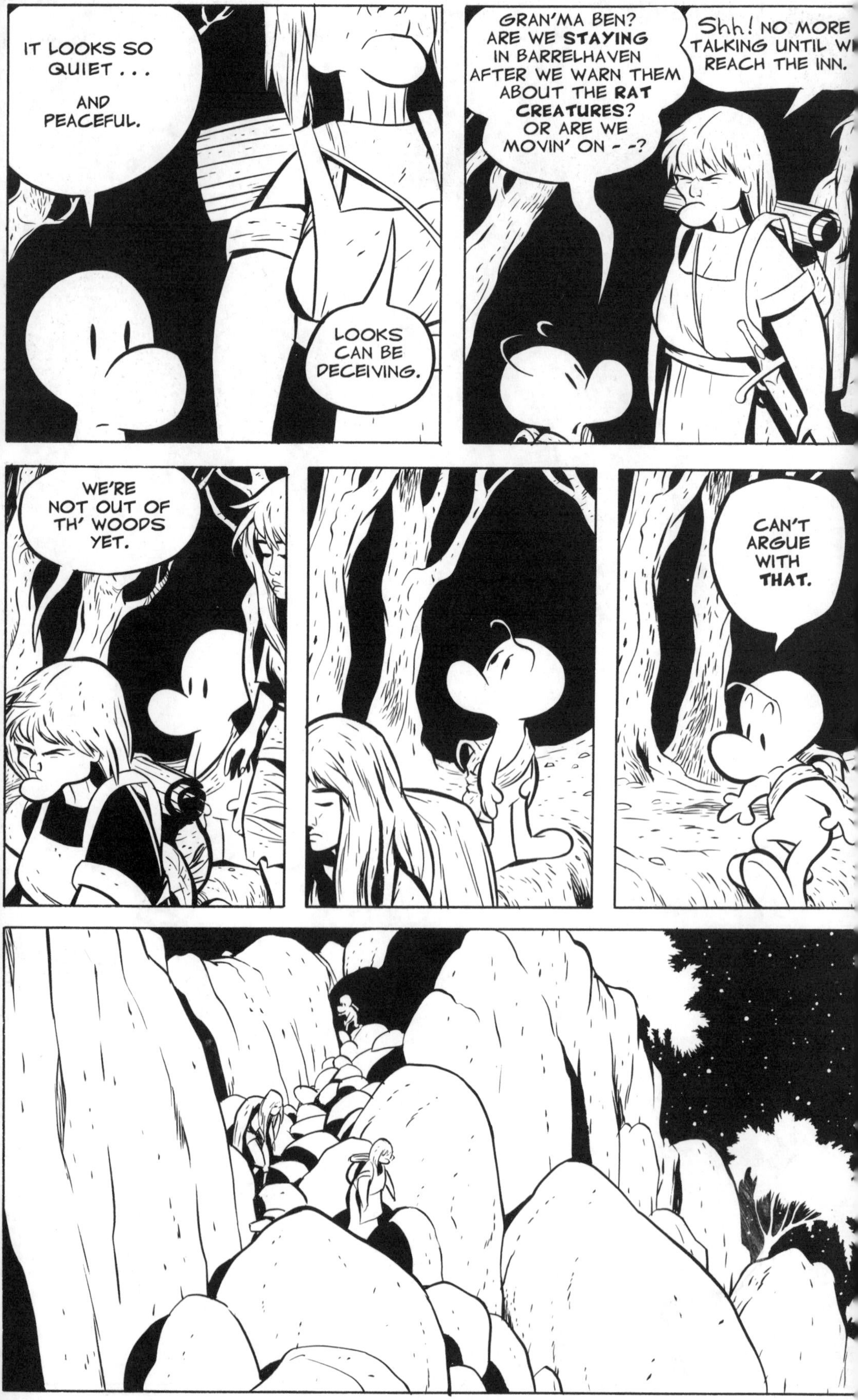
IT LOOKS SO QUIET . . .
AND PEACEFUL.
LOOKS CAN BE DECEIVING.
GRAN'MA BEN? ARE WE STAYING IN BARRELHAVEN AFTER WE WARN THEM ABOUT THE RAT CREATURES? OR ARE WE MOVIN' ON - -?
Shh! NO MORE TALKING UNTIL W REACH THE INN.
WE'RE NOT OUT OF TH' WOODS YET.
CAN'T ARGUE WITH THAT.

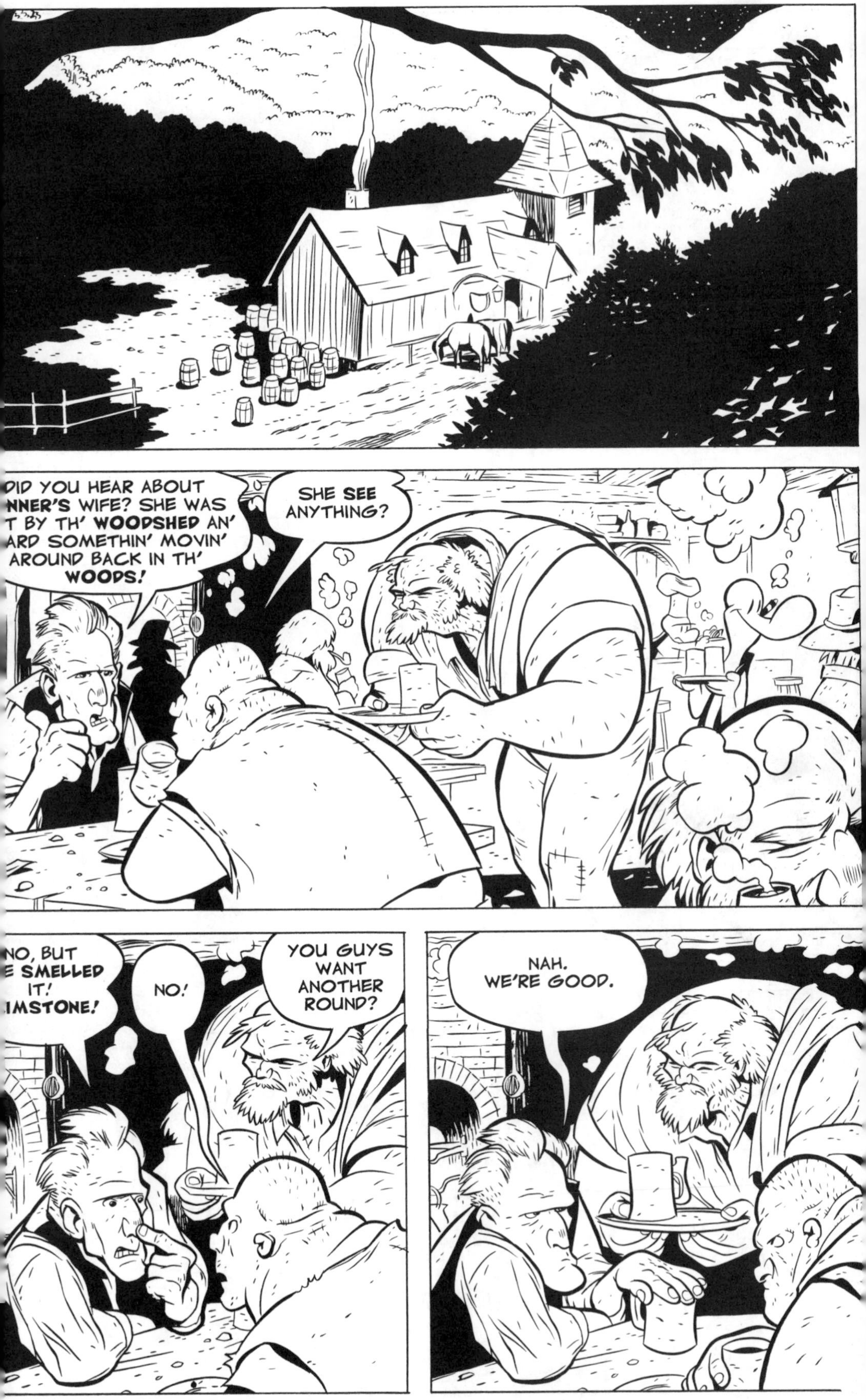
DID YOU HEAR ABOUT
NNER'S WIFE? SHE WAS
T BY TH' WOODSHED AN'
ARD SOMETHIN' MOVIN'
AROUND BACK IN TH'
WOODS!
SHE SEE ANYTHING?
NO, BUT
E SMELLED
IT!
IMSTONE!
NO!
YOU GUYS WANT ANOTHER ROUND?
NAH. WE'RE GOOD.

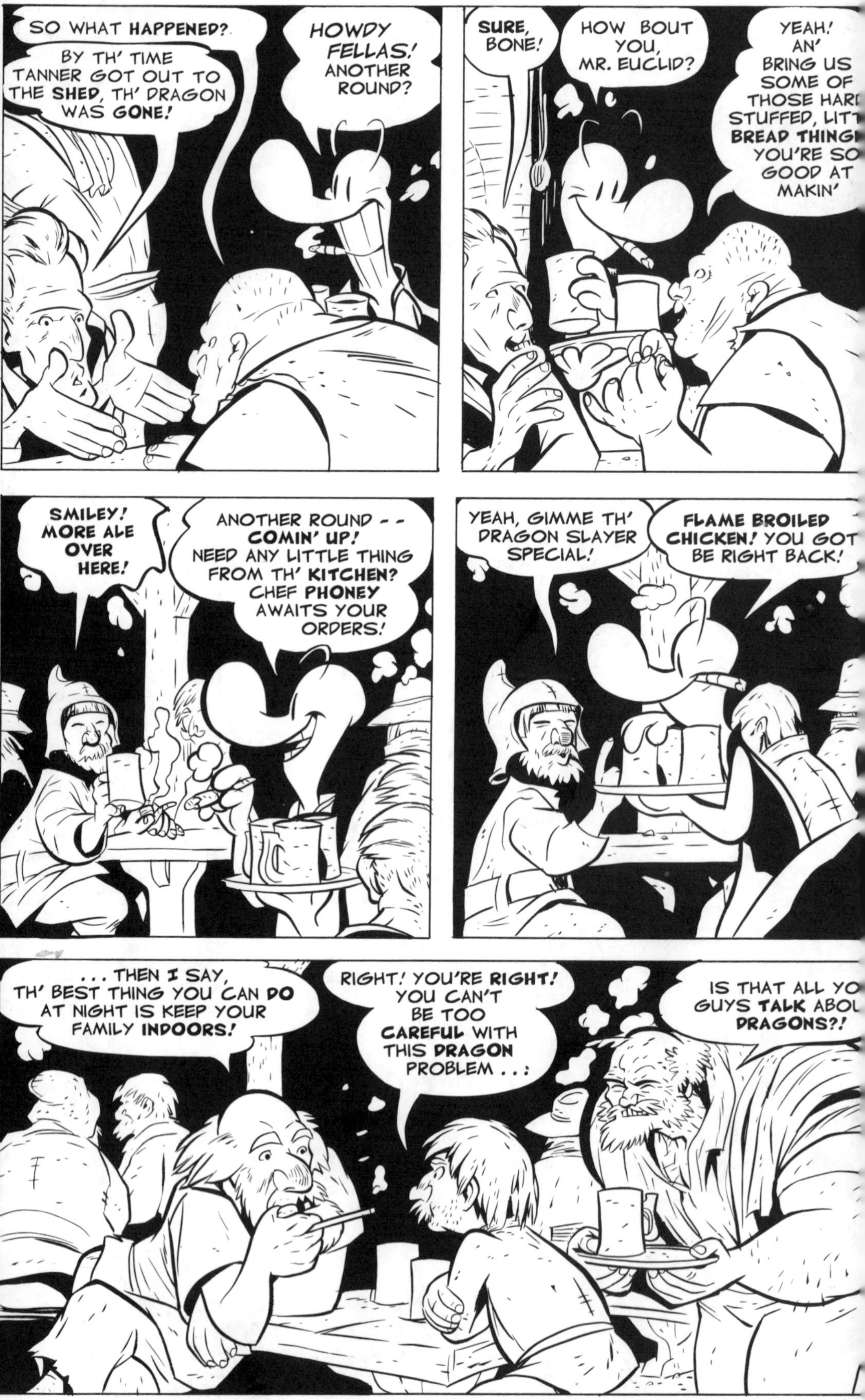
SO WHAT HAPPENED?
BY TH' TIME TANNER GOT OUT TO THE SHED, TH' DRAGON WAS GONE!
HOWDY FELLAS! ANOTHER ROUND?
SURE, BONE!
HOW BOUT YOU, MR. EUCLID?
YEAH! AN' BRING US SOME OF THOSE HARD STUFFED, LITT BREAD THING YOU'RE SO GOOD AT MAKIN'
SMILEY! MORE ALE OVER HERE!
ANOTHER ROUND - - COMIN' UP! NEED ANY LITTLE THING FROM TH' KITCHEN? CHEF PHONEY AWAITS YOUR ORDERS!
YEAH, GIMME TH' DRAGON SLAYER SPECIAL!
FLAME BROILED CHICKEN! YOU GOT BE RIGHT BACK!
. . . THEN I SAY, TH' BEST THING YOU CAN DO AT NIGHT IS KEEP YOUR FAMILY INDOORS!
RIGHT! YOU'RE RIGHT! YOU CAN'T BE TOO CAREFUL WITH THIS DRAGON PROBLEM . . :
IS THAT ALL YO GUYS TALK ABOU DRAGONS?!

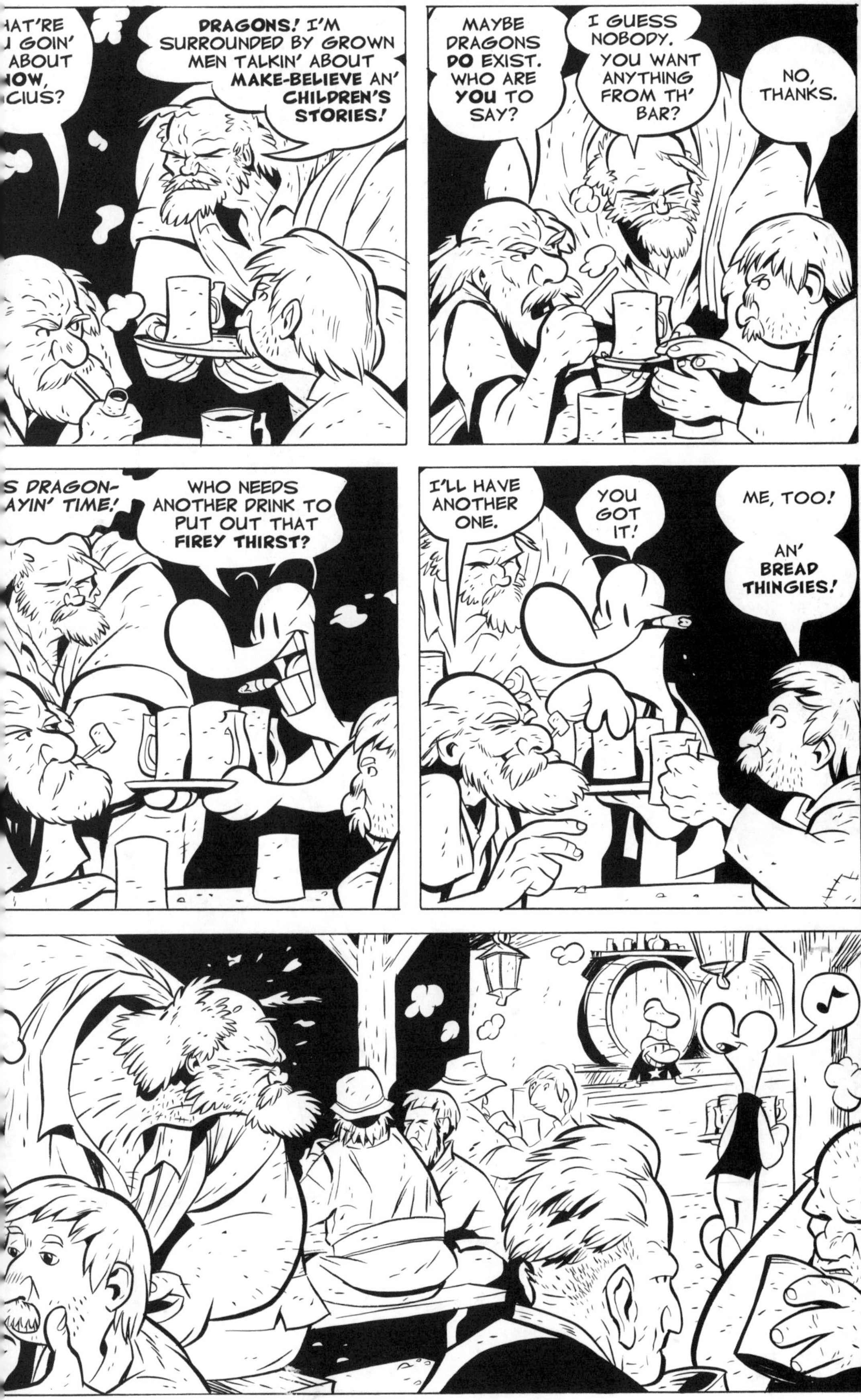
HAT'RE GOIN' ABOUT CIUS?
DRAGONS! I'M SURROUNDED BY GROWN MEN TALKIN' ABOUT MAKE-BELIEVE AN' CHILDREN'S STORIES!
MAYBE DRAGONS DO EXIST. WHO ARE YOU TO SAY?
I GUESS NOBODY.
YOU WANT ANYTHING FROM TH' BAR?
NO, THANKS.
S DRAGON-AYIN' TIME!
WHO NEEDS ANOTHER DRINK TO PUT OUT THAT FIREY THIRST?
I'LL HAVE ANOTHER ONE.
YOU GOT IT!
ME, TOO!
AN' BREAD THINGIES!

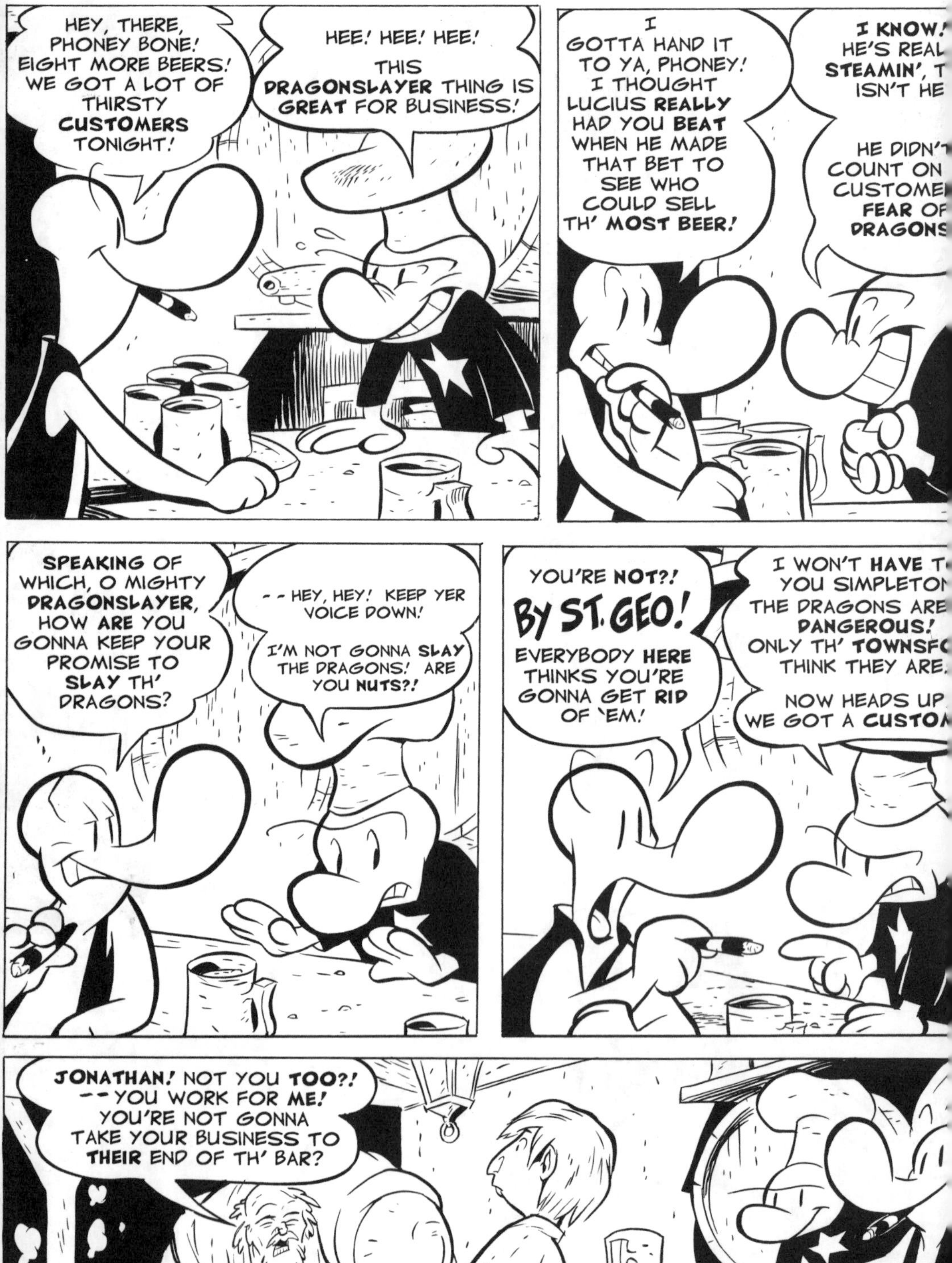

HEY, THERE, PHONEY BONE! EIGHT MORE BEERS! WE GOT A LOT OF THIRSTY **CUSTOMERS** TONIGHT!
HEE! HEE! HEE! THIS **DRAGONSLAYER** THING IS **GREAT** FOR BUSINESS!
I GOTTA HAND IT TO YA, PHONEY! I THOUGHT LUCIUS **REALLY** HAD YOU **BEAT** WHEN HE MADE THAT BET TO SEE WHO COULD SELL TH' **MOST BEER**!
I KNOW! HE'S REAL **STEAMIN'**, T ISN'T HE
HE DIDN' COUNT ON CUSTOME **FEAR OF DRAGONS**
SPEAKING OF WHICH, O MIGHTY **DRAGONSLAYER**, HOW **ARE** YOU GONNA KEEP YOUR PROMISE TO **SLAY** TH' DRAGONS?
-- HEY, HEY! KEEP YER VOICE DOWN!
I'M NOT GONNA **SLAY** THE DRAGONS! ARE YOU **NUTS**?!
YOU'RE **NOT**?! BY ST. GEO! EVERYBODY **HERE** THINKS YOU'RE GONNA GET **RID** OF 'EM!
I WON'T **HAVE** T YOU SIMPLETON THE DRAGONS ARE **DANGEROUS**! ONLY TH' **TOWNSF** THINK THEY ARE.
NOW HEADS UP WE GOT A **CUSTOM**
JONATHAN! NOT YOU **TOO**?! -- YOU WORK FOR **ME**! YOU'RE NOT GONNA TAKE YOUR BUSINESS TO **THEIR** END OF TH' BAR?
it's dragon slay time! Phoney Bone

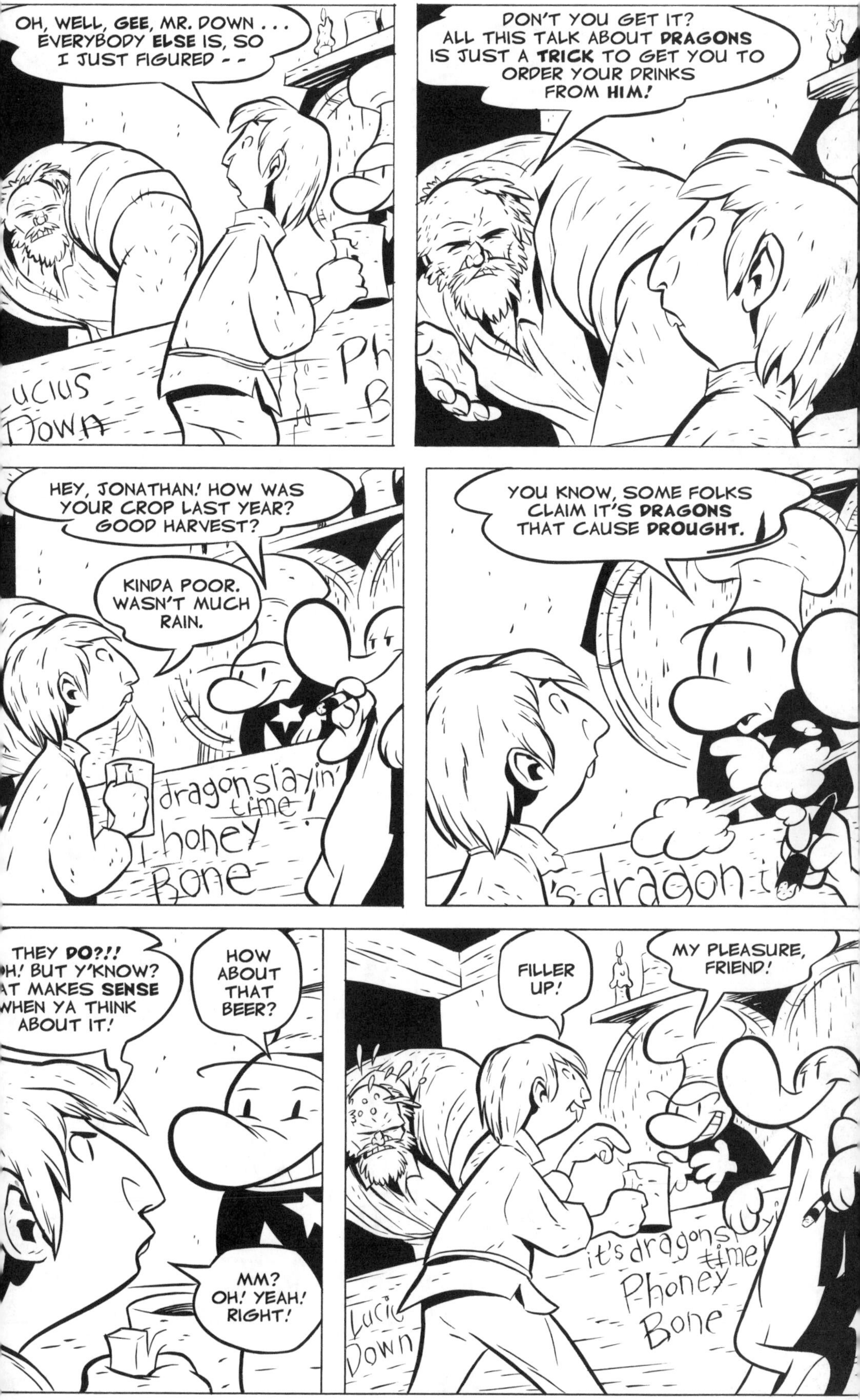

OH, WELL, GEE, MR. DOWN . . . EVERYBODY ELSE IS, SO I JUST FIGURED - -
ucius Down
DON'T YOU GET IT? ALL THIS TALK ABOUT DRAGONS IS JUST A TRICK TO GET YOU TO ORDER YOUR DRINKS FROM HIM!
HEY, JONATHAN! HOW WAS YOUR CROP LAST YEAR? GOOD HARVEST?
KINDA POOR. WASN'T MUCH RAIN.
dragonslayin' time! honey Bone
YOU KNOW, SOME FOLKS CLAIM IT'S DRAGONS THAT CAUSE DROUGHT.
THEY DO?!! OH! BUT Y'KNOW? AT MAKES SENSE WHEN YA THINK ABOUT IT!
HOW ABOUT THAT BEER?
MM? OH! YEAH! RIGHT!
FILLER UP!
MY PLEASURE, FRIEND!
it's dragons time! Phoney Bone
Down

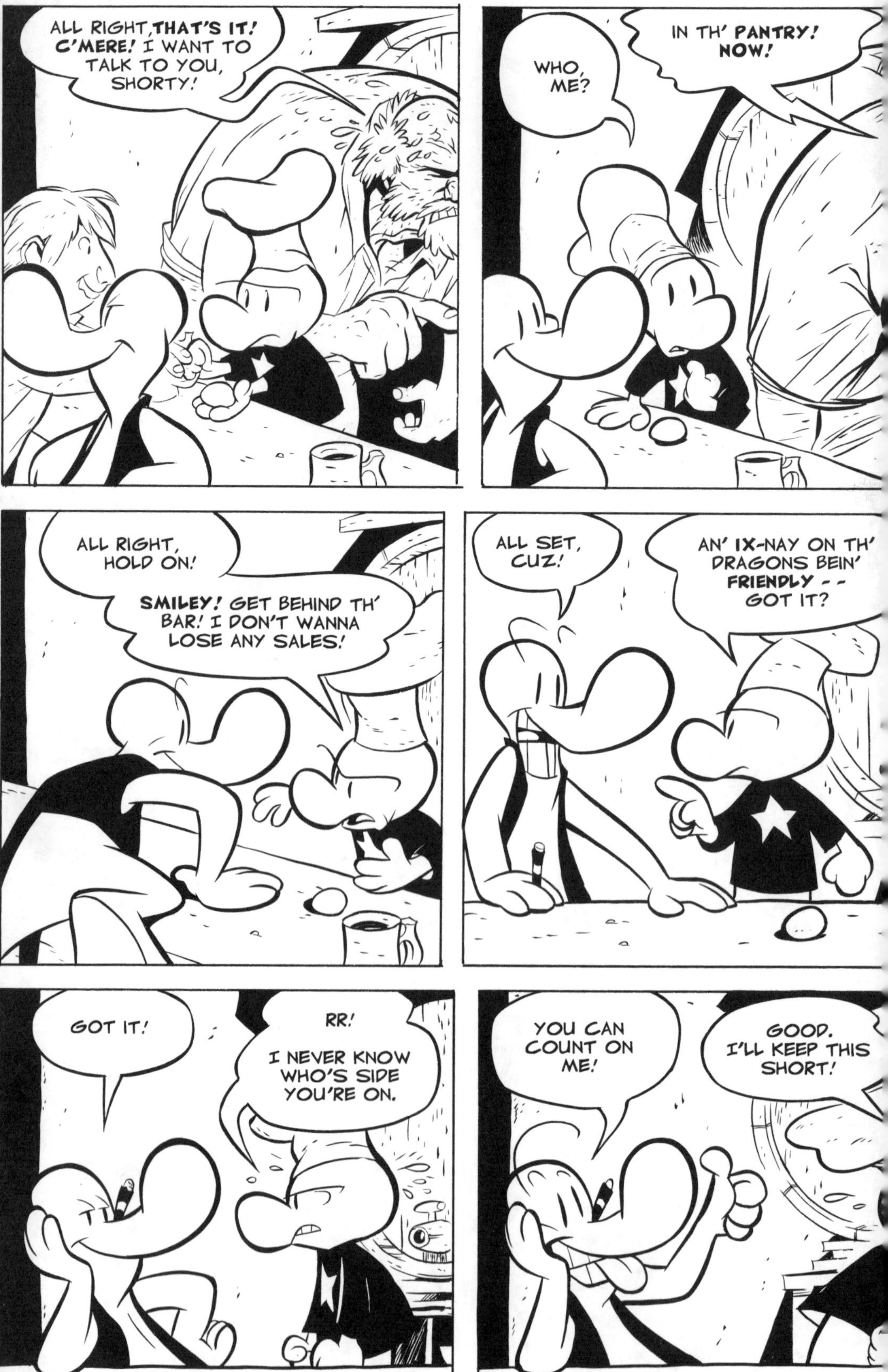
ALL RIGHT, THAT'S IT! C'MERE! I WANT TO TALK TO YOU, SHORTY!
WHO, ME?
IN TH' PANTRY! NOW!
ALL RIGHT, HOLD ON!
SMILEY! GET BEHIND TH' BAR! I DON'T WANNA LOSE ANY SALES!
ALL SET, CUZ!
AN' IX-NAY ON TH' DRAGONS BEIN' FRIENDLY - - GOT IT?
GOT IT!
RR!
I NEVER KNOW WHO'S SIDE YOU'RE ON.
YOU CAN COUNT ON ME!
GOOD. I'LL KEEP THIS SHORT!

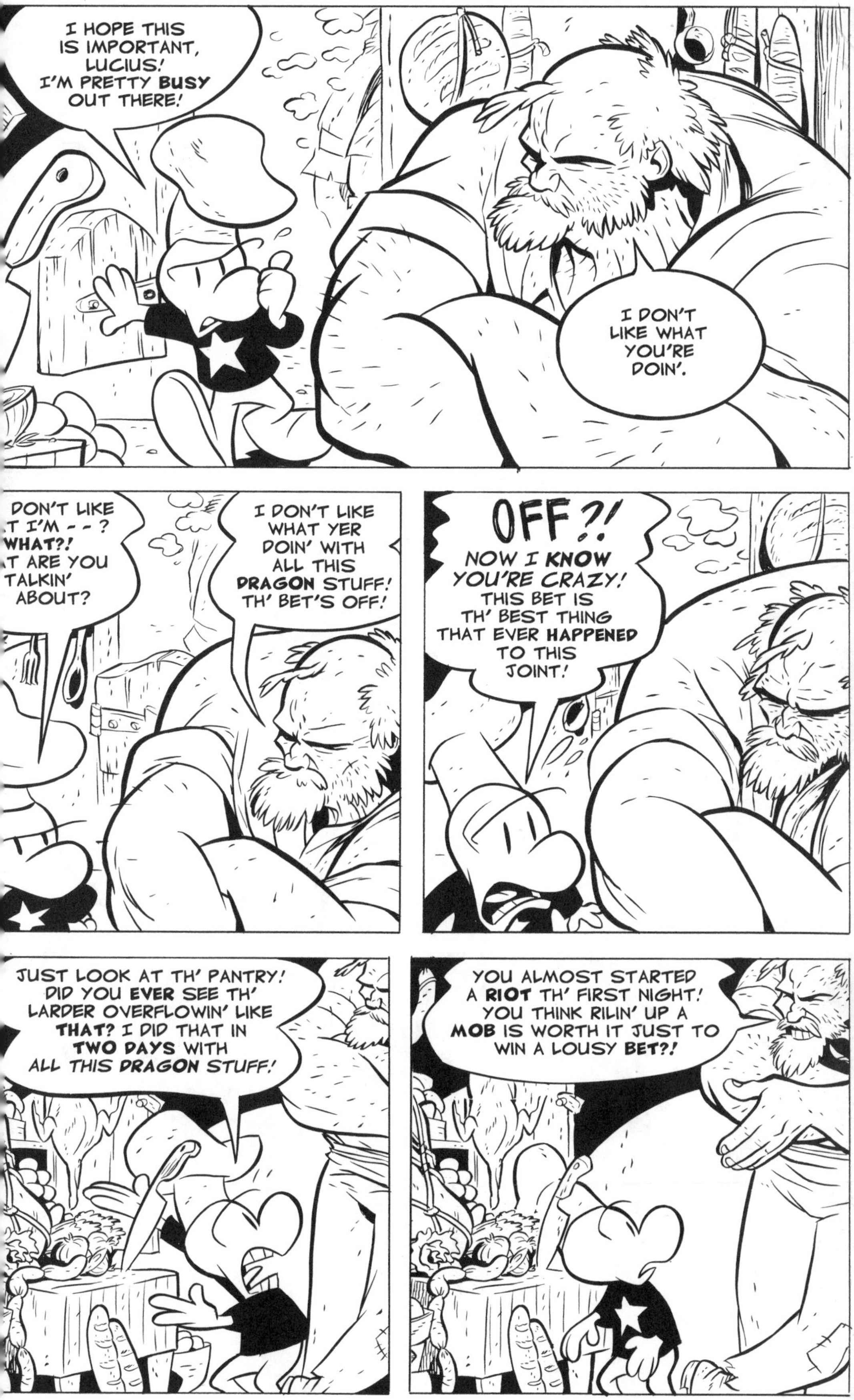
I HOPE THIS IS IMPORTANT, LUCIUS! I'M PRETTY BUSY OUT THERE!
I DON'T LIKE WHAT YOU'RE DOIN'.
DON'T LIKE T I'M - - ? WHAT?! T ARE YOU TALKIN' ABOUT?
I DON'T LIKE WHAT YER DOIN' WITH ALL THIS DRAGON STUFF! TH' BET'S OFF!
OFF?!
NOW I KNOW YOU'RE CRAZY! THIS BET IS TH' BEST THING THAT EVER HAPPENED TO THIS JOINT!
JUST LOOK AT TH' PANTRY! DID YOU EVER SEE TH' LARDER OVERFLOWIN' LIKE THAT? I DID THAT IN TWO DAYS WITH ALL THIS DRAGON STUFF!
YOU ALMOST STARTED A RIOT TH' FIRST NIGHT! YOU THINK RILIN' UP A MOB IS WORTH IT JUST TO WIN A LOUSY BET?!

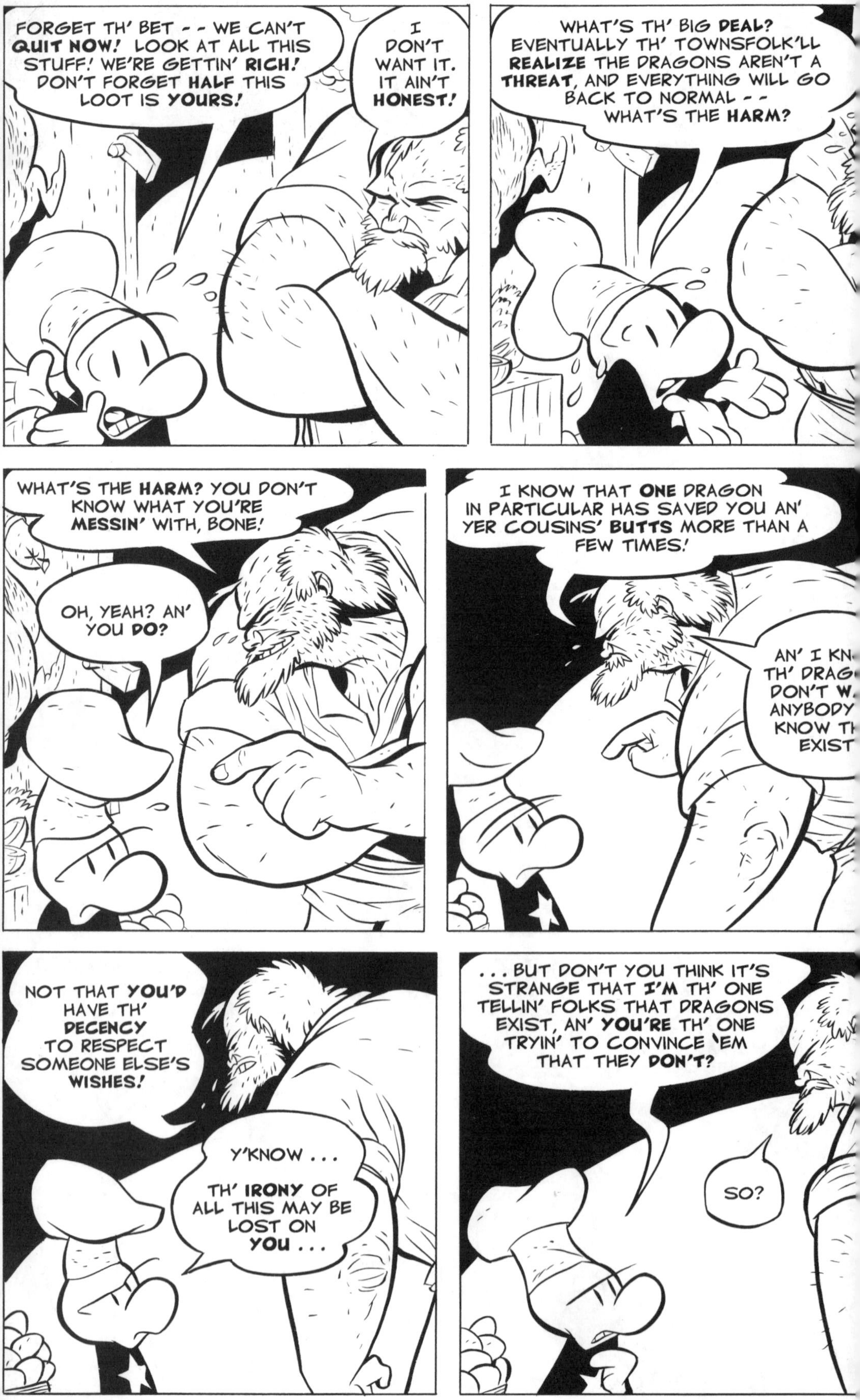
FORGET TH' BET - - WE CAN'T **QUIT NOW**! LOOK AT ALL THIS STUFF! WE'RE GETTIN' **RICH**! DON'T FORGET **HALF** THIS LOOT IS **YOURS**!
I DON'T WANT IT. IT AIN'T **HONEST**!
WHAT'S TH' BIG **DEAL**? EVENTUALLY TH' TOWNSFOLK'LL **REALIZE** THE DRAGONS AREN'T A **THREAT**, AND EVERYTHING WILL GO BACK TO NORMAL - - WHAT'S THE **HARM**?
WHAT'S THE **HARM**? YOU DON'T KNOW WHAT YOU'RE **MESSIN'** WITH, BONE!
OH, YEAH? AN' YOU **DO**?
I KNOW THAT **ONE** DRAGON IN PARTICULAR HAS SAVED YOU AN' YER COUSINS' **BUTTS** MORE THAN A FEW TIMES!
AN' I KN
TH' DRAG
DON'T W
ANYBODY
KNOW TH
EXIST
NOT THAT **YOU'D** HAVE TH' **DECENCY** TO RESPECT SOMEONE ELSE'S **WISHES**!
Y'KNOW . . .
TH' **IRONY** OF ALL THIS MAY BE LOST ON **YOU** . . .
. . . BUT DON'T YOU THINK IT'S STRANGE THAT **I'M** TH' ONE TELLIN' FOLKS THAT DRAGONS EXIST, AN' **YOU'RE** TH' ONE TRYIN' TO CONVINCE 'EM THAT THEY **DON'T**?
SO?

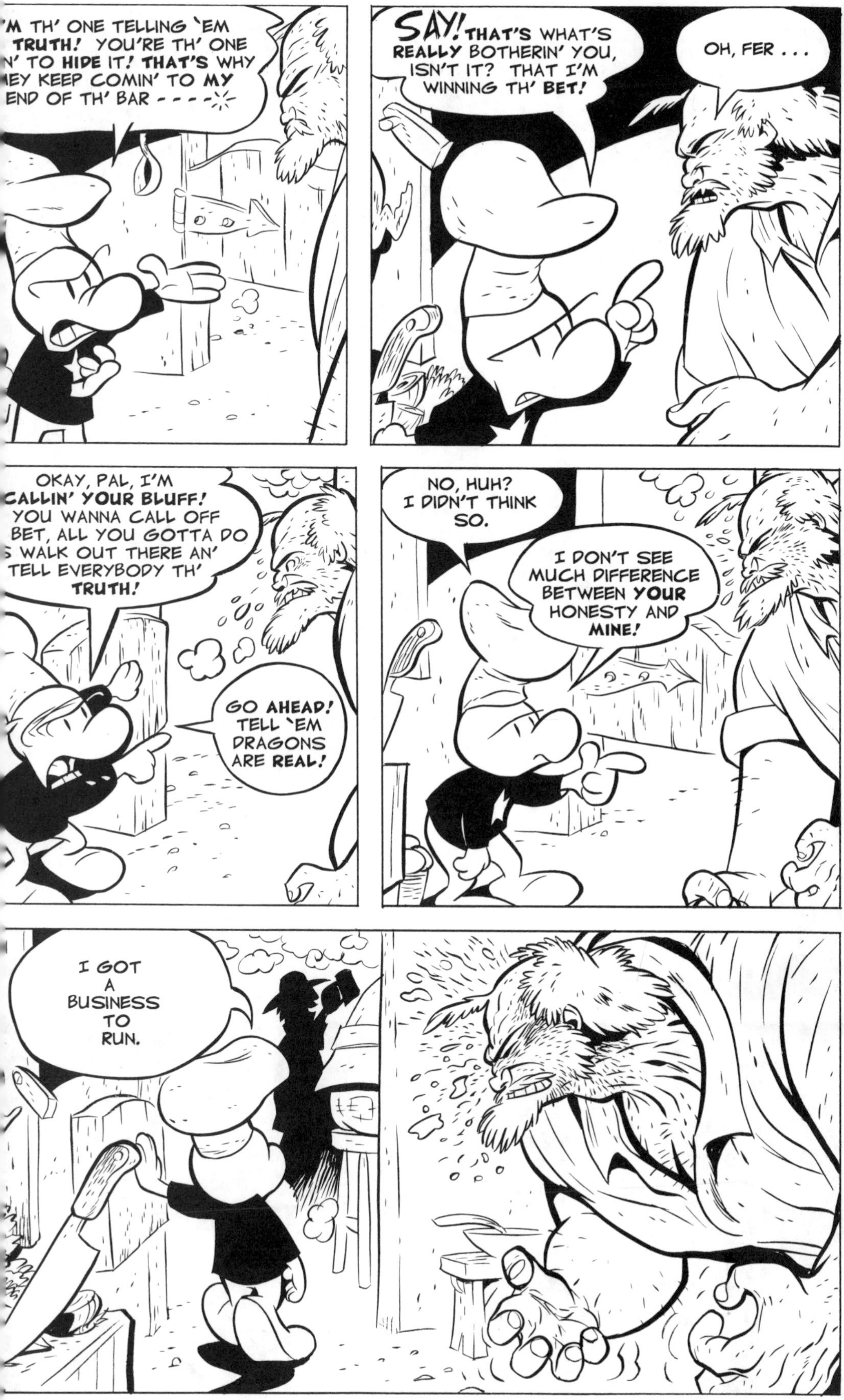
'M TH' ONE TELLING 'EM TRUTH! YOU'RE TH' ONE N' TO HIDE IT! THAT'S WHY IEY KEEP COMIN' TO MY END OF TH' BAR - - - -
SAY! THAT'S WHAT'S REALLY BOTHERIN' YOU, ISN'T IT? THAT I'M WINNING TH' BET!
OH, FER . . .
OKAY, PAL, I'M CALLIN' YOUR BLUFF! YOU WANNA CALL OFF BET, ALL YOU GOTTA DO S WALK OUT THERE AN' TELL EVERYBODY TH' TRUTH!
GO AHEAD! TELL 'EM DRAGONS ARE REAL!
NO, HUH? I DIDN'T THINK SO.
I DON'T SEE MUCH DIFFERENCE BETWEEN YOUR HONESTY AND MINE!
I GOT A BUSINESS TO RUN.

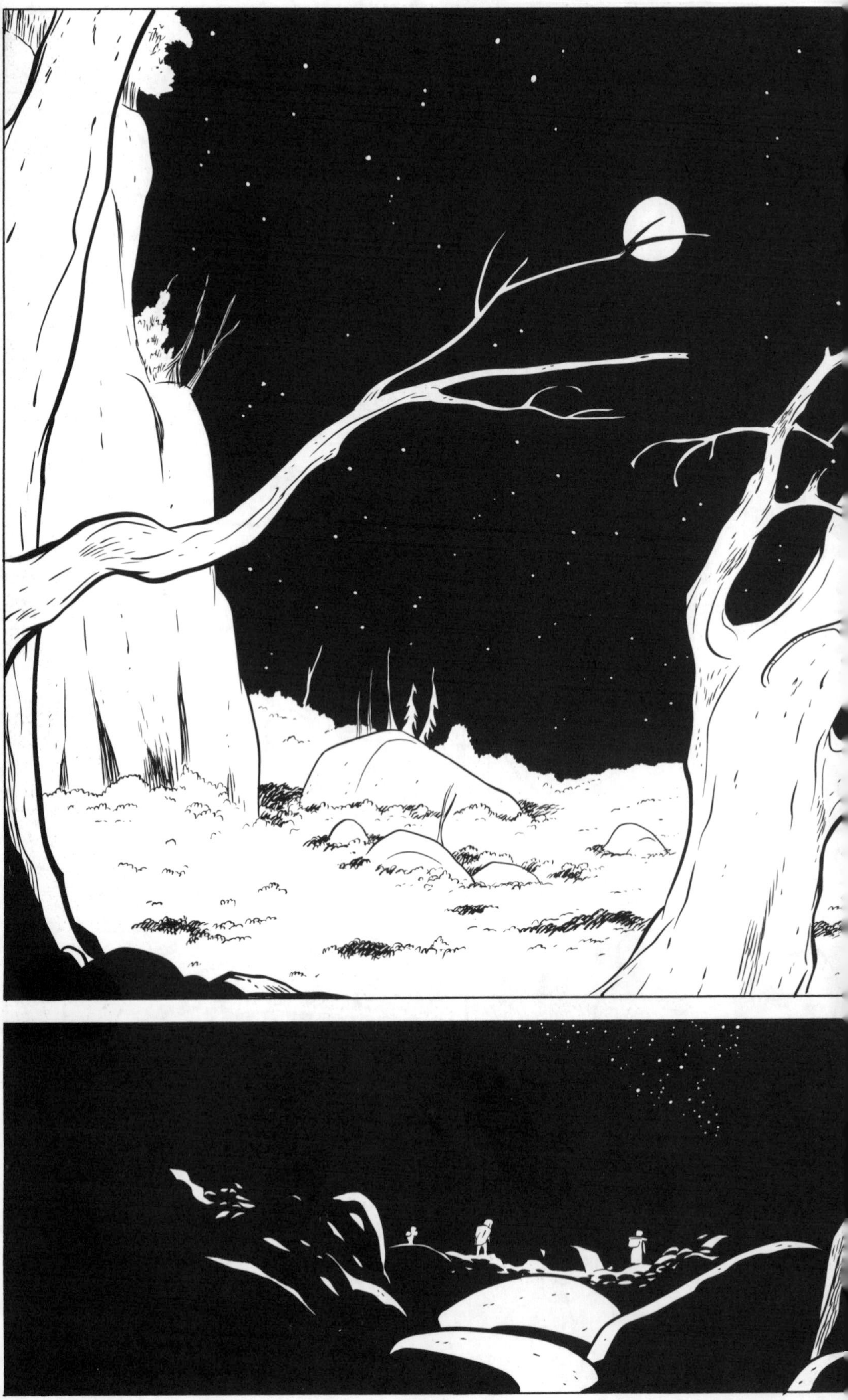

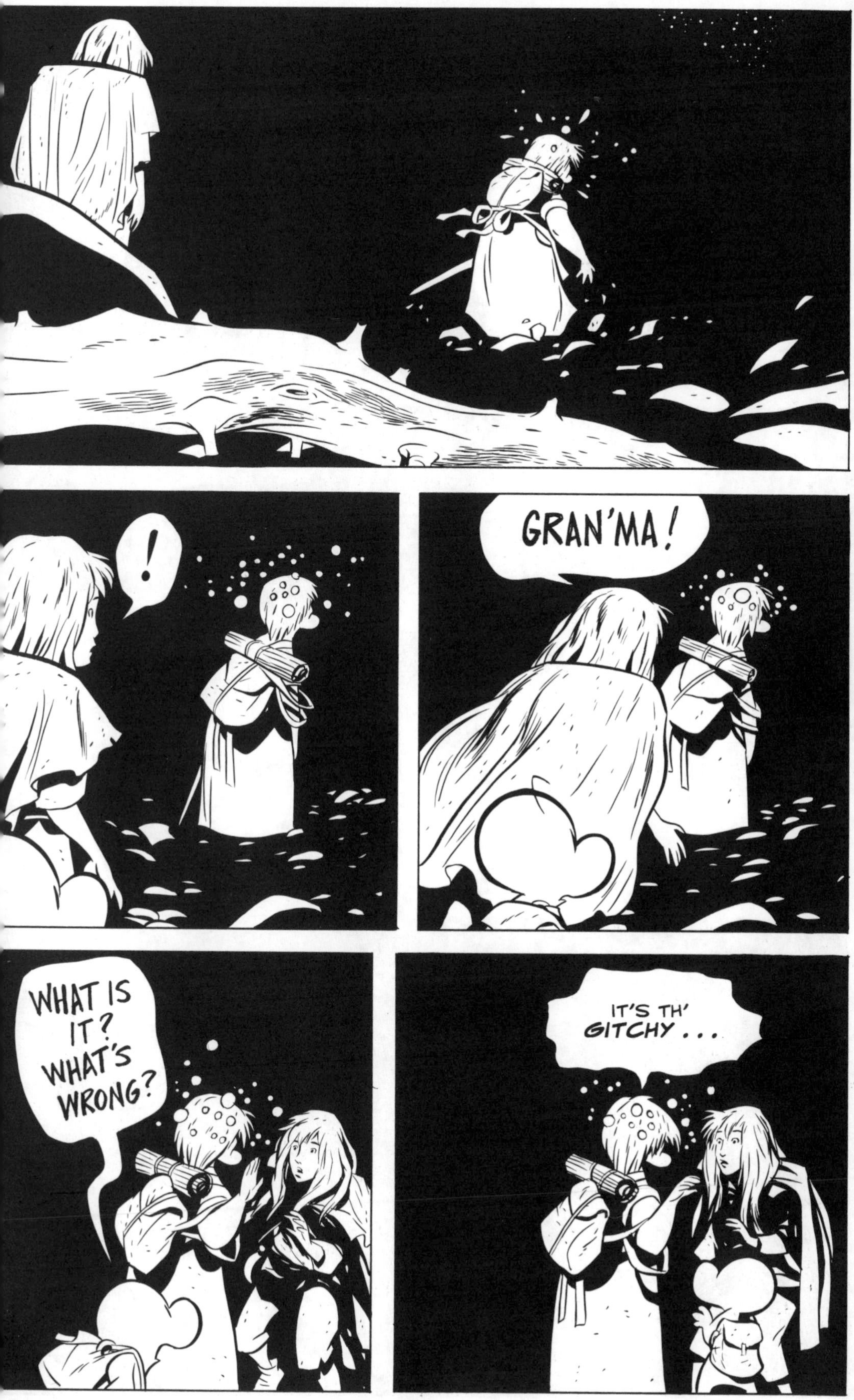
!
GRAN'MA!
WHAT IS IT? WHAT'S WRONG?
IT'S TH' GITCHY . . .

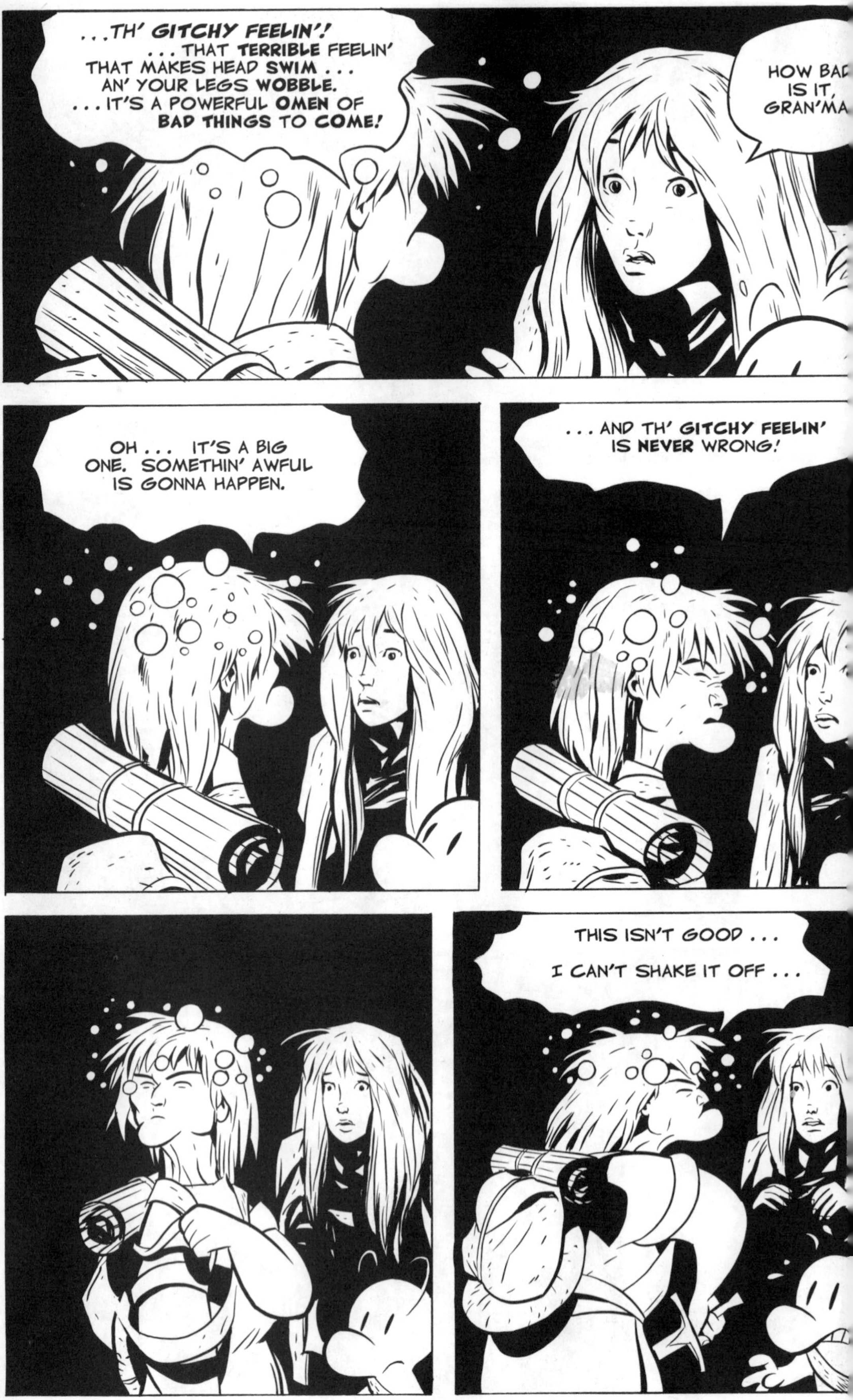
...TH' GITCHY FEELIN'! ...THAT TERRIBLE FEELIN' THAT MAKES HEAD SWIM ... AN' YOUR LEGS WOBBLE. ...IT'S A POWERFUL OMEN OF BAD THINGS TO COME!
HOW BAD IS IT, GRAN'MA
OH ... IT'S A BIG ONE. SOMETHIN' AWFUL IS GONNA HAPPEN.
...AND TH' GITCHY FEELIN' IS NEVER WRONG!
THIS ISN'T GOOD ...
I CAN'T SHAKE IT OFF ...

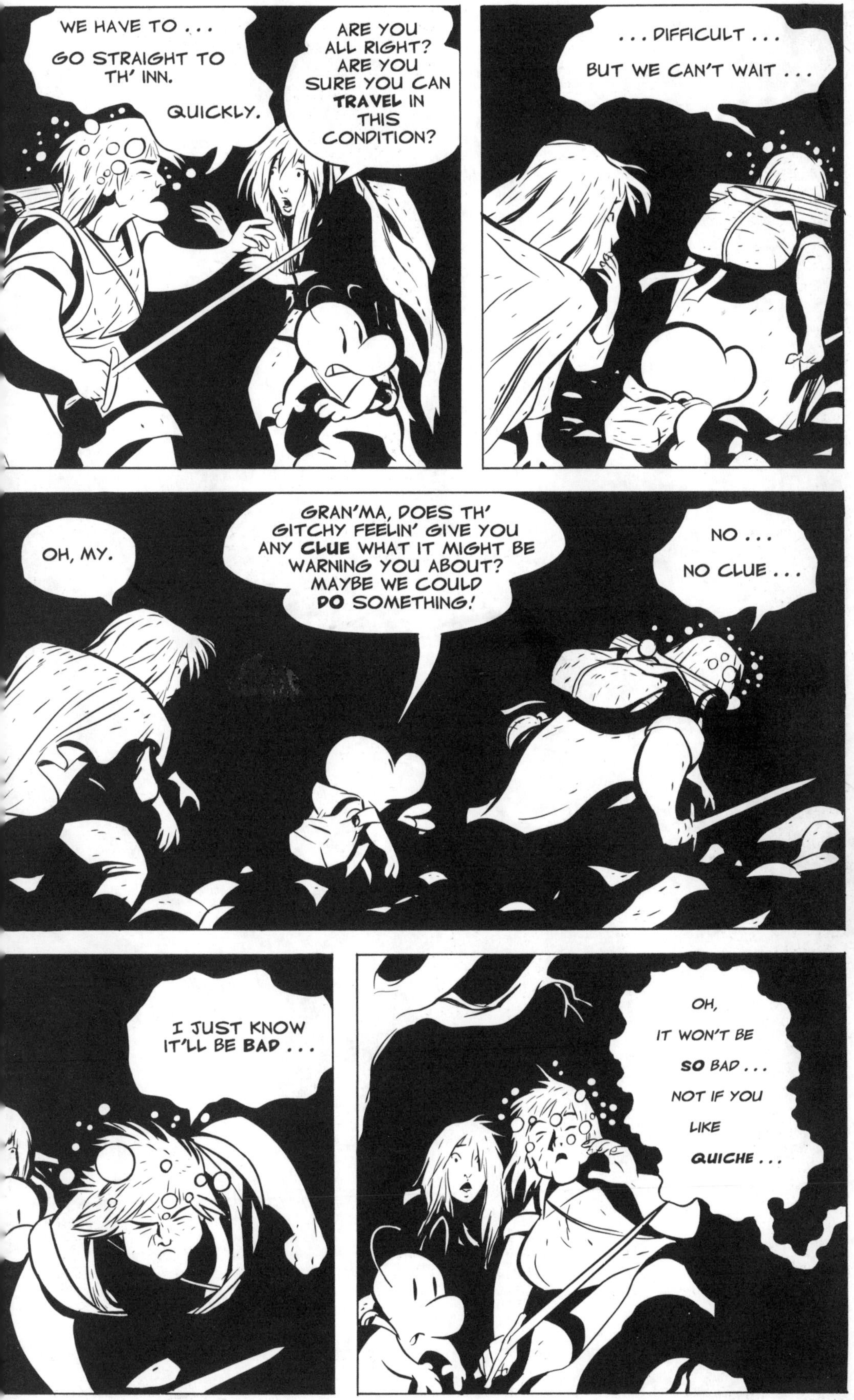
WE HAVE TO . . .
GO STRAIGHT TO TH' INN.
QUICKLY.
ARE YOU ALL RIGHT? ARE YOU SURE YOU CAN **TRAVEL** IN THIS CONDITION?
. . . DIFFICULT . . .
BUT WE CAN'T WAIT . . .
OH, MY.
GRAN'MA, DOES TH' GITCHY FEELIN' GIVE YOU ANY **CLUE** WHAT IT MIGHT BE WARNING YOU ABOUT? MAYBE WE COULD **DO** SOMETHING!
NO . . .
NO CLUE . . .
I JUST KNOW IT'LL BE **BAD** . . .
OH,
IT WON'T BE
SO BAD . . .
NOT IF YOU
LIKE
QUICHE . . .

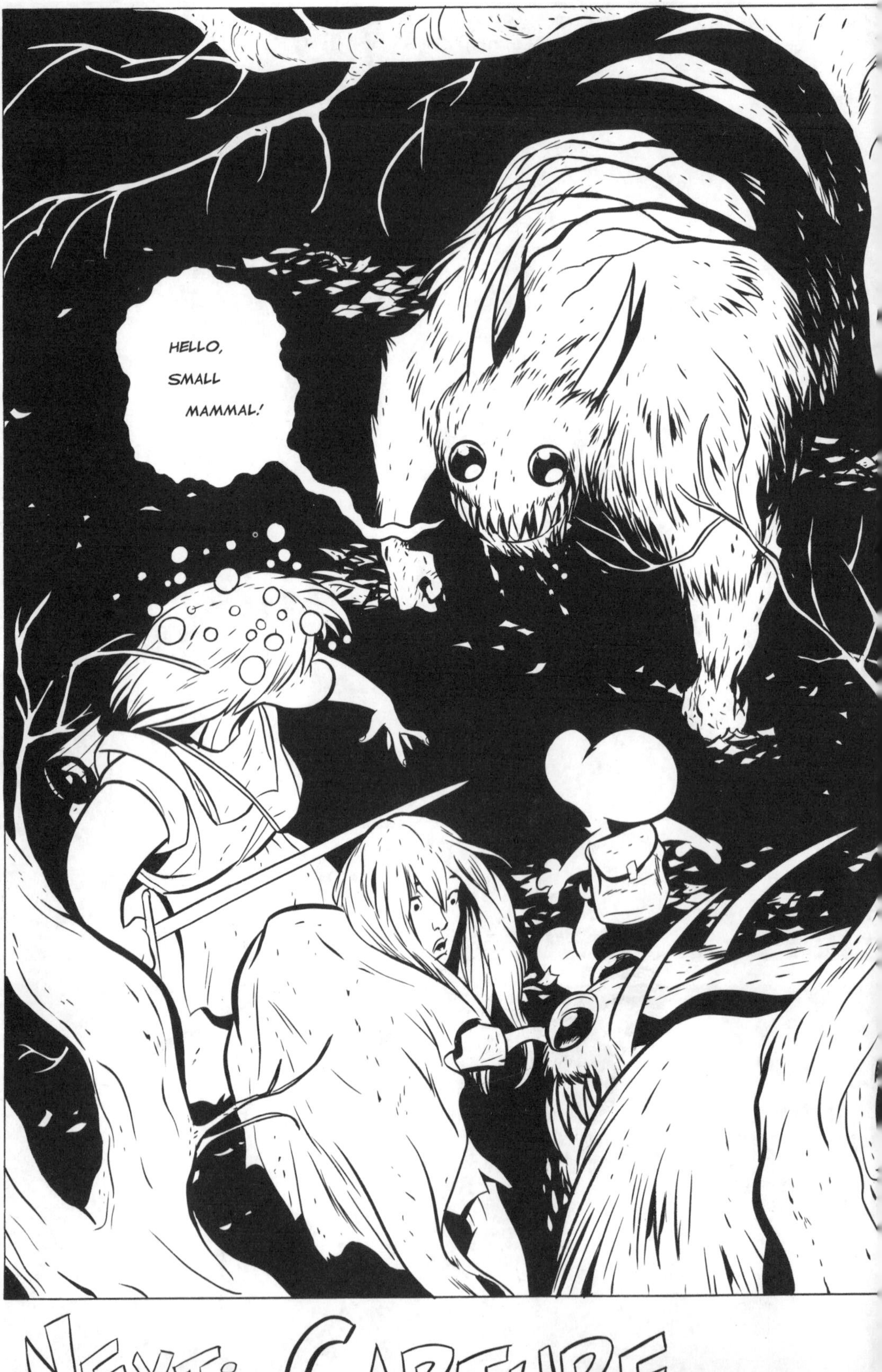
HELLO, SMALL MAMMAL!

NEXT: CAPTURE

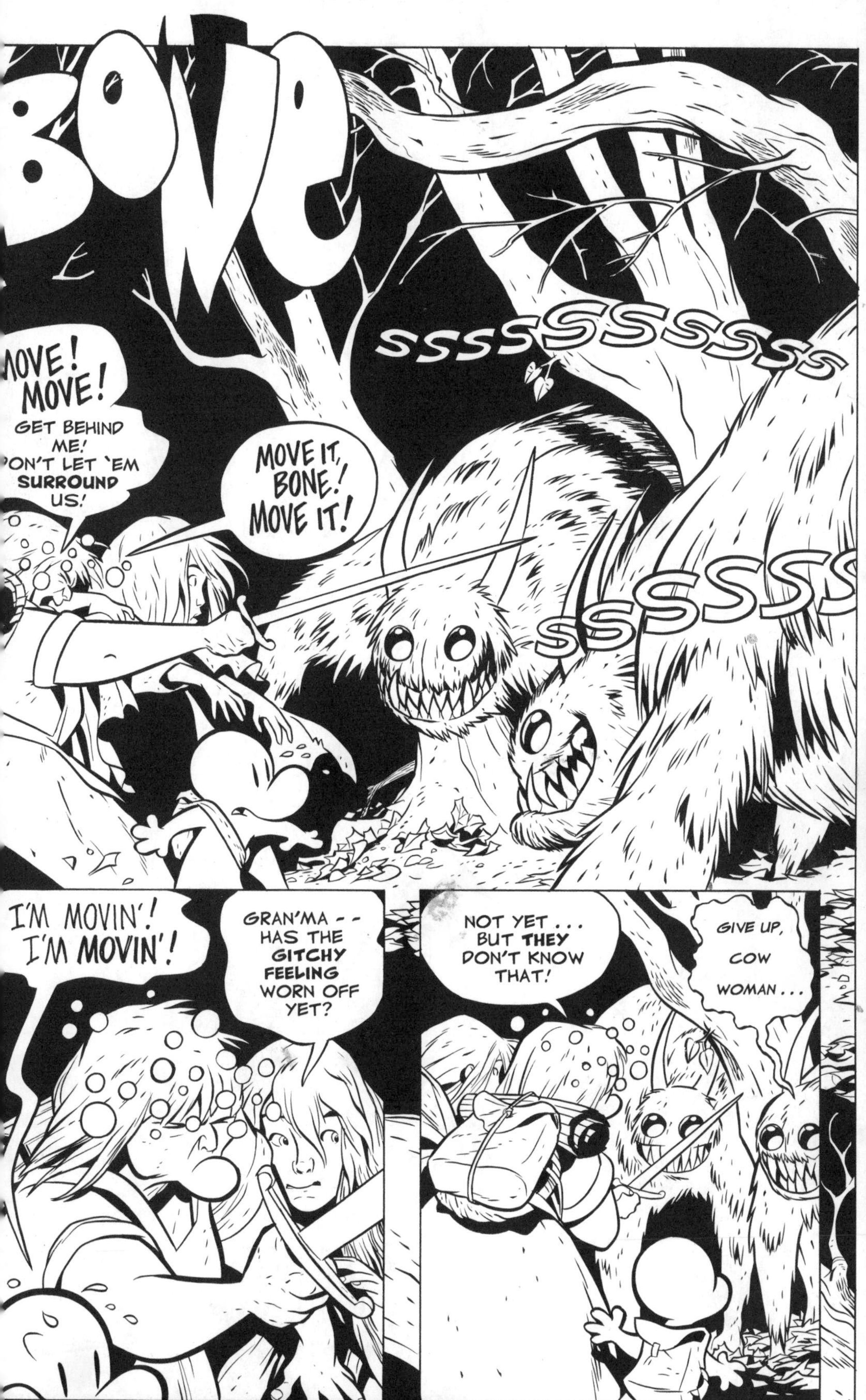
BONE
SSSSSSSSSSSSS
MOVE! MOVE! GET BEHIND ME! DON'T LET 'EM SURROUND US!
MOVE IT, BONE! MOVE IT!
SSSSSSSS
I'M MOVIN'! I'M MOVIN'!
GRAN'MA -- HAS THE GITCHY FEELING WORN OFF YET?
NOT YET ... BUT THEY DON'T KNOW THAT!
GIVE UP, COW WOMAN...

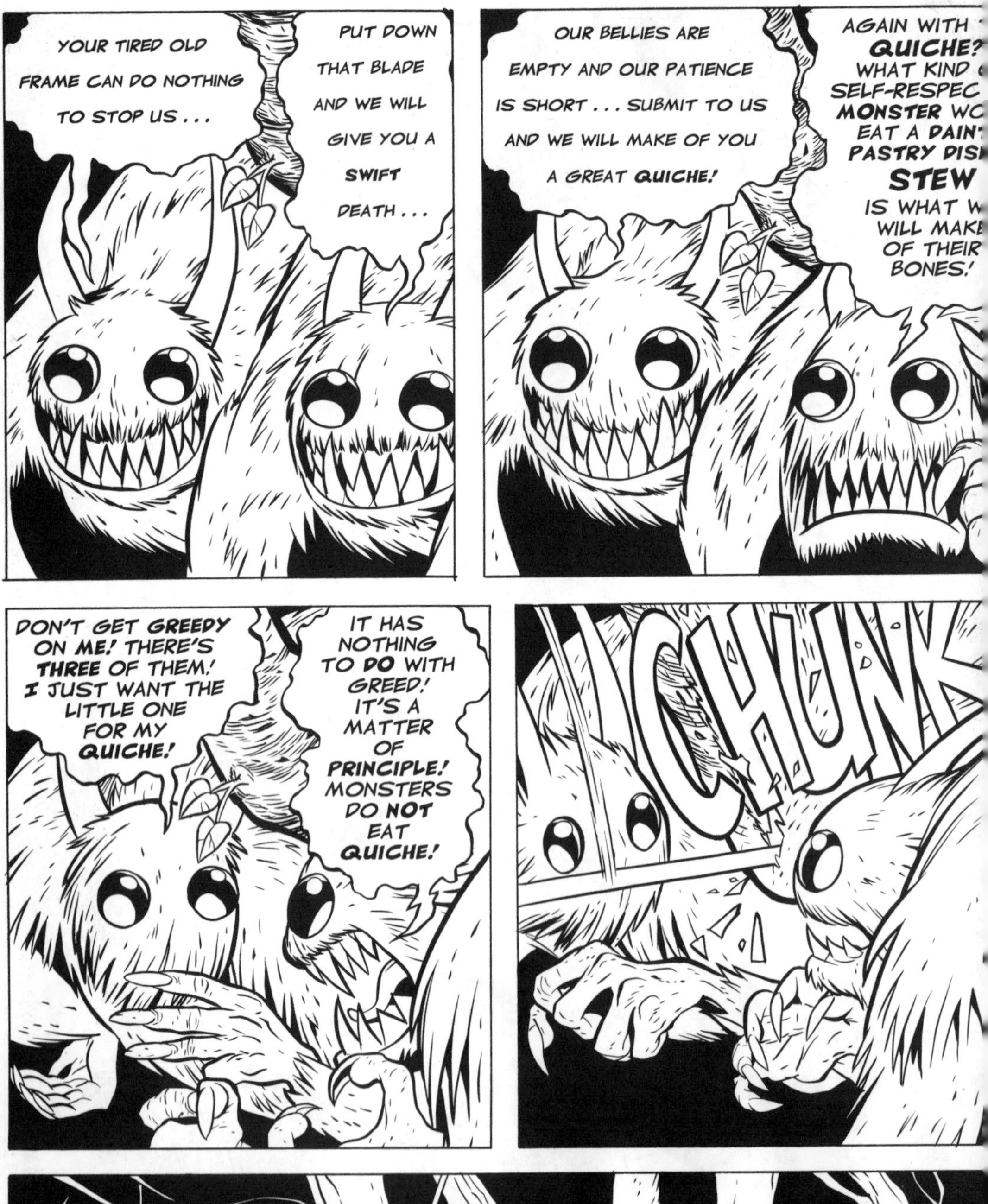
YOUR TIRED OLD FRAME CAN DO NOTHING TO STOP US . . .
PUT DOWN THAT BLADE AND WE WILL GIVE YOU A SWIFT DEATH . . .
OUR BELLIES ARE EMPTY AND OUR PATIENCE IS SHORT . . . SUBMIT TO US AND WE WILL MAKE OF YOU A GREAT QUICHE!
AGAIN WITH QUICHE? WHAT KIND SELF-RESPEC MONSTER WO EAT A DAIN PASTRY DIS STEW IS WHAT W WILL MAKE OF THEIR BONES!
DON'T GET GREEDY ON ME! THERE'S THREE OF THEM! I JUST WANT THE LITTLE ONE FOR MY QUICHE!
IT HAS NOTHING TO DO WITH GREED! IT'S A MATTER OF PRINCIPLE! MONSTERS DO NOT EAT QUICHE!
CHUNK
DID I HIT ONE?
NO. YOU MISSED.

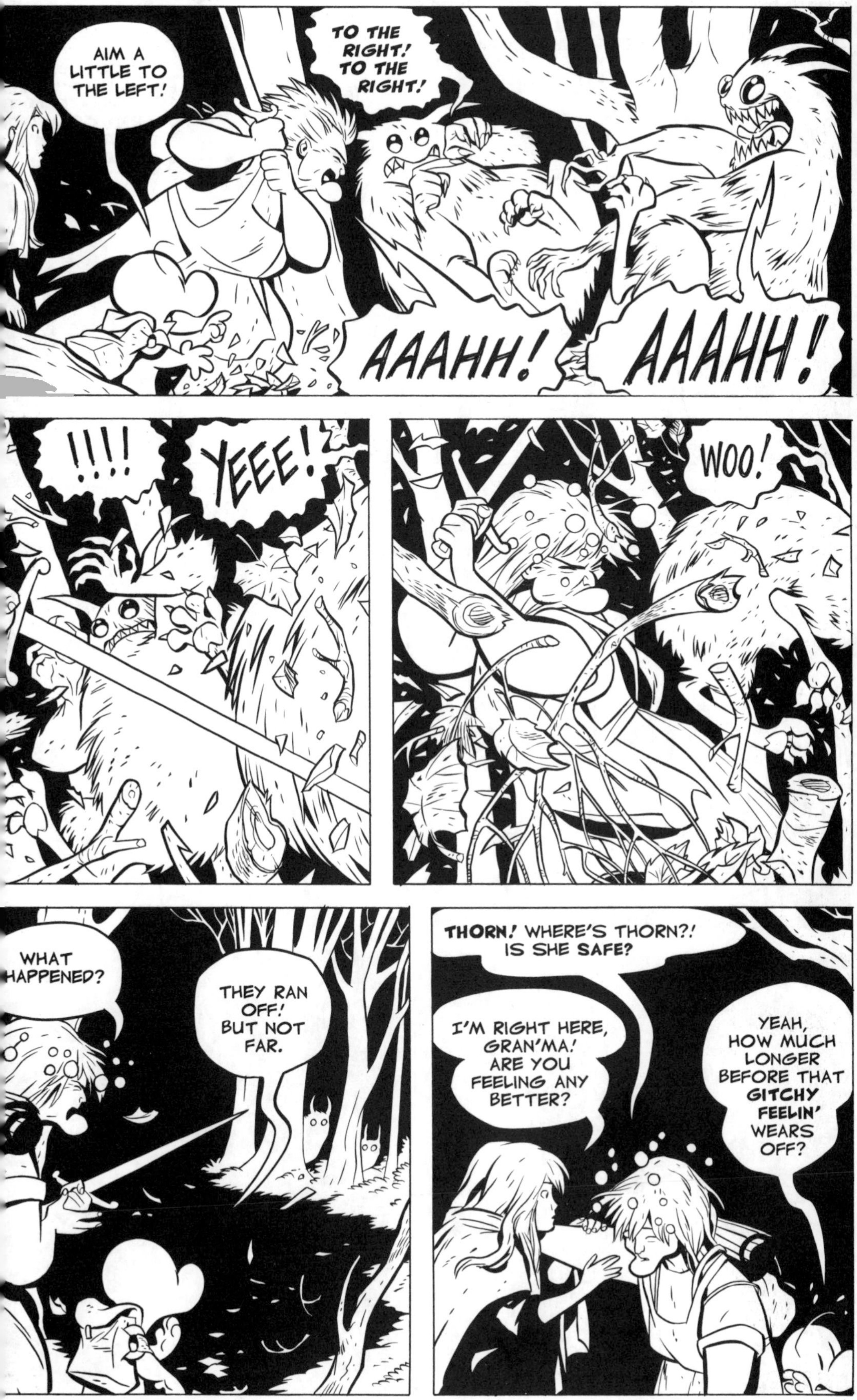
AIM A LITTLE TO THE LEFT!
TO THE RIGHT! TO THE RIGHT!
AAAHH!
AAAHH!
!!!!
YEEE!
WOO!
WHAT HAPPENED?
THEY RAN OFF! BUT NOT FAR.
THORN! WHERE'S THORN?! IS SHE SAFE?
I'M RIGHT HERE, GRAN'MA! ARE YOU FEELING ANY BETTER?
YEAH, HOW MUCH LONGER BEFORE THAT GITCHY FEELIN' WEARS OFF?

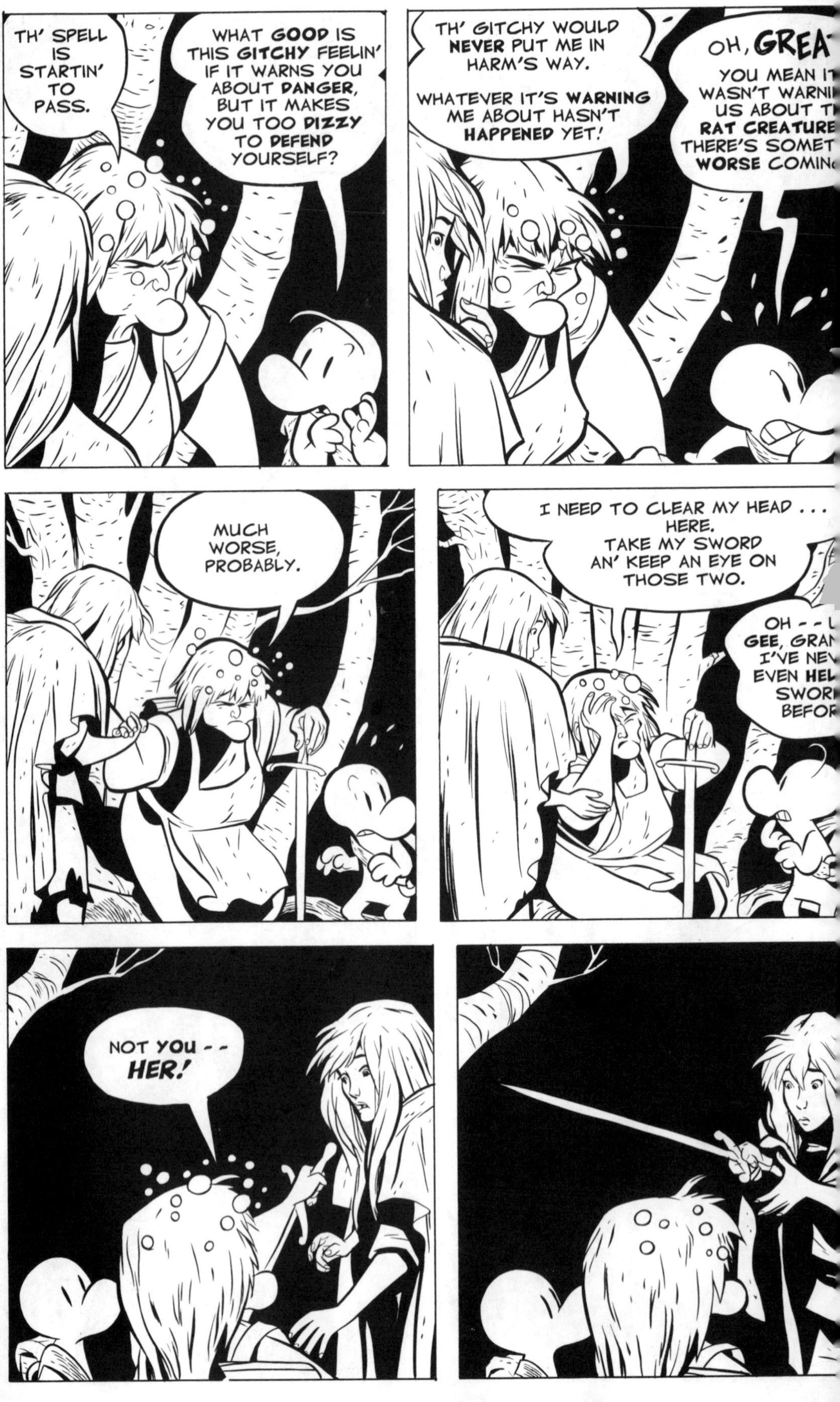
TH' SPELL IS STARTIN' TO PASS.
WHAT GOOD IS THIS GITCHY FEELIN' IF IT WARNS YOU ABOUT DANGER, BUT IT MAKES YOU TOO DIZZY TO DEFEND YOURSELF?
TH' GITCHY WOULD NEVER PUT ME IN HARM'S WAY.
WHATEVER IT'S WARNING ME ABOUT HASN'T HAPPENED YET!
OH, GREA
YOU MEAN IT WASN'T WARNI US ABOUT T RAT CREATURE THERE'S SOMET WORSE COMIN
MUCH WORSE, PROBABLY.
I NEED TO CLEAR MY HEAD . . . HERE. TAKE MY SWORD AN' KEEP AN EYE ON THOSE TWO.
OH - - U GEE, GRAN I'VE NEV EVEN HEL SWOR BEFOR
NOT YOU - - HER!

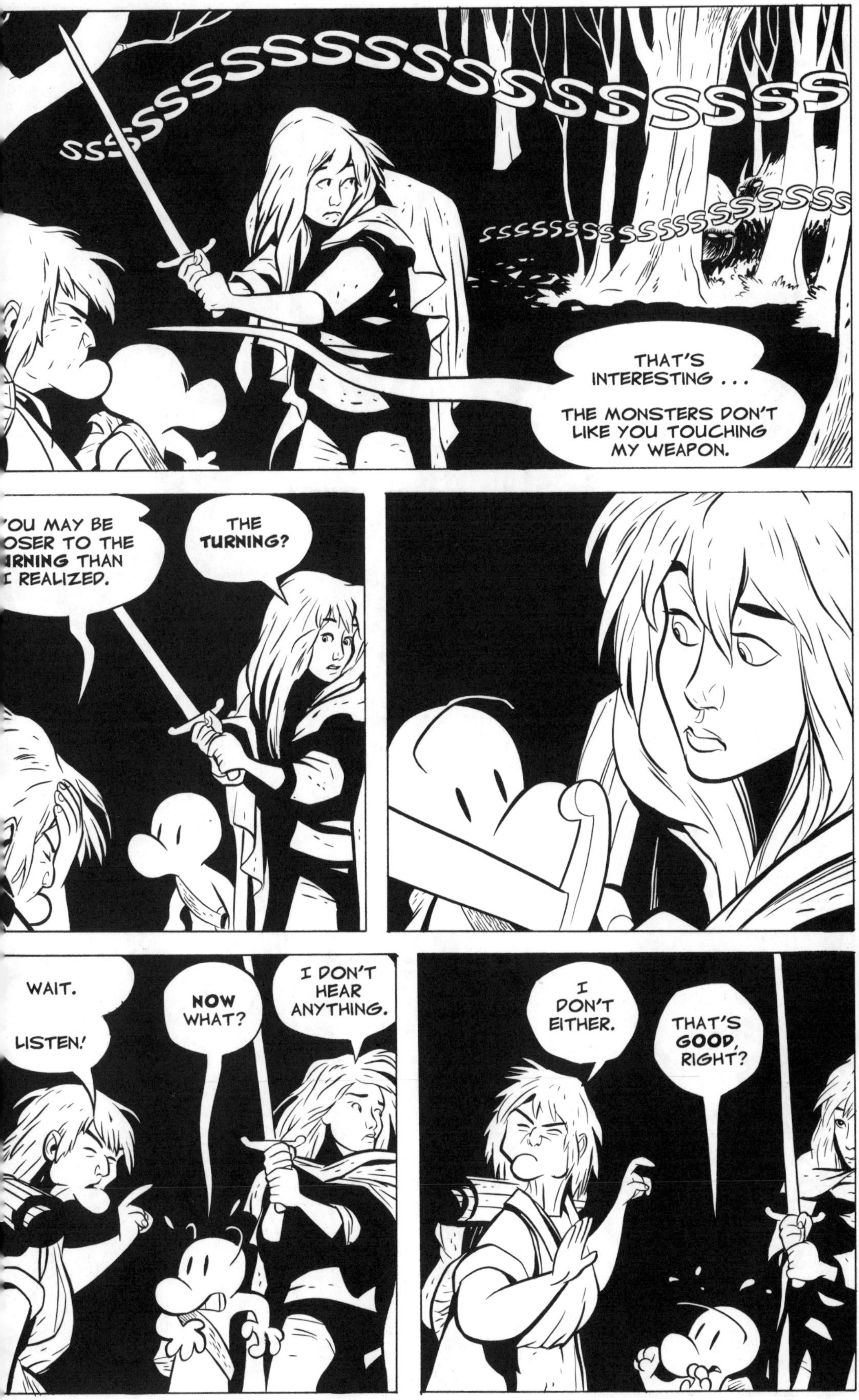
SSSSSSSSSSSSSSSSSSSSSS
SSSSSSSSSSSSSSSSSSSSSS
THAT'S INTERESTING . . .
THE MONSTERS DON'T LIKE YOU TOUCHING MY WEAPON.
OU MAY BE OSER TO THE RNING THAN REALIZED.
THE TURNING?
WAIT.
LISTEN!
NOW WHAT?
I DON'T HEAR ANYTHING.
I DON'T EITHER.
THAT'S GOOD, RIGHT?

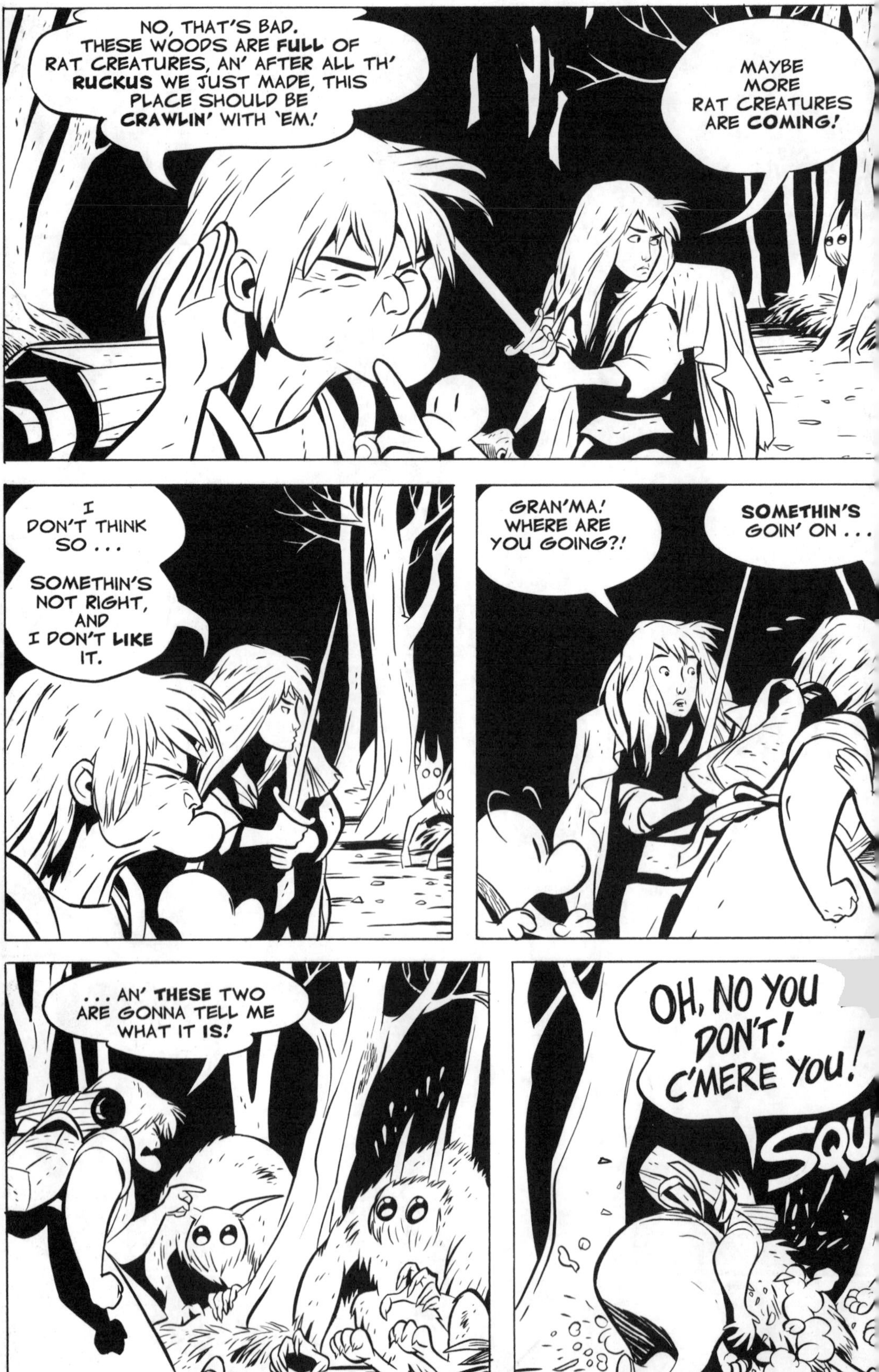
NO, THAT'S BAD. THESE WOODS ARE **FULL** OF RAT CREATURES, AN' AFTER ALL TH' **RUCKUS** WE JUST MADE, THIS PLACE SHOULD BE **CRAWLIN'** WITH 'EM!
MAYBE MORE RAT CREATURES ARE **COMING!**
I DON'T THINK SO . . .
SOMETHIN'S NOT RIGHT, AND I DON'T **LIKE** IT.
GRAN'MA! WHERE ARE YOU GOING?!
SOMETHIN'S GOIN' ON . . .
. . . AN' **THESE** TWO ARE GONNA TELL ME WHAT IT **IS!**
OH, NO YOU DON'T! C'MERE YOU!
SQU

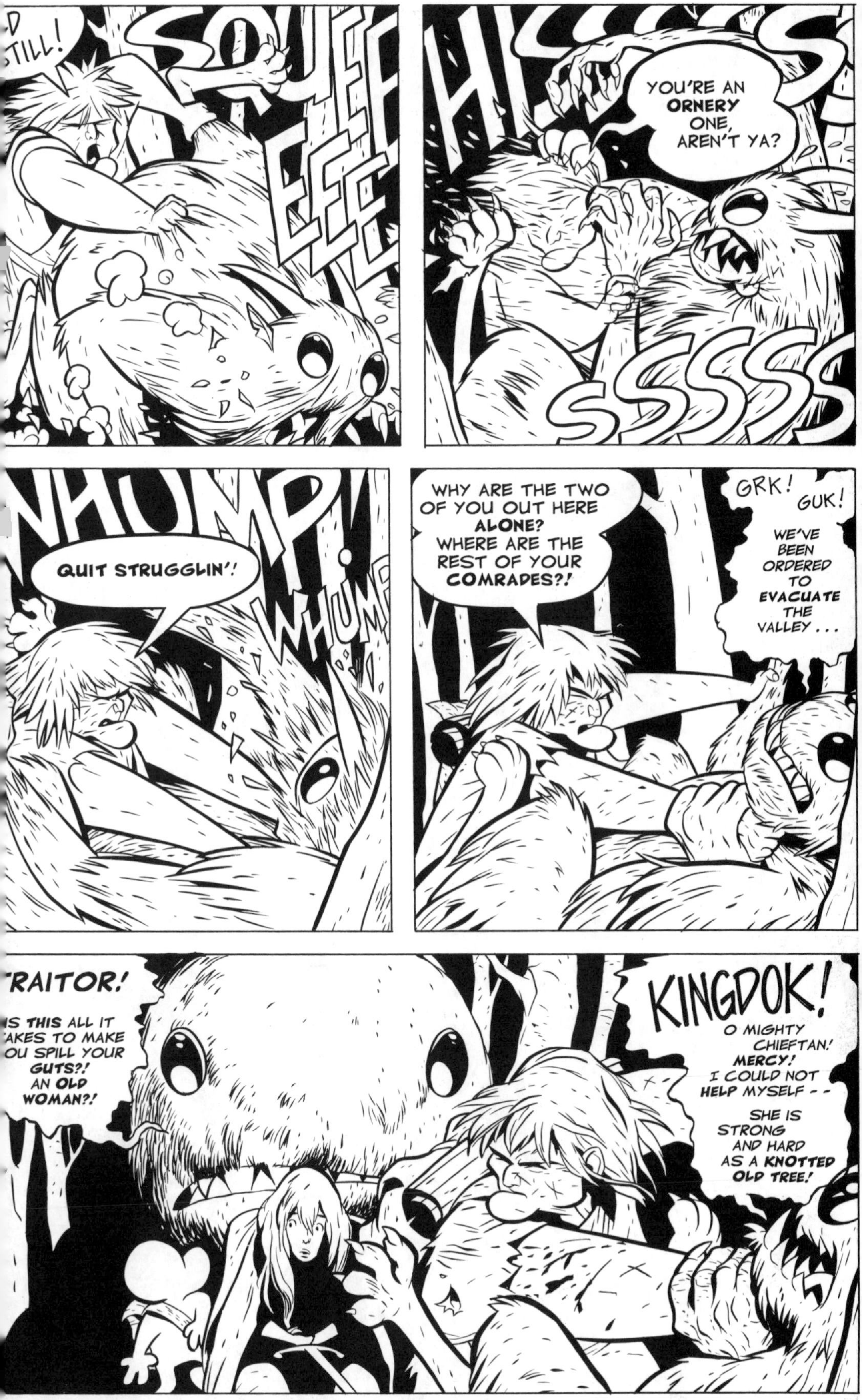

D STILL!
SQUEEEEE
HISSSS
YOU'RE AN **ORNERY** ONE, AREN'T YA?
SSSSS
WHUMP!
QUIT STRUGGLIN'!
WHUMP
WHY ARE THE TWO OF YOU OUT HERE **ALONE?** WHERE ARE THE REST OF YOUR **COMRADES?!**
GRK!
GUK!
WE'VE BEEN ORDERED TO **EVACUATE** THE VALLEY . . .
TRAITOR!
IS **THIS** ALL IT TAKES TO MAKE YOU SPILL YOUR **GUTS?!** AN **OLD WOMAN?!**
KINGDOK!
O MIGHTY CHIEFTAN! **MERCY!** I COULD NOT **HELP** MYSELF - -
SHE IS STRONG AND HARD AS A **KNOTTED OLD TREE!**

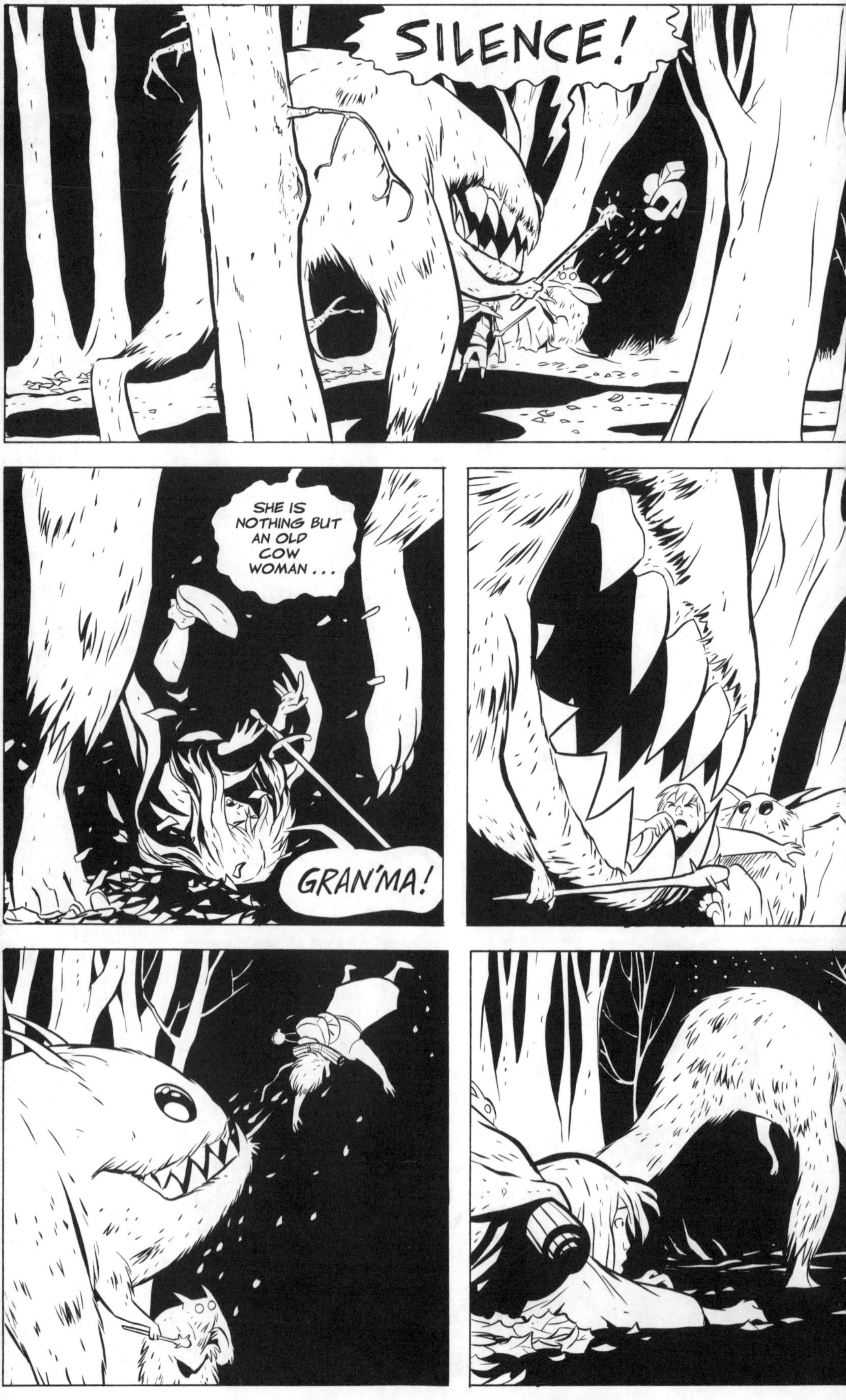
SILENCE!
SHE IS NOTHING BUT AN OLD COW WOMAN...
GRAN'MA!

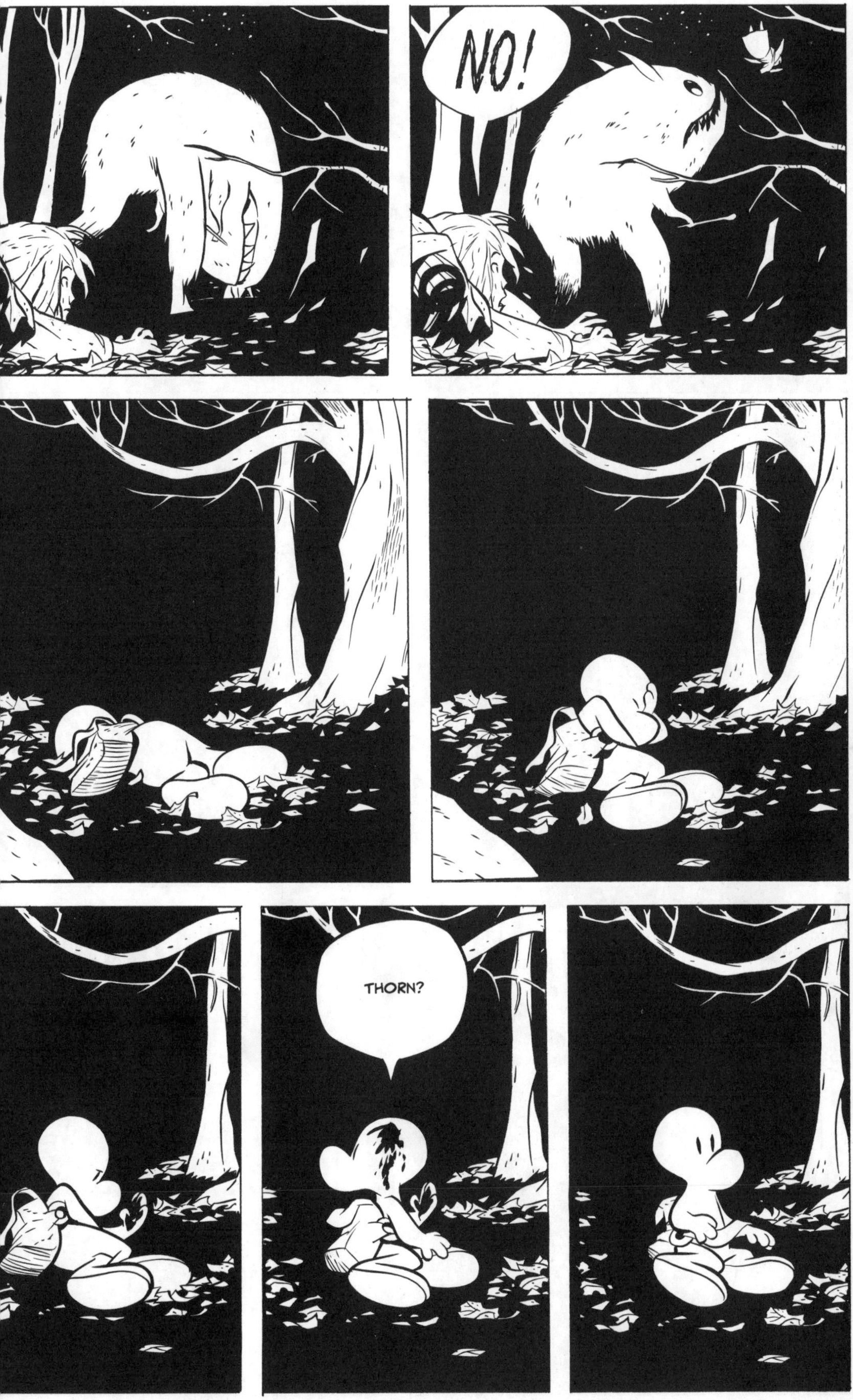
NO!
THORN?

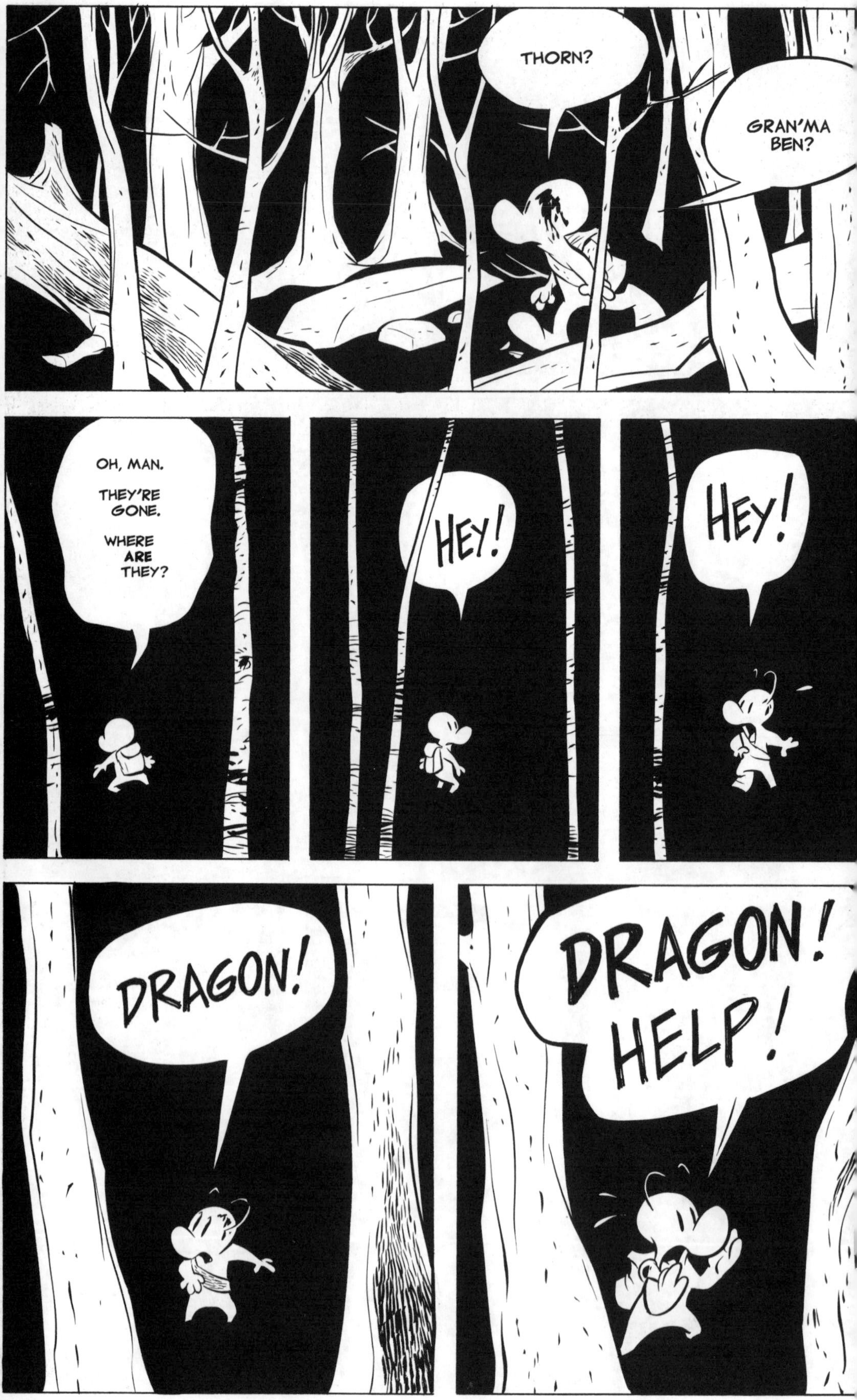
THORN?
GRAN'MA BEN?
OH, MAN.
THEY'RE GONE.
WHERE ARE THEY?
HEY!
HEY!
DRAGON!
DRAGON! HELP!

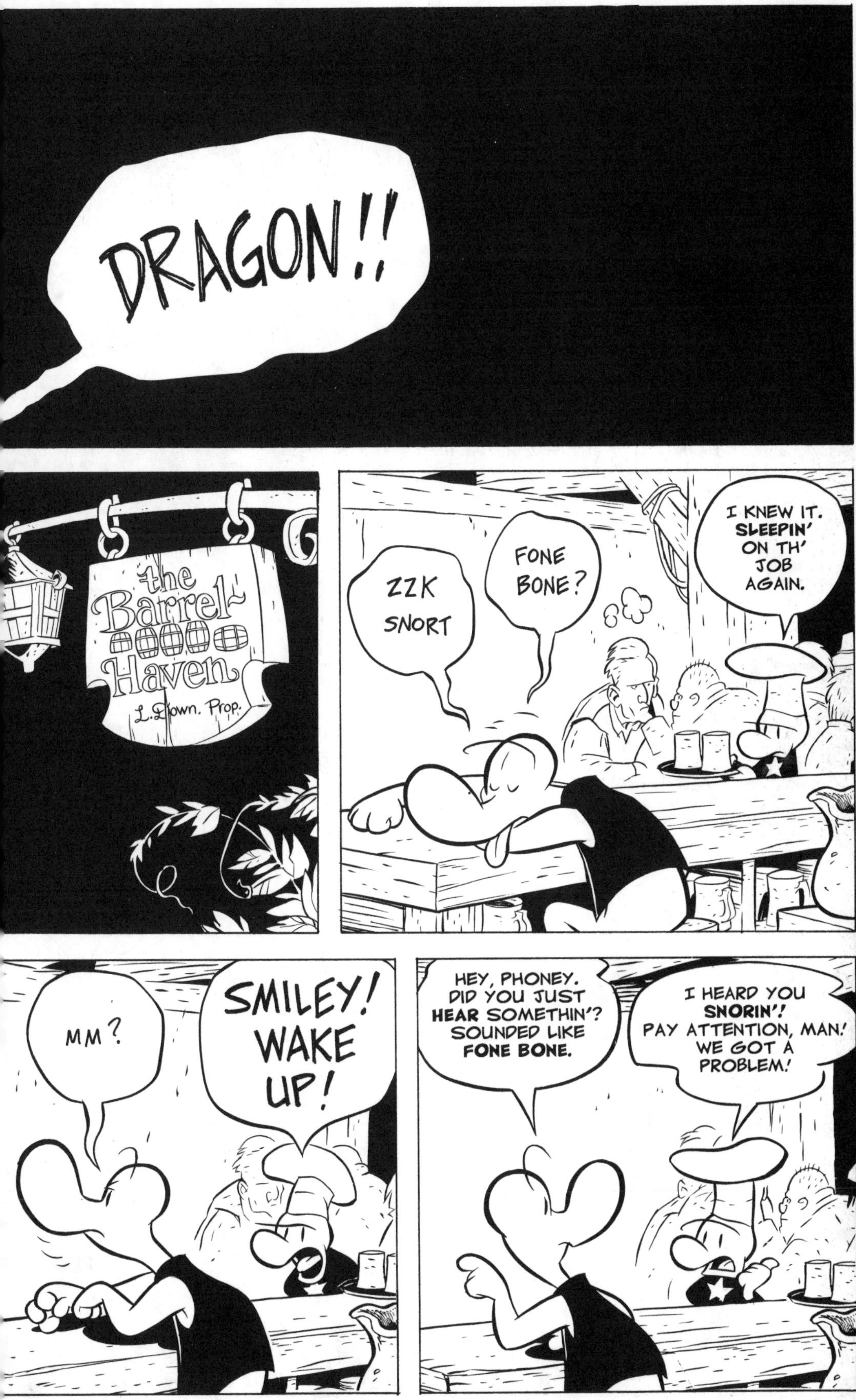

DRAGON!!
the Barrel Haven
L. Down. Prop.
ZZK SNORT
FONE BONE?
I KNEW IT. SLEEPIN' ON TH' JOB AGAIN.
MM?
SMILEY! WAKE UP!
HEY, PHONEY. DID YOU JUST HEAR SOMETHIN'? SOUNDED LIKE FONE BONE.
I HEARD YOU SNORIN'! PAY ATTENTION, MAN! WE GOT A PROBLEM!

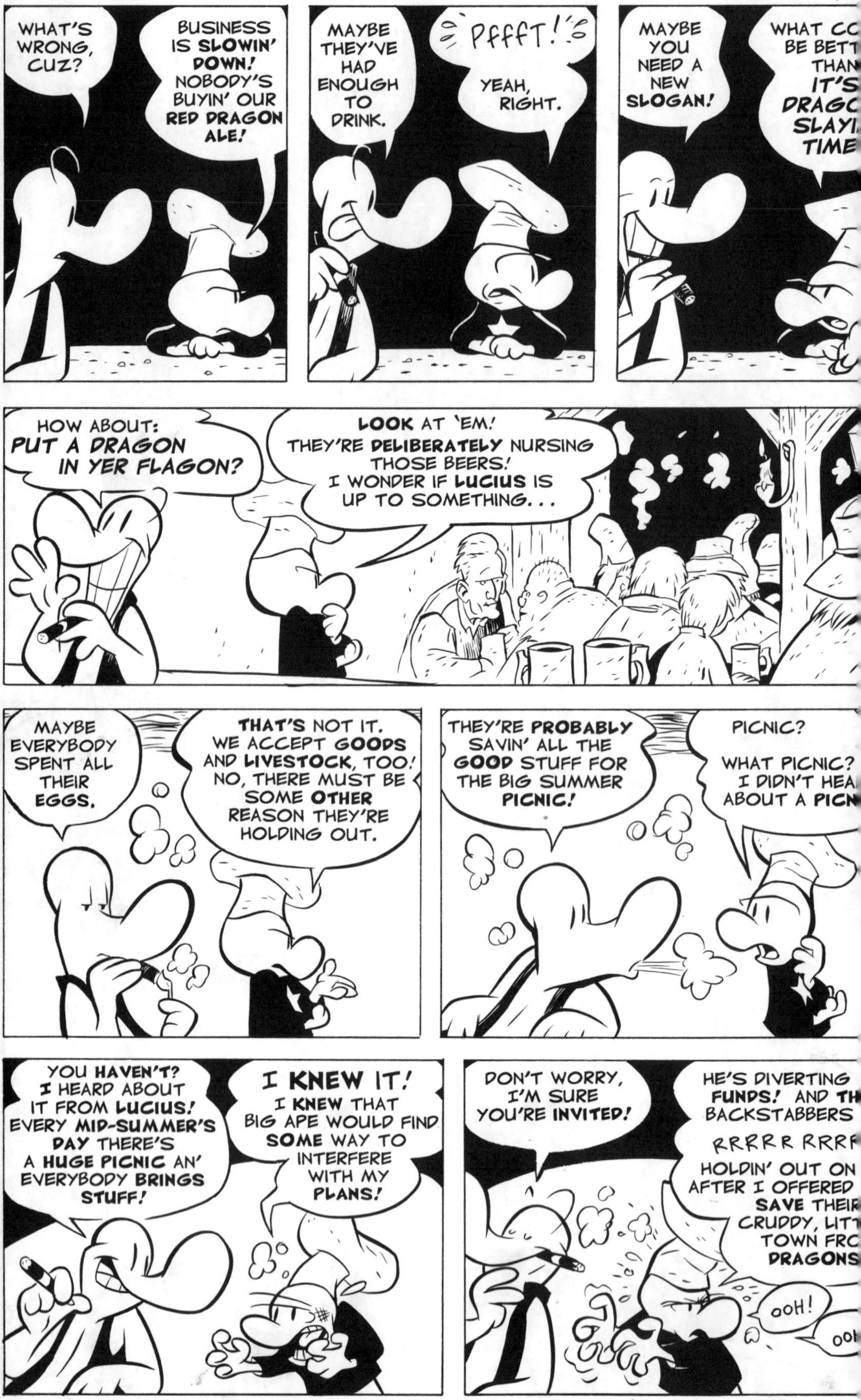
WHAT'S WRONG, CUZ?
BUSINESS IS SLOWIN' DOWN! NOBODY'S BUYIN' OUR RED DRAGON ALE!
MAYBE THEY'VE HAD ENOUGH TO DRINK.
PFFFT!
YEAH, RIGHT.
MAYBE YOU NEED A NEW SLOGAN!
WHAT CO BE BETT THAN IT'S DRAGO SLAYI TIME
HOW ABOUT: PUT A DRAGON IN YER FLAGON?
LOOK AT 'EM! THEY'RE DELIBERATELY NURSING THOSE BEERS! I WONDER IF LUCIUS IS UP TO SOMETHING...
MAYBE EVERYBODY SPENT ALL THEIR EGGS.
THAT'S NOT IT. WE ACCEPT GOODS AND LIVESTOCK, TOO! NO, THERE MUST BE SOME OTHER REASON THEY'RE HOLDING OUT.
THEY'RE PROBABLY SAVIN' ALL THE GOOD STUFF FOR THE BIG SUMMER PICNIC!
PICNIC? WHAT PICNIC? I DIDN'T HEA ABOUT A PICN
YOU HAVEN'T? I HEARD ABOUT IT FROM LUCIUS! EVERY MID-SUMMER'S DAY THERE'S A HUGE PICNIC AN' EVERYBODY BRINGS STUFF!
I KNEW IT! I KNEW THAT BIG APE WOULD FIND SOME WAY TO INTERFERE WITH MY PLANS!
DON'T WORRY, I'M SURE YOU'RE INVITED!
HE'S DIVERTING FUNDS! AND TH BACKSTABBERS
RRRRR RRRR
HOLDIN' OUT ON AFTER I OFFERED SAVE THEIR CRUDDY, LITT TOWN FRO DRAGONS
OOH!
OO

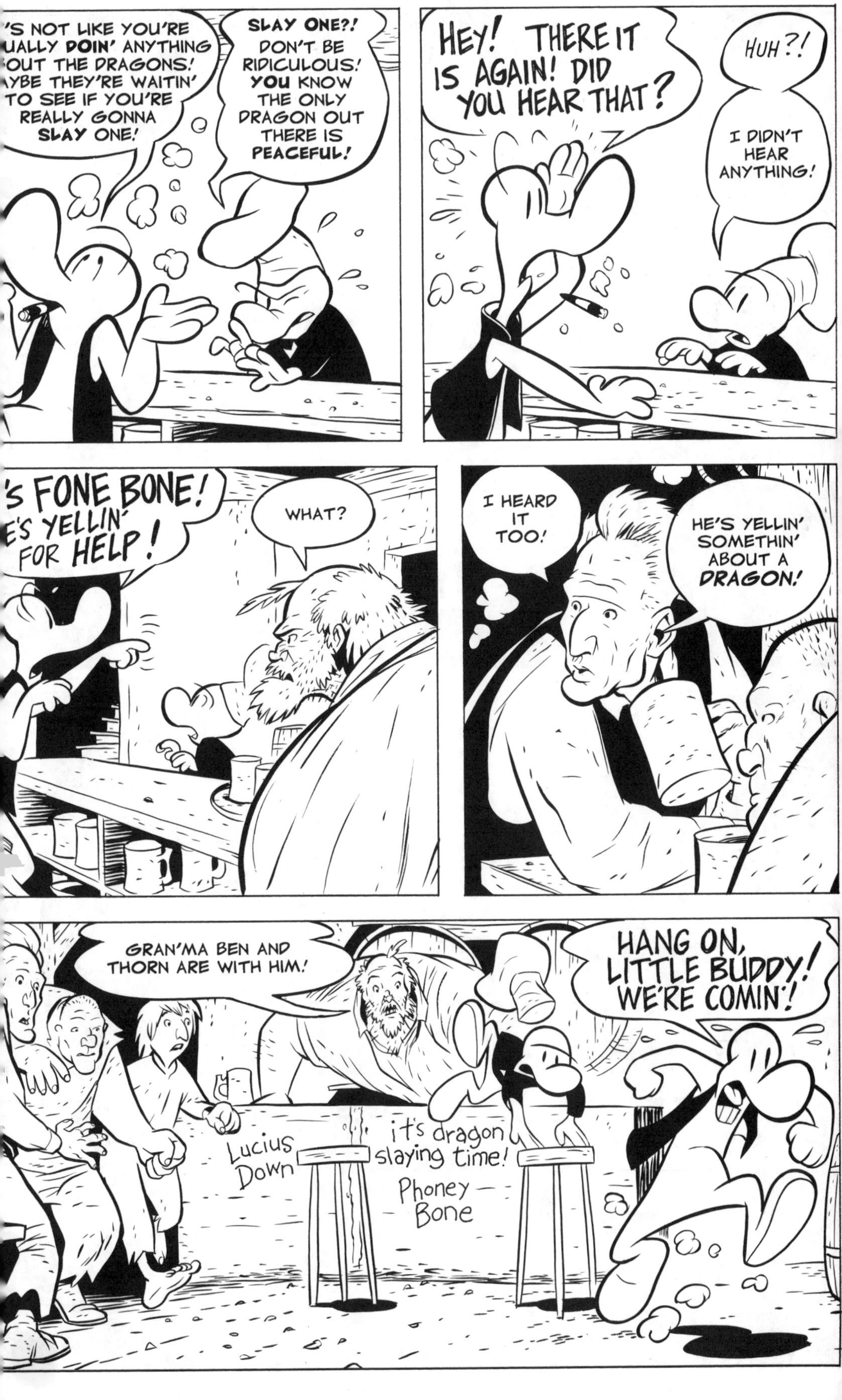
'S NOT LIKE YOU'RE UALLY DOIN' ANYTHING OUT THE DRAGONS! AYBE THEY'RE WAITIN' TO SEE IF YOU'RE REALLY GONNA SLAY ONE!
SLAY ONE?! DON'T BE RIDICULOUS! YOU KNOW THE ONLY DRAGON OUT THERE IS PEACEFUL!
HEY! THERE IT IS AGAIN! DID YOU HEAR THAT?
HUH?!
I DIDN'T HEAR ANYTHING!
'S FONE BONE! E'S YELLIN' FOR HELP!
WHAT?
I HEARD IT TOO!
HE'S YELLIN' SOMETHIN' ABOUT A DRAGON!
GRAN'MA BEN AND THORN ARE WITH HIM!
HANG ON, LITTLE BUDDY! WE'RE COMIN'!
Lucius Down
it's dragon slaying time! Phoney Bone

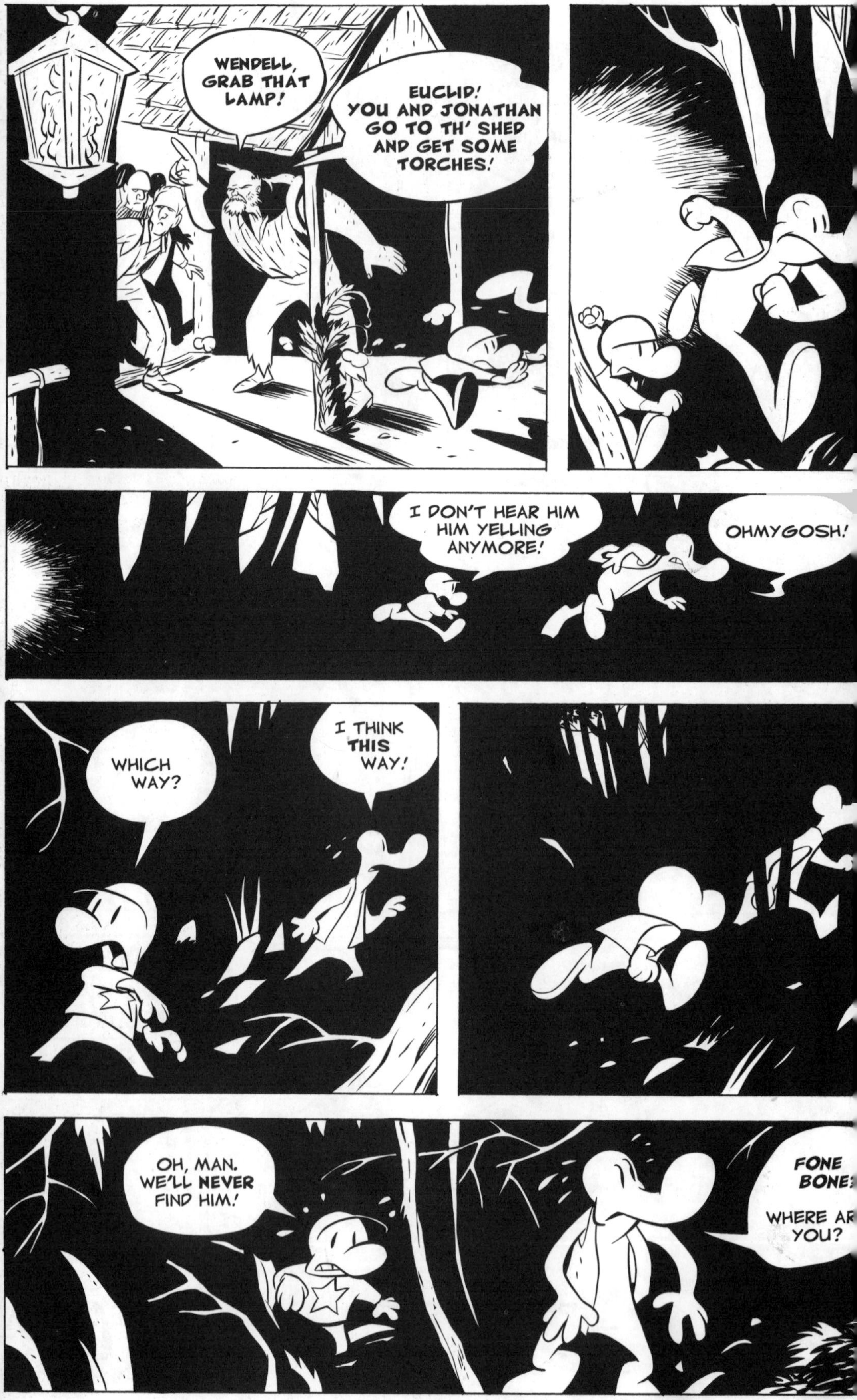
WENDELL, GRAB THAT LAMP!
EUCLID! YOU AND JONATHAN GO TO TH' SHED AND GET SOME TORCHES!
I DON'T HEAR HIM HIM YELLING ANYMORE!
OHMYGOSH!
WHICH WAY?
I THINK THIS WAY!
OH, MAN. WE'LL NEVER FIND HIM!
FONE BONE
WHERE AR YOU?

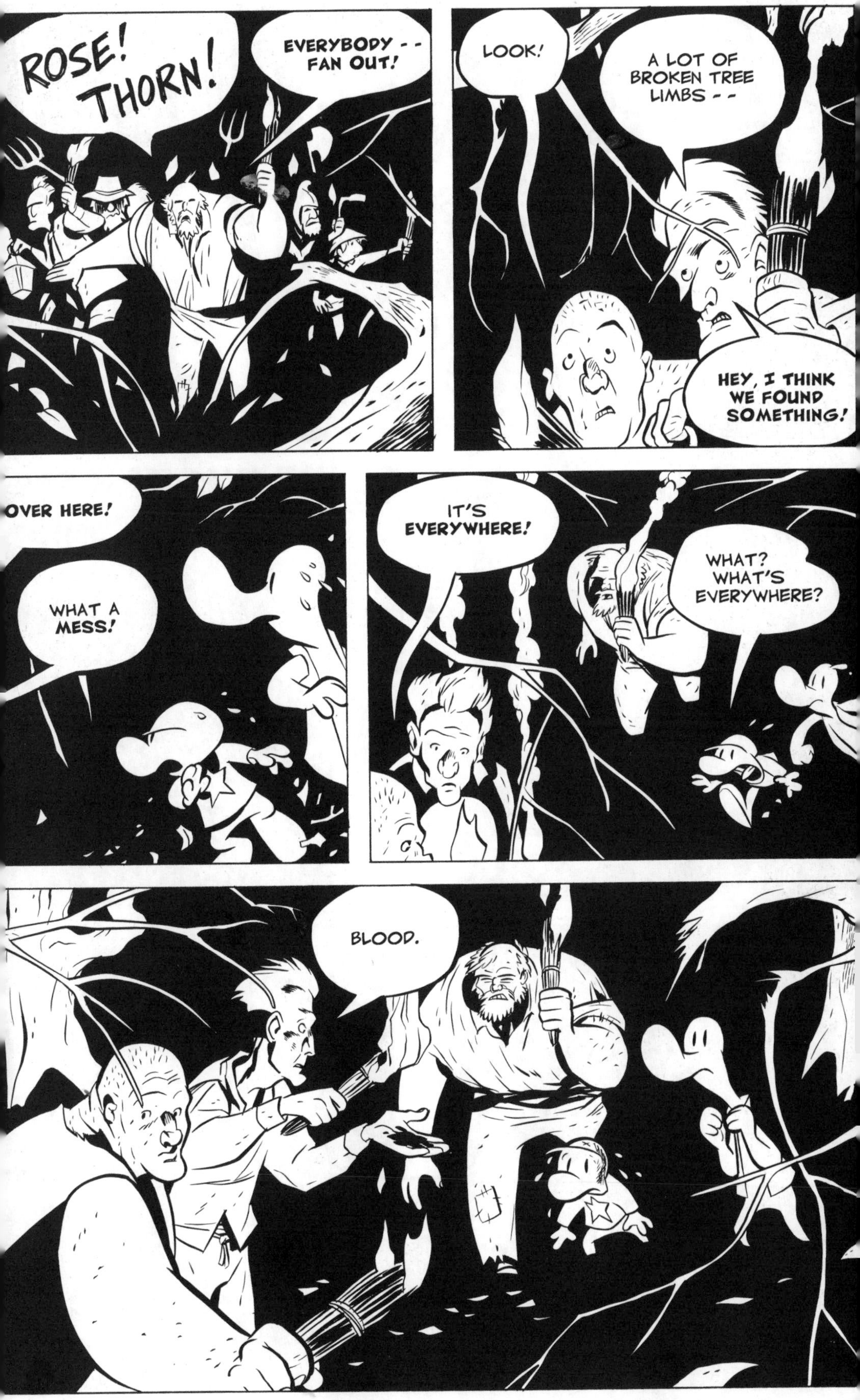
ROSE! THORN!
EVERYBODY - - FAN OUT!
LOOK!
A LOT OF BROKEN TREE LIMBS - -
HEY, I THINK WE FOUND SOMETHING!
OVER HERE!
WHAT A MESS!
IT'S EVERYWHERE!
WHAT? WHAT'S EVERYWHERE?
BLOOD.

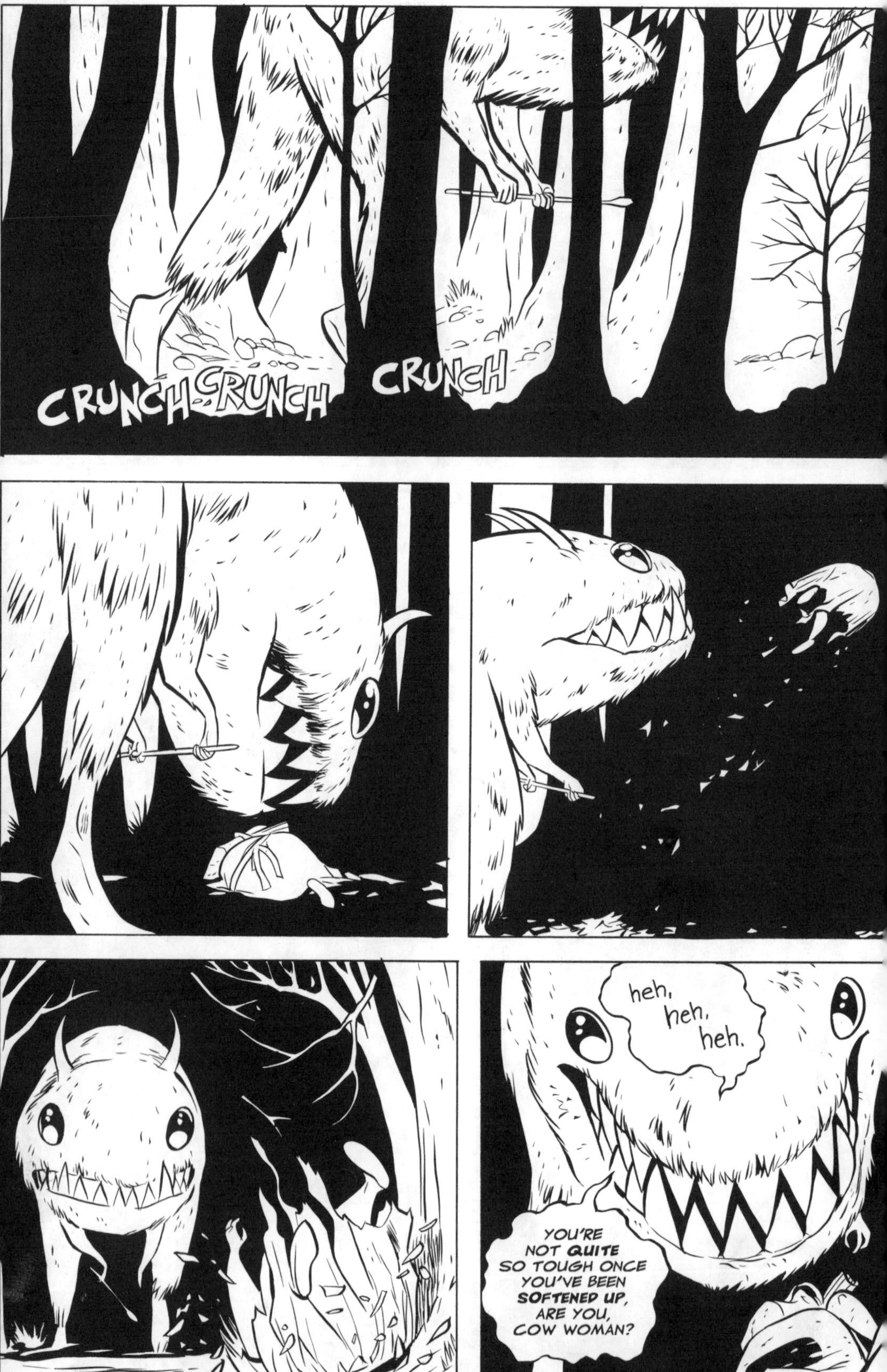

CRUNCH-CRUNCH
CRUNCH
heh, heh, heh.
YOU'RE NOT QUITE SO TOUGH ONCE YOU'VE BEEN SOFTENED UP, ARE YOU, COW WOMAN?

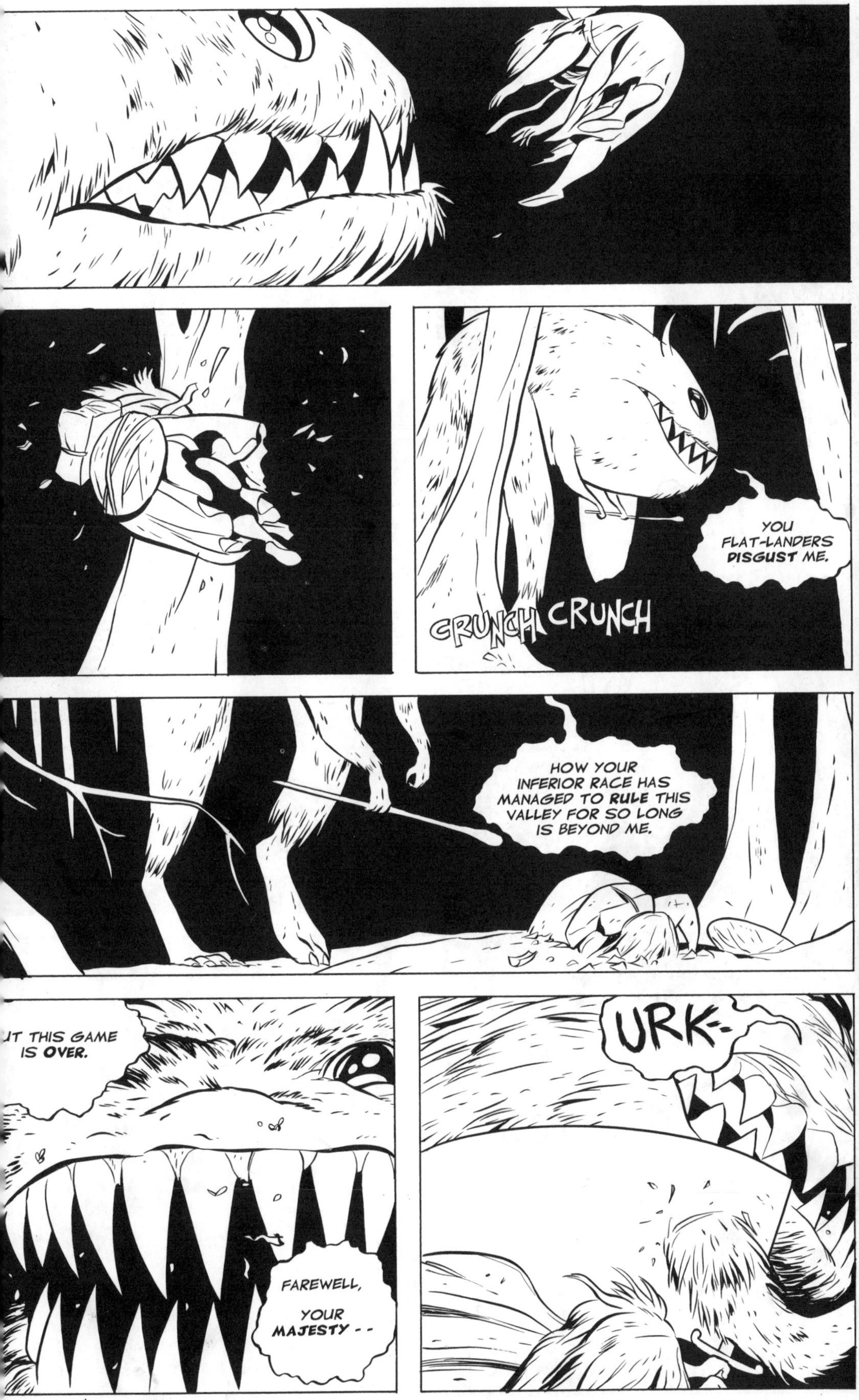

YOU FLAT-LANDERS DISGUST ME.
CRUNCH CRUNCH
HOW YOUR INFERIOR RACE HAS MANAGED TO RULE THIS VALLEY FOR SO LONG IS BEYOND ME.
UT THIS GAME IS OVER.
FAREWELL, YOUR MAJESTY - -
URK-

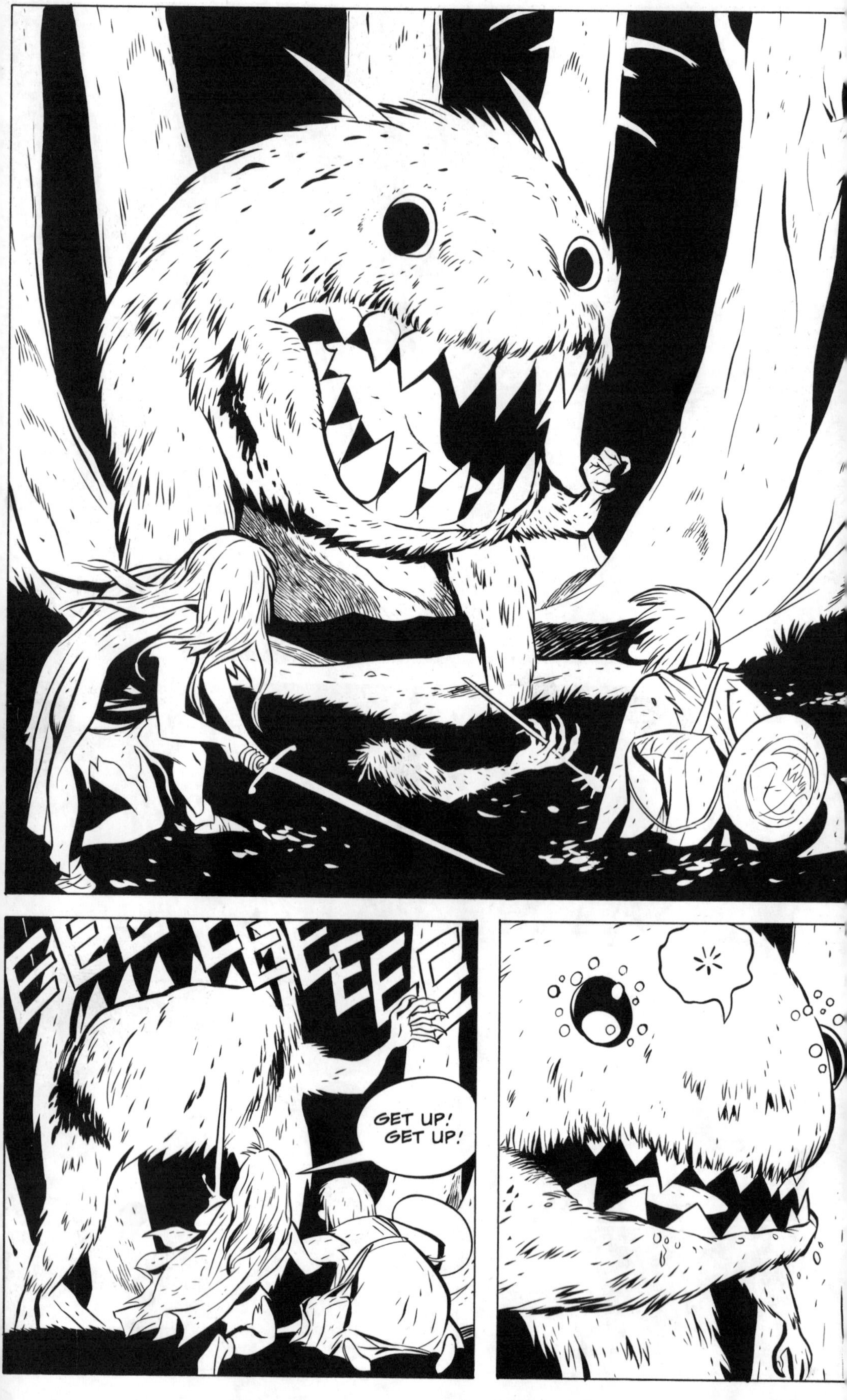
EEE EEEEEEE
GET UP! GET UP!
*!

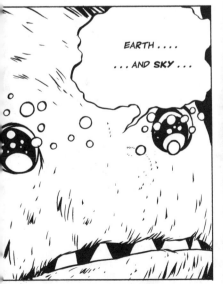

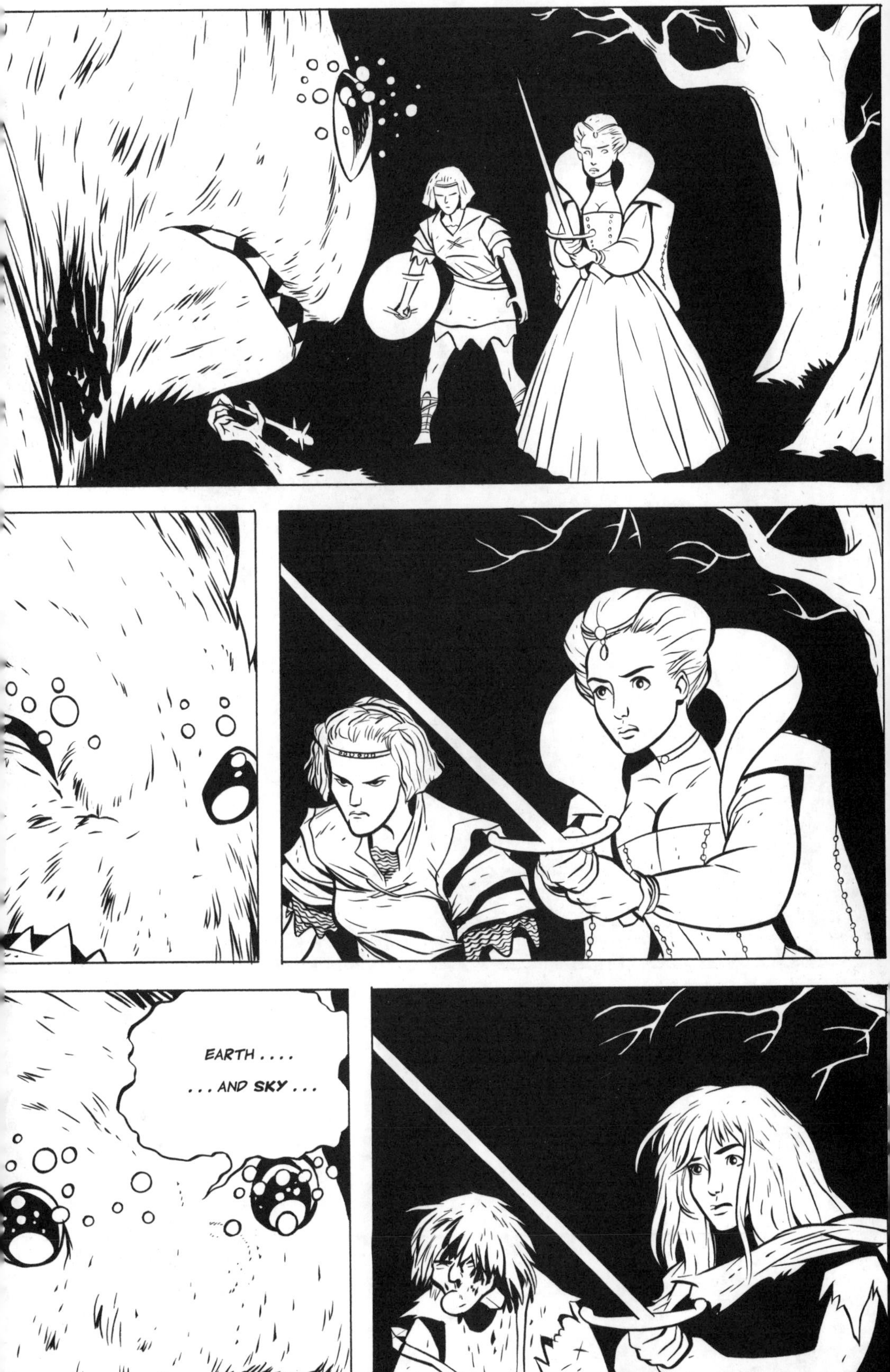
EARTH ....
... AND SKY ...

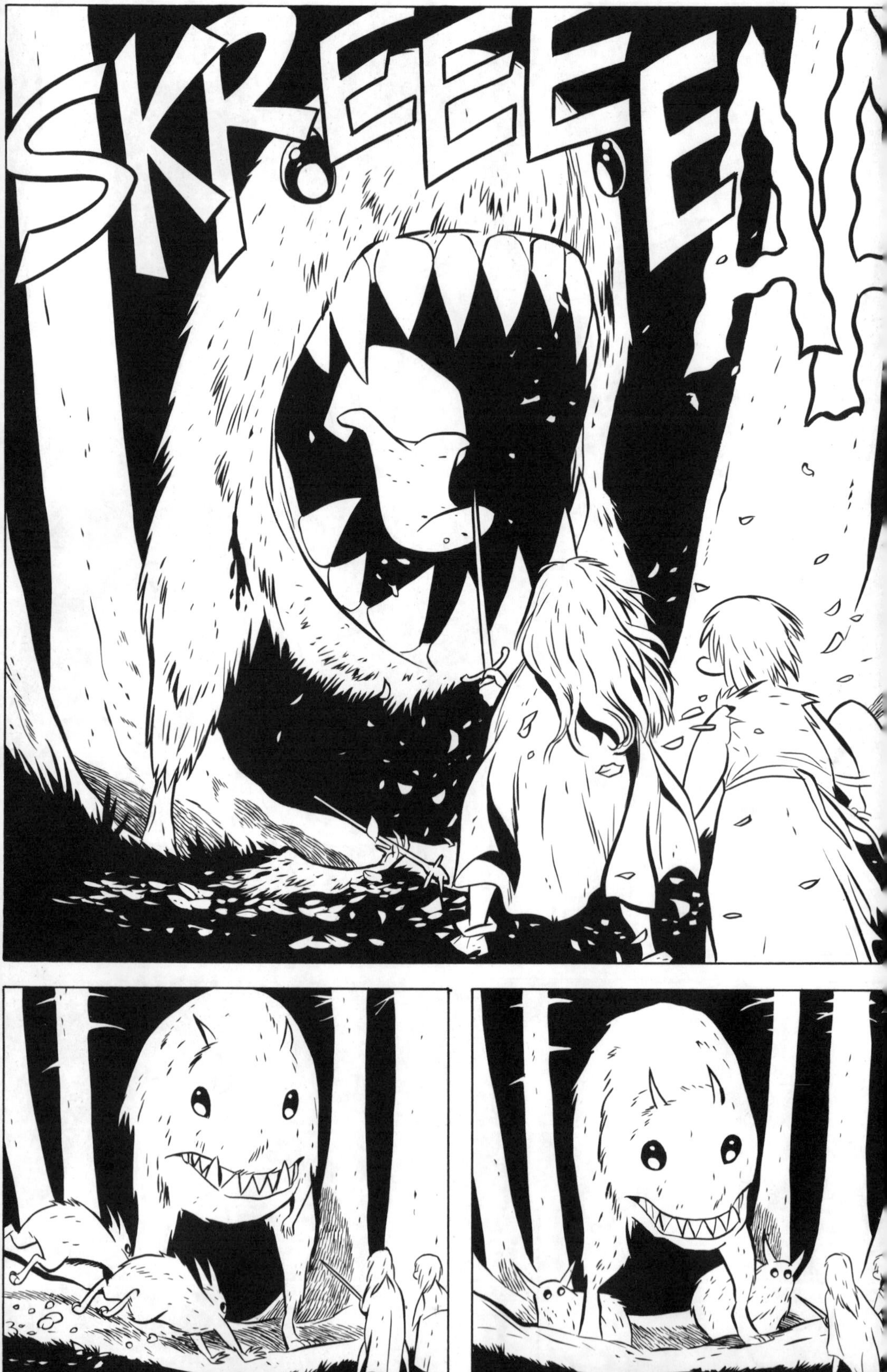
SKREEEEA

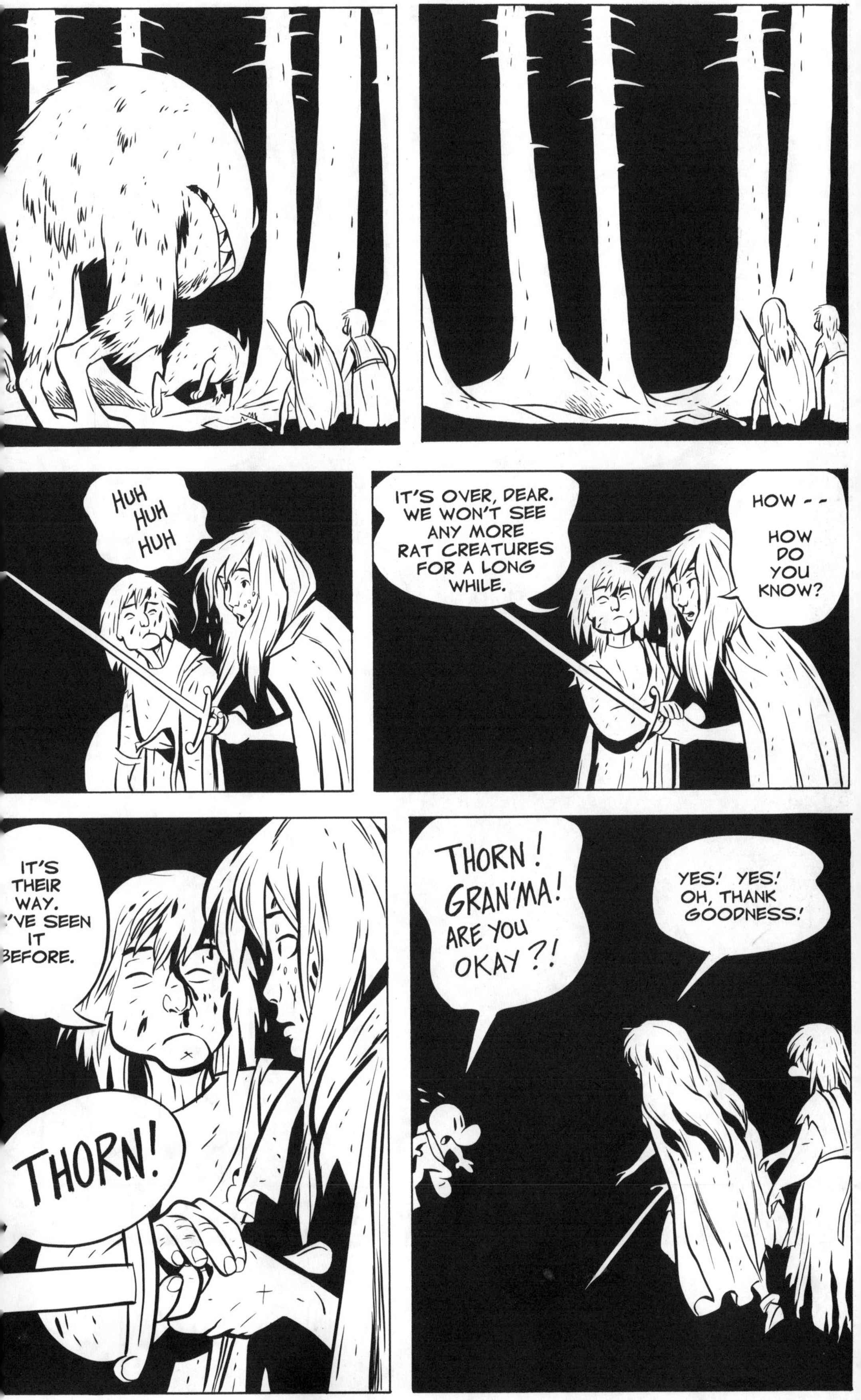
HUH HUH HUH
IT'S OVER, DEAR. WE WON'T SEE ANY MORE RAT CREATURES FOR A LONG WHILE.
HOW - - HOW DO YOU KNOW?
IT'S THEIR WAY. I'VE SEEN IT BEFORE.
THORN!
THORN! GRAN'MA! ARE YOU OKAY?!
YES! YES! OH, THANK GOODNESS!

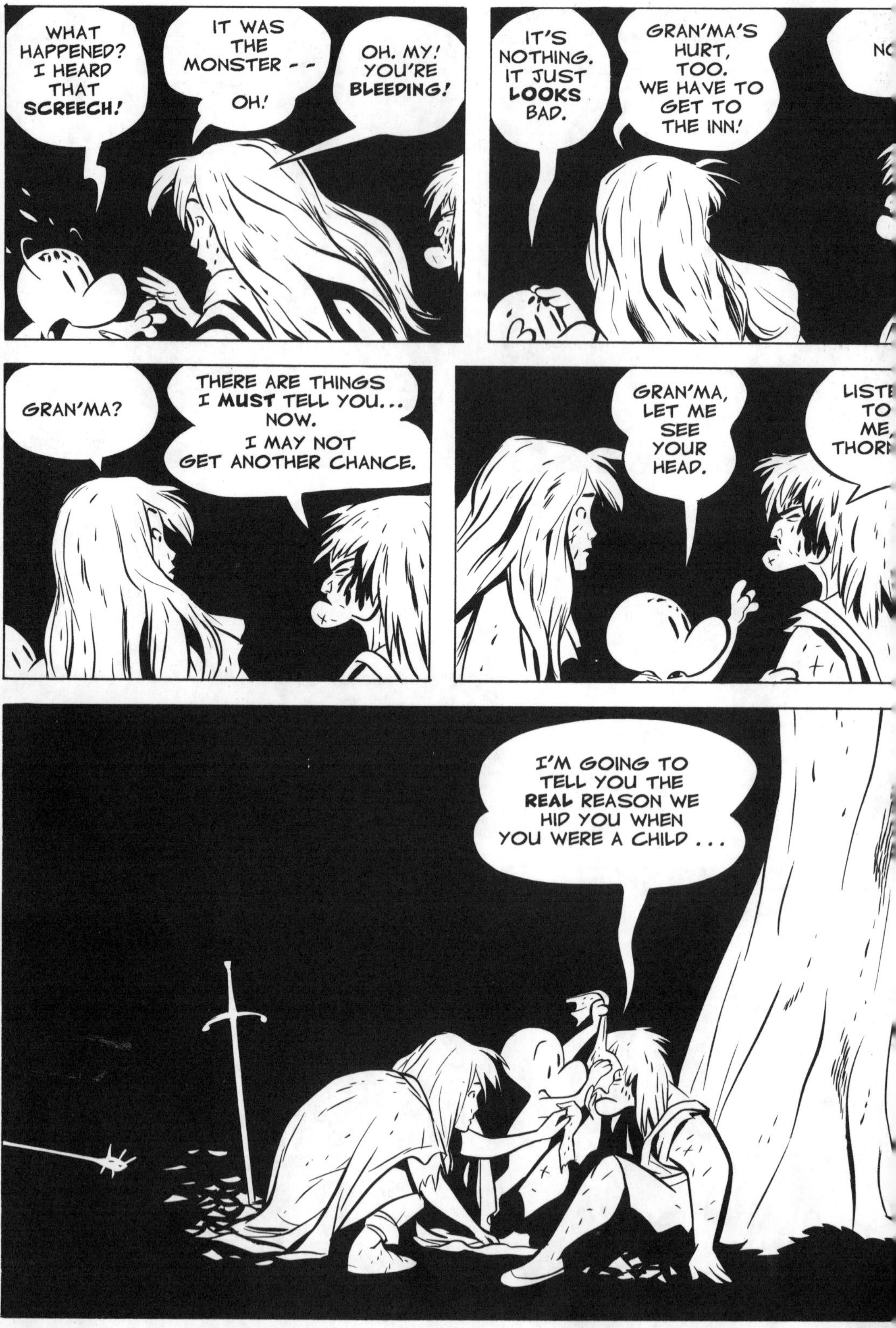
WHAT HAPPENED? I HEARD THAT SCREECH!
IT WAS THE MONSTER - - OH!
OH. MY! YOU'RE BLEEDING!
IT'S NOTHING. IT JUST LOOKS BAD.
GRAN'MA'S HURT, TOO. WE HAVE TO GET TO THE INN!
GRAN'MA?
THERE ARE THINGS I MUST TELL YOU... NOW. I MAY NOT GET ANOTHER CHANCE.
GRAN'MA, LET ME SEE YOUR HEAD.
I'M GOING TO TELL YOU THE REAL REASON WE HID YOU WHEN YOU WERE A CHILD . . .
NEXT: COUNCIL IN THE DARK

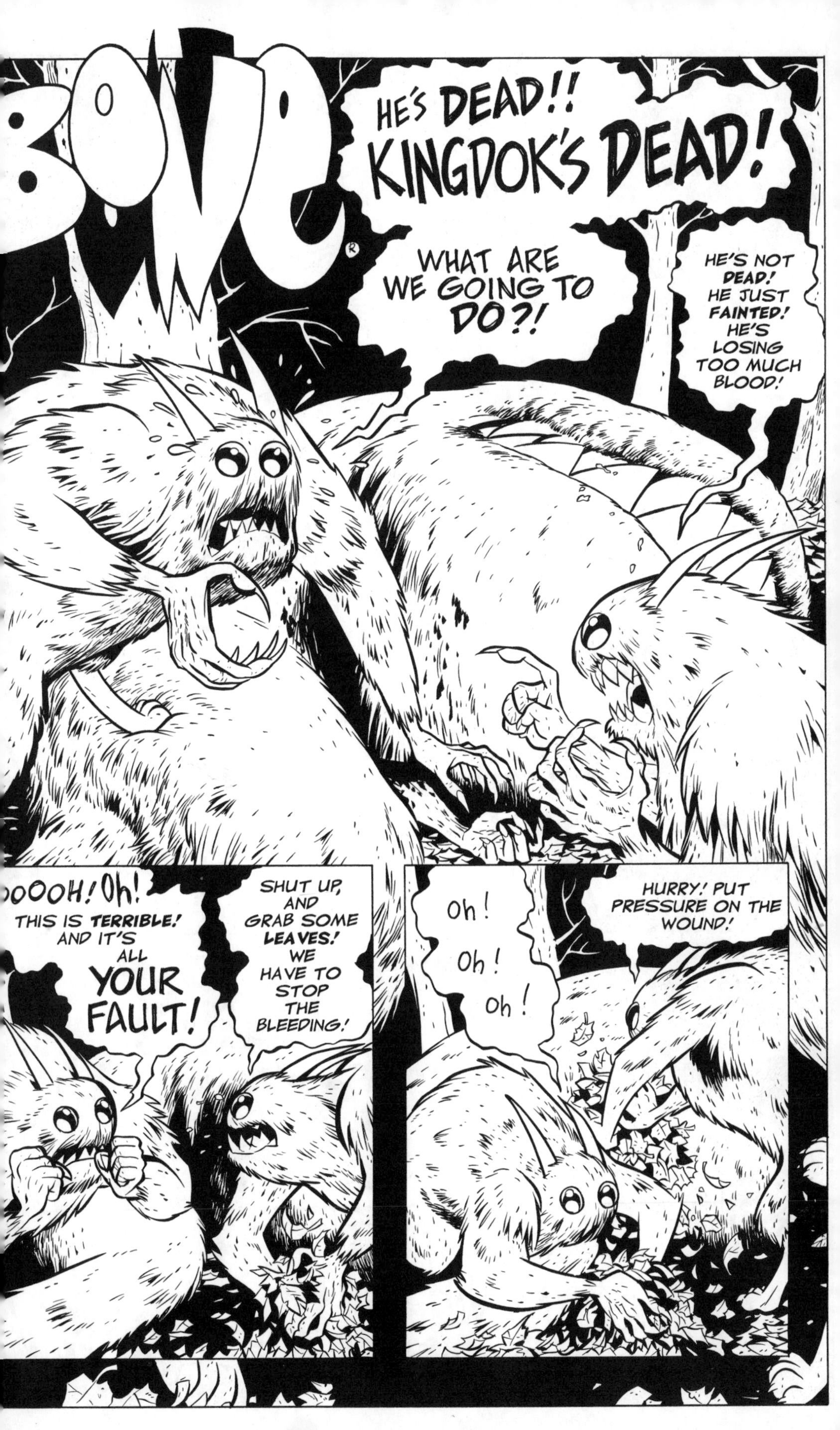
BONE®
HE'S DEAD!! KINGDOK'S DEAD!
WHAT ARE WE GOING TO DO?!
HE'S NOT DEAD! HE JUST FAINTED! HE'S LOSING TOO MUCH BLOOD!
OOOOH! Oh! THIS IS TERRIBLE! AND IT'S ALL YOUR FAULT!
SHUT UP, AND GRAB SOME LEAVES! WE HAVE TO STOP THE BLEEDING!
Oh! Oh! Oh!
HURRY! PUT PRESSURE ON THE WOUND!

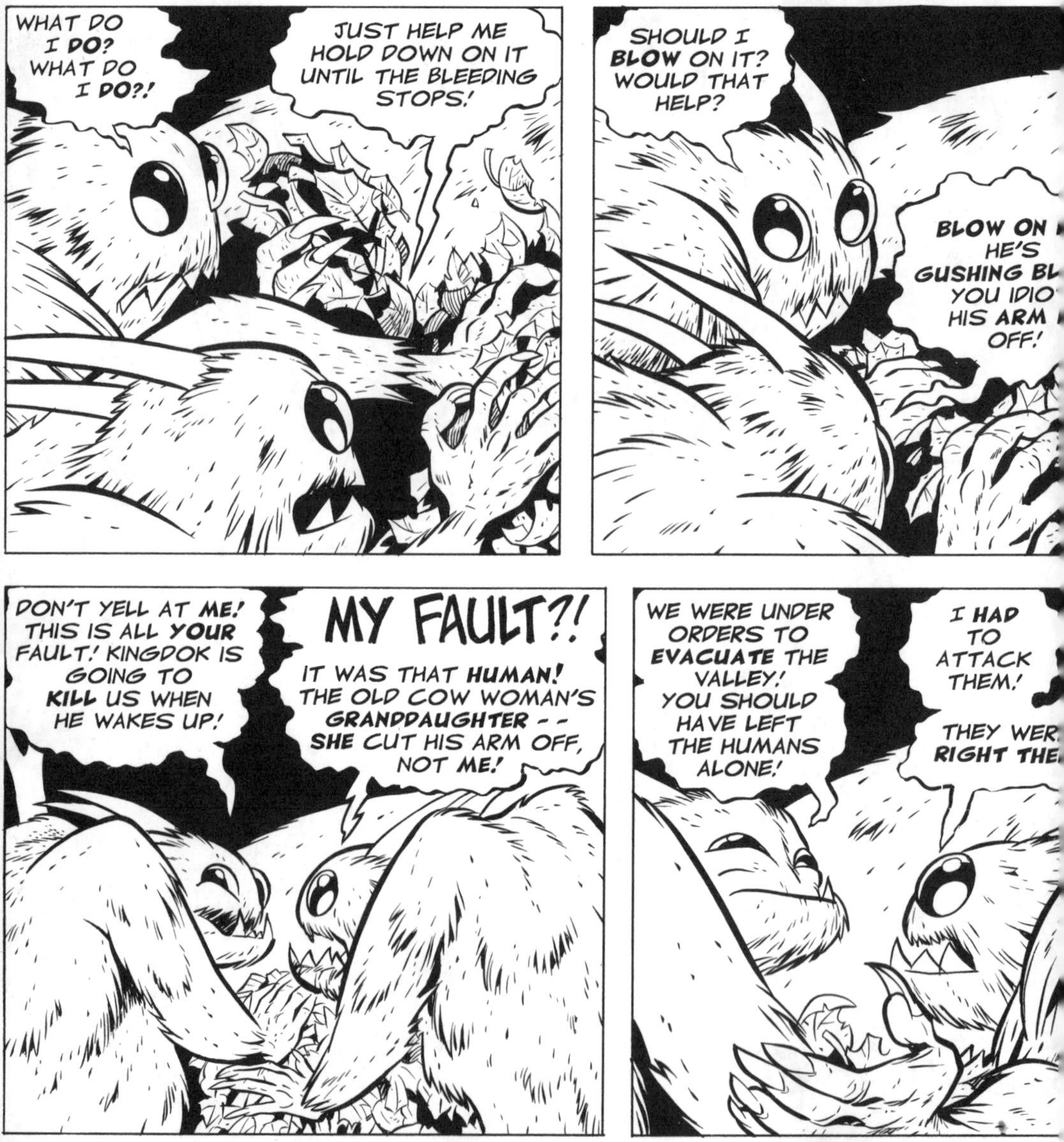

WHAT DO I DO? WHAT DO I DO?!
JUST HELP ME HOLD DOWN ON IT UNTIL THE BLEEDING STOPS!
SHOULD I BLOW ON IT? WOULD THAT HELP?
BLOW ON HE'S GUSHING B YOU IDIO HIS ARM OFF!
DON'T YELL AT ME! THIS IS ALL YOUR FAULT! KINGDOK IS GOING TO KILL US WHEN HE WAKES UP!
MY FAULT?!
IT WAS THAT HUMAN! THE OLD COW WOMAN'S GRANDDAUGHTER -- SHE CUT HIS ARM OFF, NOT ME!
WE WERE UNDER ORDERS TO EVACUATE THE VALLEY! YOU SHOULD HAVE LEFT THE HUMANS ALONE!
I HAD TO ATTACK THEM!
THEY WER RIGHT THE
YOU DISOBEYED ORDERS!
I COULDN'T HELP IT! THAT LITTLE BONE GUY WAS WITH THEM!
...MMMM....
SUCCULENT, MARBLED WITH FAT, LITTLE BONE GUY...
SOMEDAY WE'LL CATCH HIM AND STUFF HIM IN A QUICHE!
SEE? YOU WANTED T EAT HIM, T

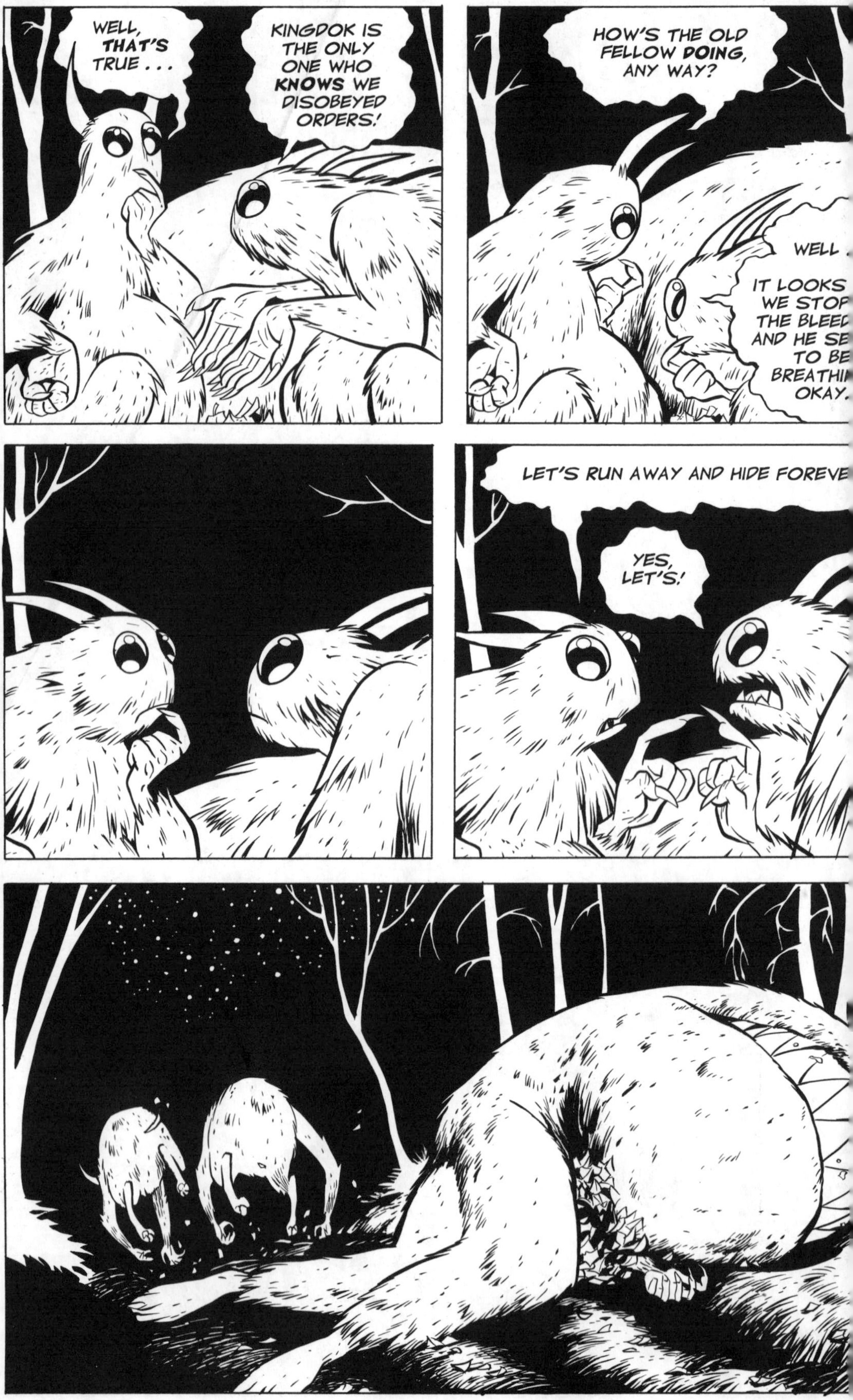
WELL, THAT'S TRUE . . .
KINGDOK IS THE ONLY ONE WHO KNOWS WE DISOBEYED ORDERS!
HOW'S THE OLD FELLOW DOING, ANY WAY?
LET'S RUN AWAY AND HIDE FOREVE
YES, LET'S!

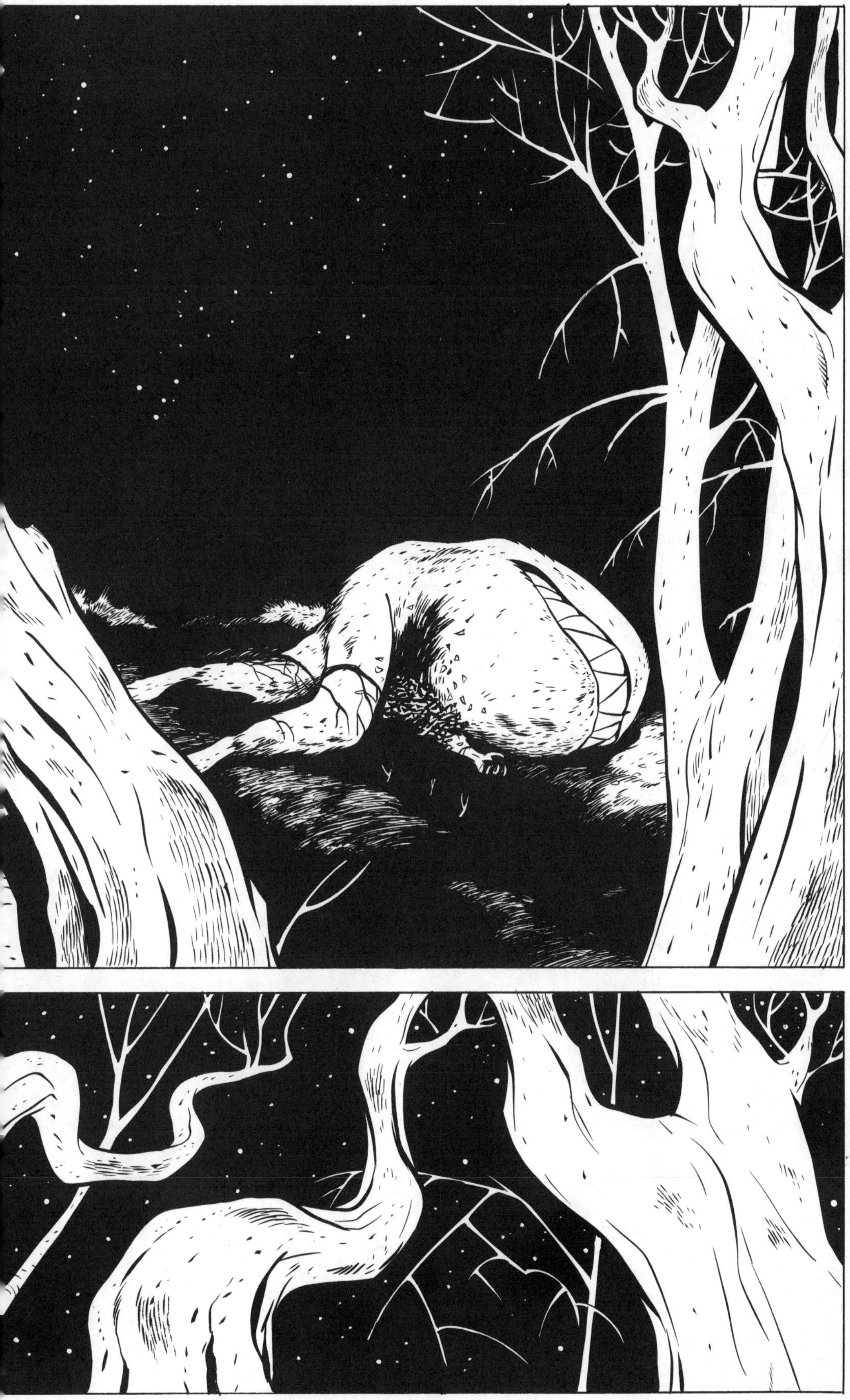

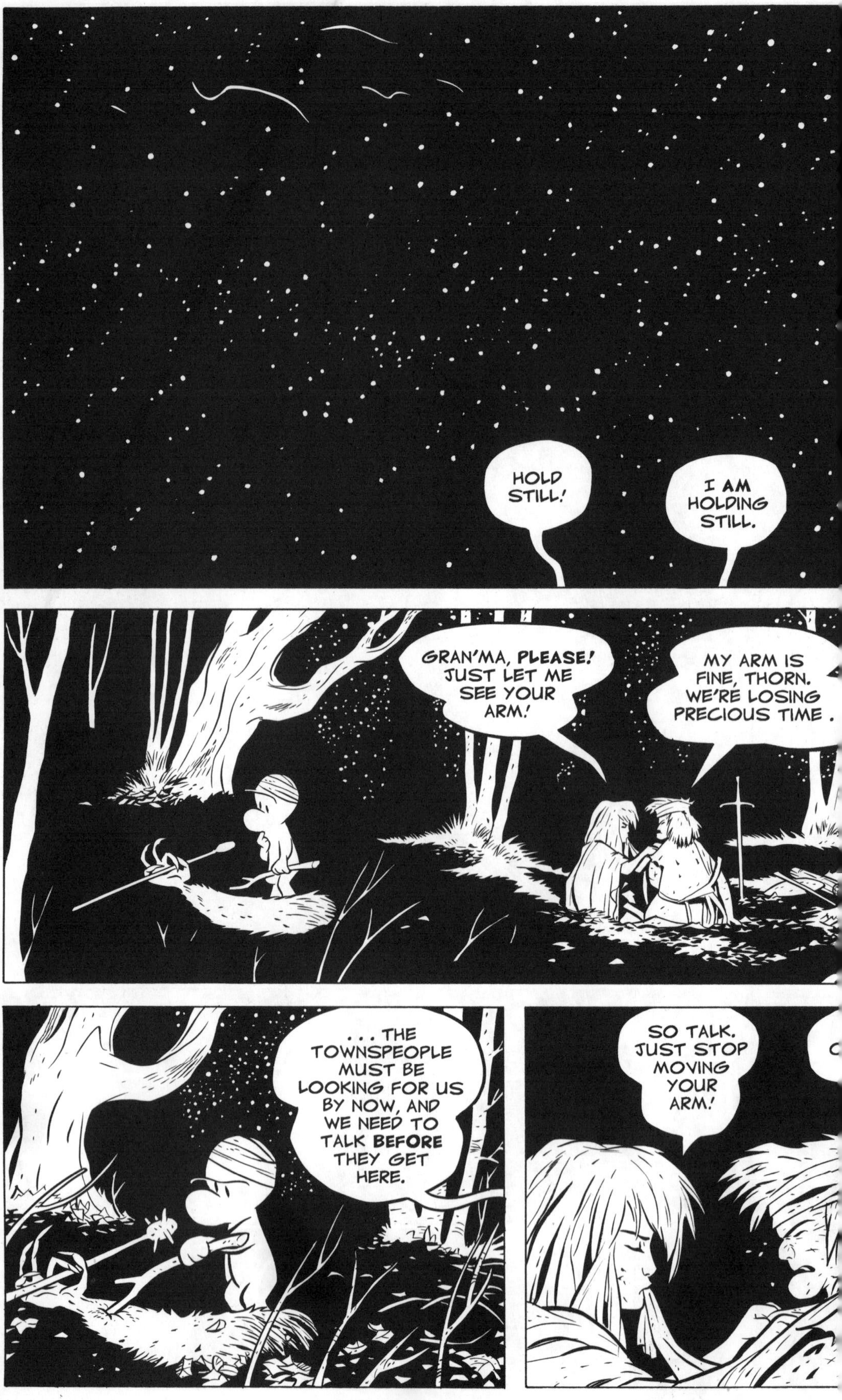
HOLD STILL!
I AM HOLDING STILL.
GRAN'MA, PLEASE! JUST LET ME SEE YOUR ARM!
MY ARM IS FINE, THORN. WE'RE LOSING PRECIOUS TIME . . .
. . . THE TOWNSPEOPLE MUST BE LOOKING FOR US BY NOW, AND WE NEED TO TALK BEFORE THEY GET HERE.
SO TALK. JUST STOP MOVING YOUR ARM!

SEE? YOU ENED UP THAT T AGAIN!

LISTEN TO ME, THORN . . .

EENNH!

TAKE IT EASY, THERE WILL YOU?

WHAT I'M ABOUT TO TELL YOU, DEAR, CONCERNS NOT ONLY **YOU**, BUT **EVERYONE** WHO LIVES IN THE VALLEY. YOU SEE, YOU ARE NOT **LIKE** OTHER PEOPLE . . . YOU ARE VERY **SPECIAL** --

OW!

YES, I KNOW. I'M A **PRINCESS**. YOU ALREADY TOLD ME.

NO.

THAT'S NOT WHAT I'M TALKING ABOUT.

THERE WERE PRINCESSES **BEFORE** YOU, AND THERE WILL BE PRINCESSES **AFTER** YOU -- LIKE GRAINS OF SAND ON THE BEACH, OR **STARS** IN THE SKY . . .

. . . I SHOULD KNOW. I WAS ONE OF THEM.

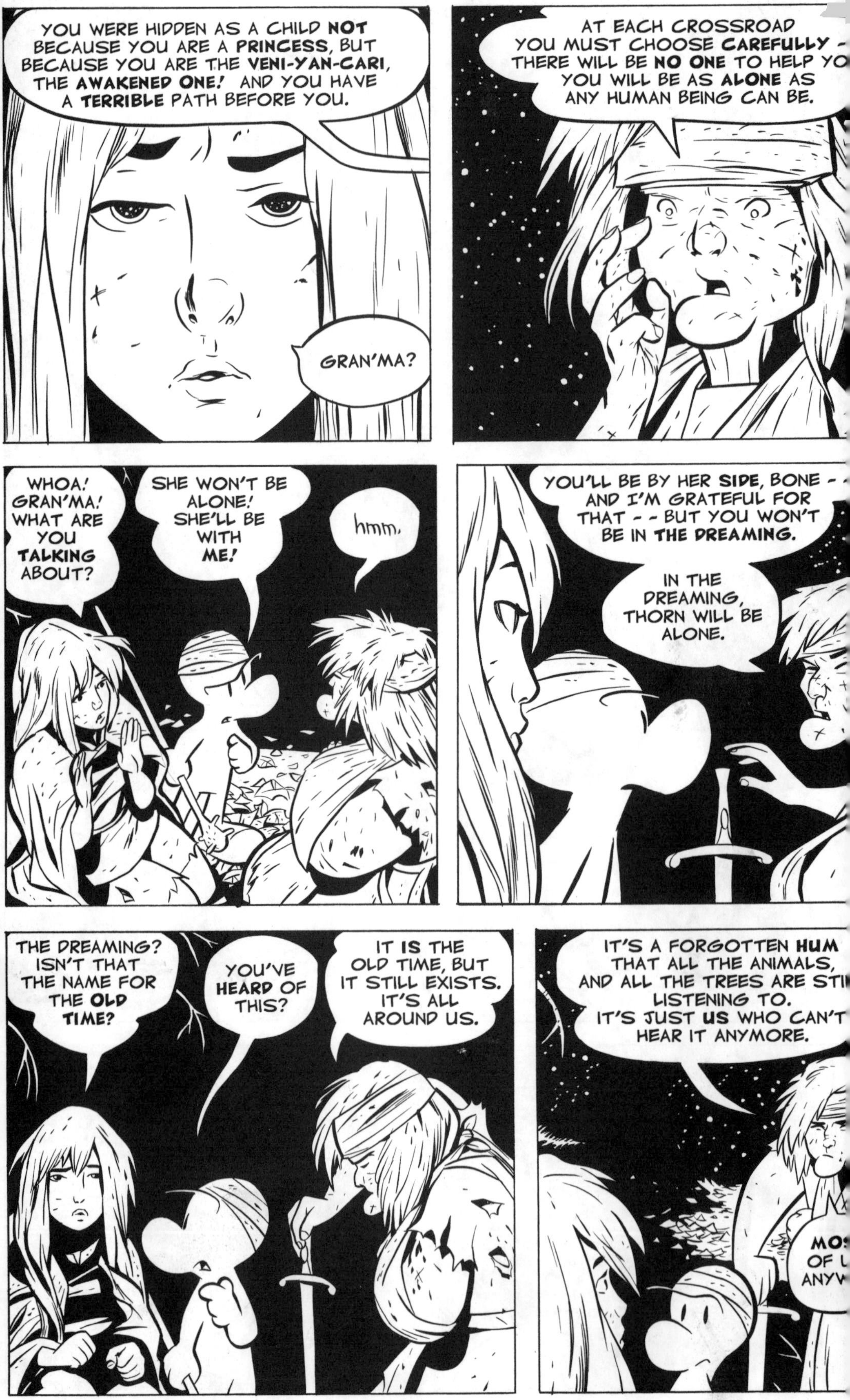
YOU WERE HIDDEN AS A CHILD NOT BECAUSE YOU ARE A PRINCESS, BUT BECAUSE YOU ARE THE VENI-YAN-CARI, THE AWAKENED ONE! AND YOU HAVE A TERRIBLE PATH BEFORE YOU.
GRAN'MA?
AT EACH CROSSROAD YOU MUST CHOOSE CAREFULLY - THERE WILL BE NO ONE TO HELP YO YOU WILL BE AS ALONE AS ANY HUMAN BEING CAN BE.
WHOA! GRAN'MA! WHAT ARE YOU TALKING ABOUT?
SHE WON'T BE ALONE! SHE'LL BE WITH ME!
hmm.
YOU'LL BE BY HER SIDE, BONE - - AND I'M GRATEFUL FOR THAT - - BUT YOU WON'T BE IN THE DREAMING.
IN THE DREAMING, THORN WILL BE ALONE.
THE DREAMING? ISN'T THAT THE NAME FOR THE OLD TIME?
YOU'VE HEARD OF THIS?
IT IS THE OLD TIME, BUT IT STILL EXISTS. IT'S ALL AROUND US.
IT'S A FORGOTTEN HUM THAT ALL THE ANIMALS, AND ALL THE TREES ARE STI LISTENING TO. IT'S JUST US WHO CAN'T HEAR IT ANYMORE.
MOS OF U ANYW

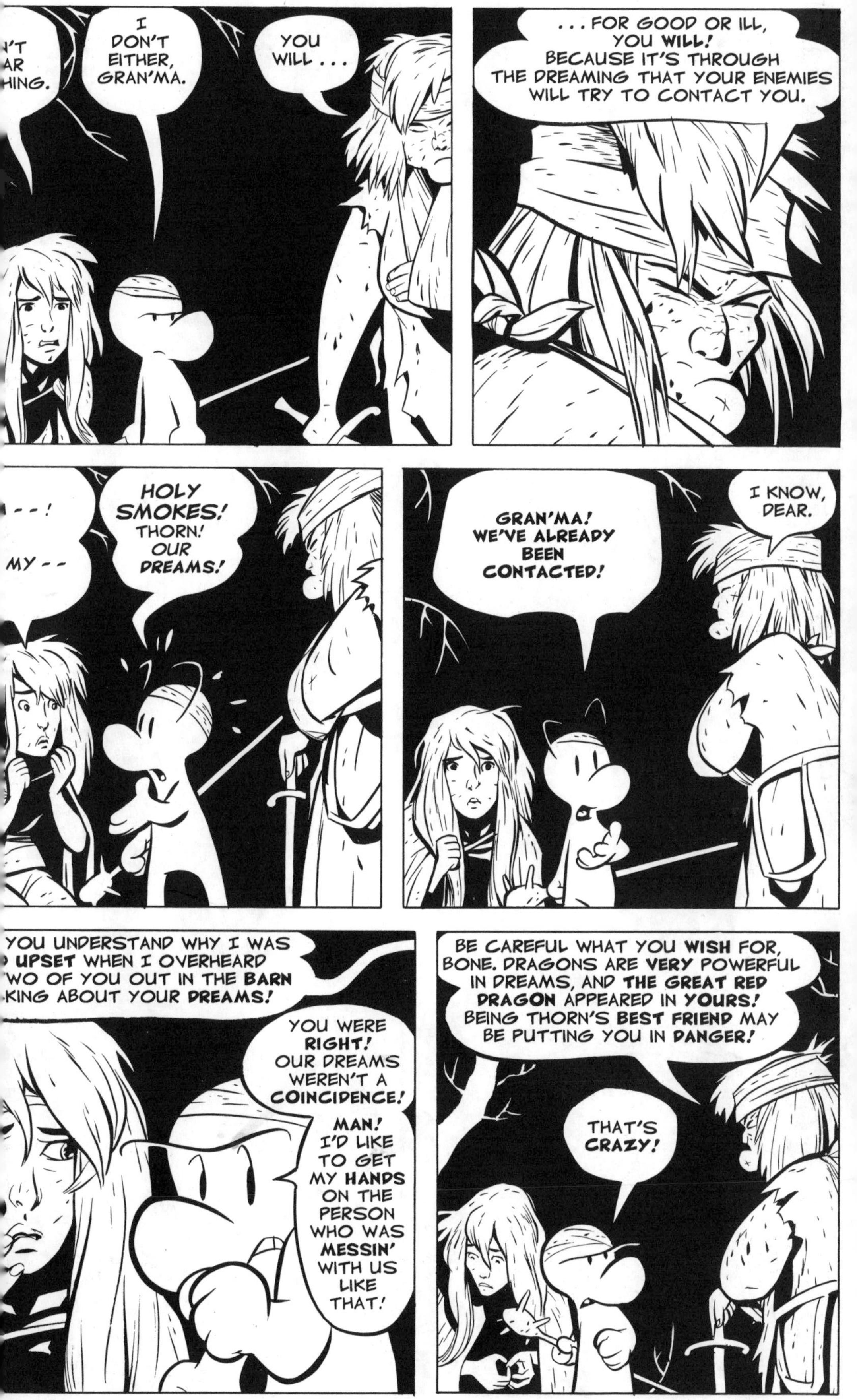
I DON'T EITHER, GRAN'MA.
YOU WILL . . .
. . . FOR GOOD OR ILL, YOU WILL! BECAUSE IT'S THROUGH THE DREAMING THAT YOUR ENEMIES WILL TRY TO CONTACT YOU.
HOLY SMOKES! THORN! OUR DREAMS!
GRAN'MA! WE'VE ALREADY BEEN CONTACTED!
I KNOW, DEAR.
YOU UNDERSTAND WHY I WAS UPSET WHEN I OVERHEARD WO OF YOU OUT IN THE BARN KING ABOUT YOUR DREAMS!
YOU WERE RIGHT! OUR DREAMS WEREN'T A COINCIDENCE!
MAN! I'D LIKE TO GET MY HANDS ON THE PERSON WHO WAS MESSIN' WITH US LIKE THAT!
BE CAREFUL WHAT YOU WISH FOR, BONE. DRAGONS ARE VERY POWERFUL IN DREAMS, AND THE GREAT RED DRAGON APPEARED IN YOURS! BEING THORN'S BEST FRIEND MAY BE PUTTING YOU IN DANGER!
THAT'S CRAZY!

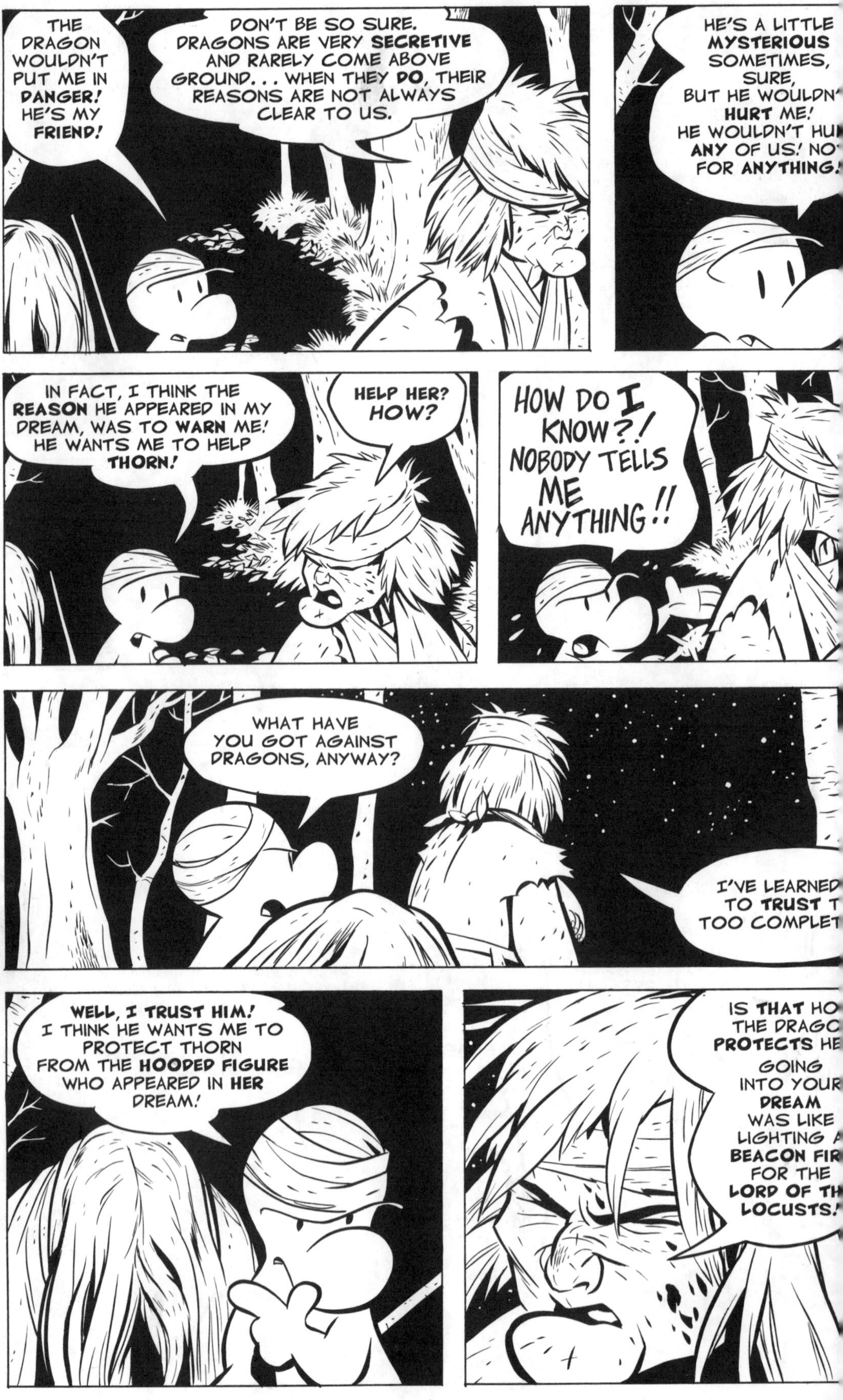
THE DRAGON WOULDN'T PUT ME IN DANGER! HE'S MY FRIEND!
DON'T BE SO SURE. DRAGONS ARE VERY SECRETIVE AND RARELY COME ABOVE GROUND. . . WHEN THEY DO, THEIR REASONS ARE NOT ALWAYS CLEAR TO US.
HE'S A LITTLE MYSTERIOUS SOMETIMES, SURE, BUT HE WOULDN' HURT ME! HE WOULDN'T HU ANY OF US! NO FOR ANYTHING!
IN FACT, I THINK THE REASON HE APPEARED IN MY DREAM, WAS TO WARN ME! HE WANTS ME TO HELP THORN!
HELP HER? HOW?
HOW DO I KNOW?! NOBODY TELLS ME ANYTHING!!
WHAT HAVE YOU GOT AGAINST DRAGONS, ANYWAY?
I'VE LEARNED TO TRUST T TOO COMPLET
WELL, I TRUST HIM! I THINK HE WANTS ME TO PROTECT THORN FROM THE HOODED FIGURE WHO APPEARED IN HER DREAM!
IS THAT HO THE DRAGO PROTECTS HE GOING INTO YOUR DREAM WAS LIKE LIGHTING A BEACON FIR FOR THE LORD OF TH LOCUSTS!

WHY?

ACCORDING TO THEIR BELIEFS, A **VISITATION** CAN ONLY BE ACCOMPLISHED IN **TWO WAYS.**

ONE IS WITH THE HELP OF THE DRAGONS -- WHICH IS **FORBIDDEN** BY THE **TREATY** --

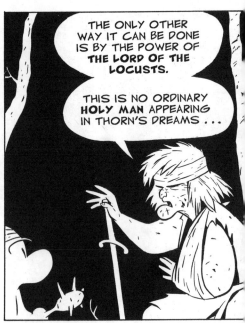

THE ONLY OTHER WAY IT CAN BE DONE IS BY THE POWER OF **THE LORD OF THE LOCUSTS.**

THIS IS NO ORDINARY **HOLY MAN** APPEARING IN THORN'S DREAMS . . .

WHOEVER THIS HOODED PERSON IS . . . IF HE IS USING THE **POWER** OF THE LORD OF THE LOCUSTS . . . THEN HE MAY VERY WELL **BECOME** THE LOCUST KING ON EARTH.

WHOA.

THAT DOESN'T SOUND GOOD.

I'VE KNOWN FOR A **LONG T** THAT THE RAT CREATURES A NEW LEADER -- BUT I NE **IMAGINED** THAT HE WAS POSSESED BY THE SPIRIT THE ANCIENT LORD **HIMSELF.**

AND NOW HE IS GATHERING AN **ARMY!** THAT IS WHY WE HAVE TO GO **SOUTH!** WE MUST GET THORN AS **FAR** AWAY FROM THE **EASTERN MOUNTAINS** AS POSSIBLE!

OUR ONLY HOPE NOW IS TO GET HER INTO THE HANDS OF THE PEOPLE OF **ATHEIA** --

I'
NO
GO
ANYW

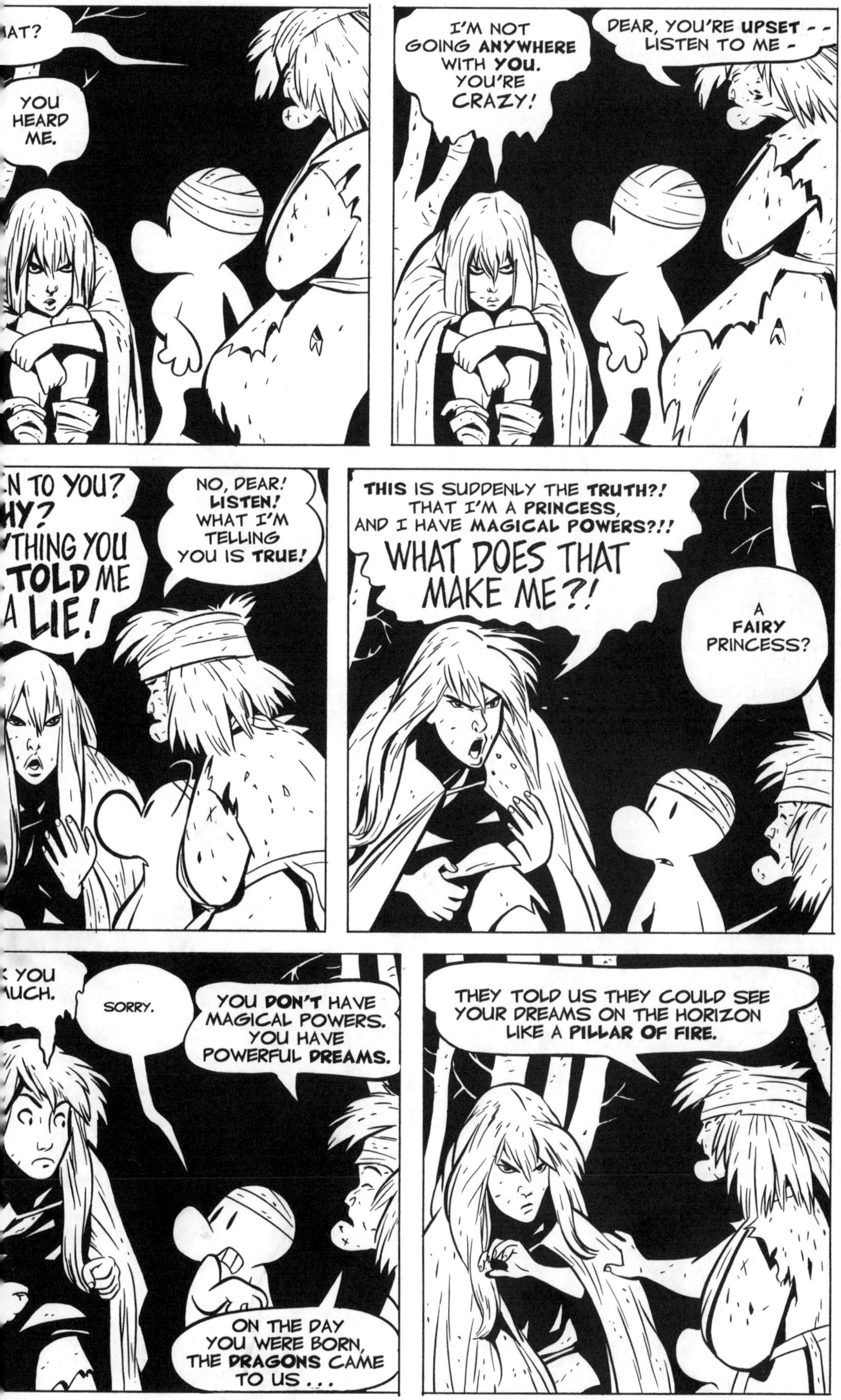

AT?
YOU HEARD ME.
I'M NOT GOING ANYWHERE WITH YOU. YOU'RE CRAZY!
DEAR, YOU'RE UPSET - - LISTEN TO ME -
N TO YOU? HY? THING YOU TOLD ME A LIE!
NO, DEAR! LISTEN! WHAT I'M TELLING YOU IS TRUE!
THIS IS SUDDENLY THE TRUTH?! THAT I'M A PRINCESS, AND I HAVE MAGICAL POWERS?!!
WHAT DOES THAT MAKE ME?!
A FAIRY PRINCESS?
YOU UCH.
SORRY.
YOU DON'T HAVE MAGICAL POWERS. YOU HAVE POWERFUL DREAMS.
ON THE DAY YOU WERE BORN, THE DRAGONS CAME TO US . . .
THEY TOLD US THEY COULD SEE YOUR DREAMS ON THE HORIZON LIKE A PILLAR OF FIRE.

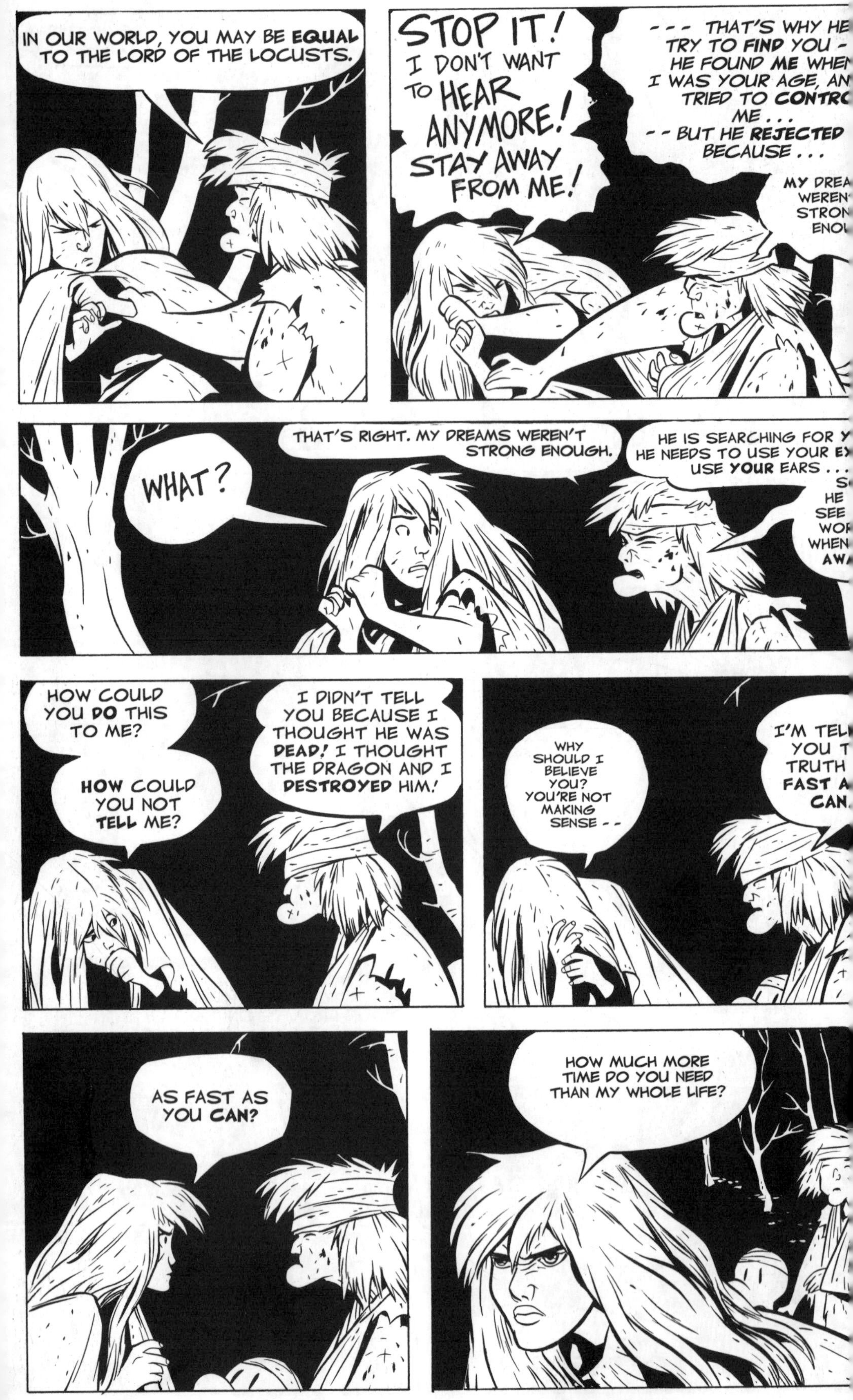
IN OUR WORLD, YOU MAY BE EQUAL TO THE LORD OF THE LOCUSTS.
STOP IT! I DON'T WANT TO HEAR ANYMORE! STAY AWAY FROM ME!
--- THAT'S WHY HE TRY TO FIND YOU - HE FOUND ME WHEN I WAS YOUR AGE, AN TRIED TO CONTR ME... -- BUT HE REJECTED BECAUSE...
MY DREA WEREN STRON ENOU
WHAT?
THAT'S RIGHT. MY DREAMS WEREN'T STRONG ENOUGH.
HE IS SEARCHING FOR Y HE NEEDS TO USE YOUR E USE YOUR EARS ...
HOW COULD YOU DO THIS TO ME?
HOW COULD YOU NOT TELL ME?
I DIDN'T TELL YOU BECAUSE I THOUGHT HE WAS DEAD! I THOUGHT THE DRAGON AND I DESTROYED HIM!
WHY SHOULD I BELIEVE YOU? YOU'RE NOT MAKING SENSE --
I'M TEL YOU T TRUTH FAST A CAN.
AS FAST AS YOU CAN?
HOW MUCH MORE TIME DO YOU NEED THAN MY WHOLE LIFE?

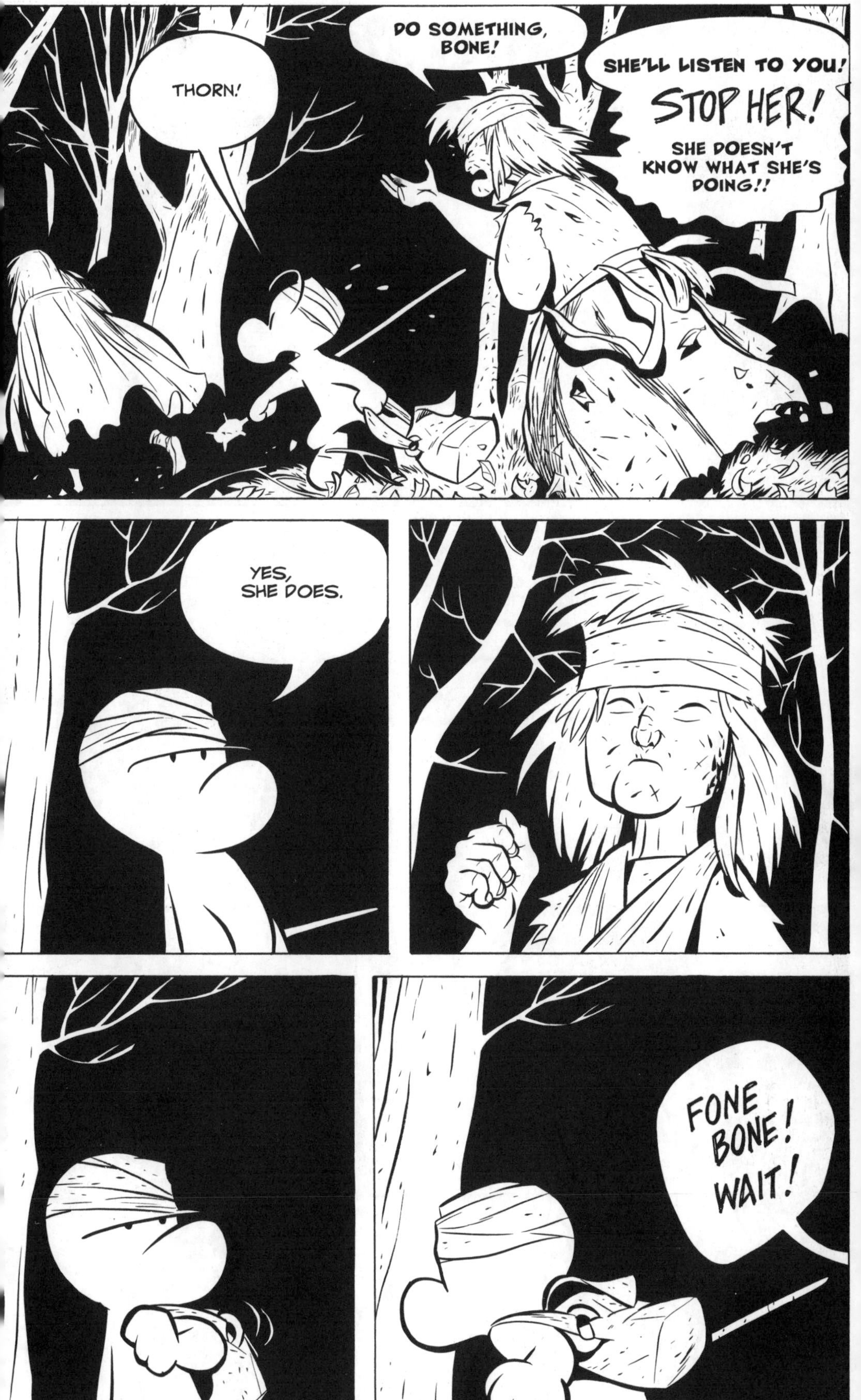

THORN!
DO SOMETHING, BONE!
SHE'LL LISTEN TO YOU! STOP HER! SHE DOESN'T KNOW WHAT SHE'S DOING!!
YES, SHE DOES.
FONE BONE! WAIT!

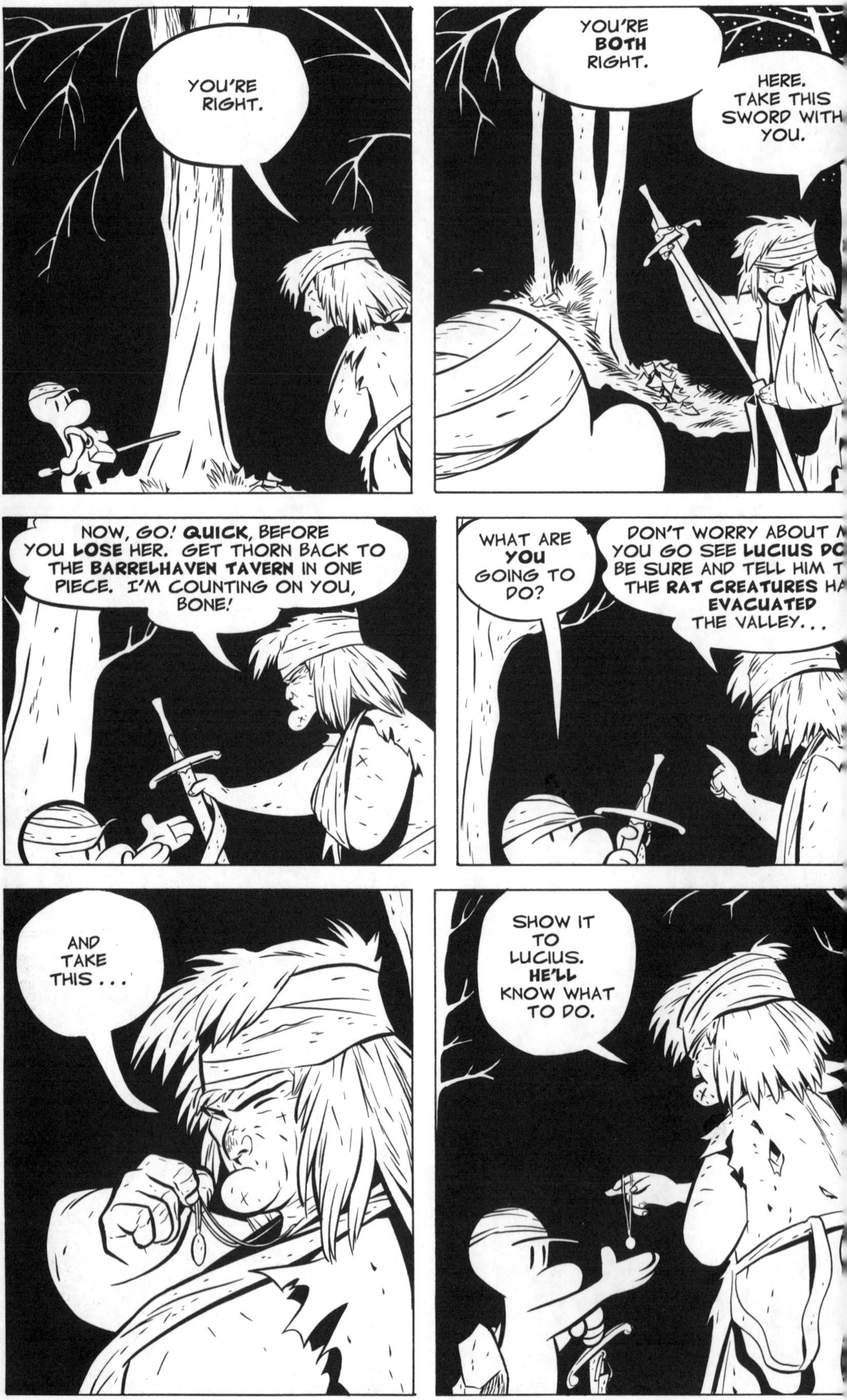

YOU'RE RIGHT.
YOU'RE BOTH RIGHT.
HERE. TAKE THIS SWORD WITH YOU.
NOW, GO! QUICK, BEFORE YOU LOSE HER. GET THORN BACK TO THE BARRELHAVEN TAVERN IN ONE PIECE. I'M COUNTING ON YOU, BONE!
WHAT ARE YOU GOING TO DO?
DON'T WORRY ABOUT M YOU GO SEE LUCIUS DO BE SURE AND TELL HIM T THE RAT CREATURES HA EVACUATED THE VALLEY...
AND TAKE THIS...
SHOW IT TO LUCIUS. HE'LL KNOW WHAT TO DO.

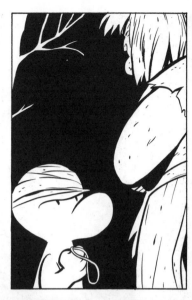

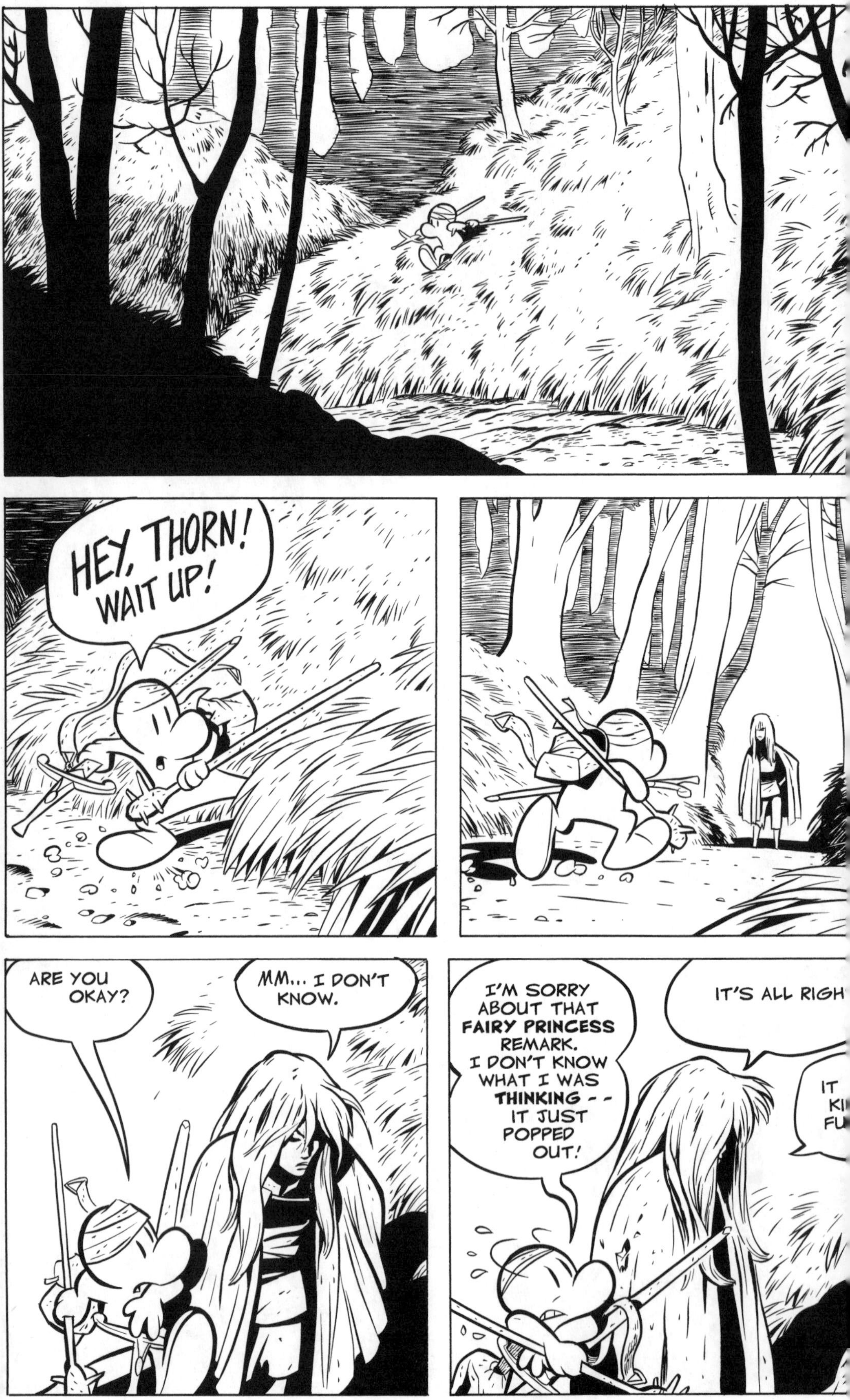
HEY, THORN! WAIT UP!
ARE YOU OKAY?
MM... I DON'T KNOW.
I'M SORRY ABOUT THAT **FAIRY PRINCESS** REMARK. I DON'T KNOW WHAT I WAS **THINKING** -- IT JUST POPPED OUT!
IT'S ALL RIGH

I'LL TELL YOU WHAT YOU CAN DO - -
JONATHAN. WHO GAVE YOU THESE ORDERS?
UM . . . THE NEW BOSS DID!
WHO'S THE NEW BOSS?
HE IS!
NEXT: THE ORPHAN

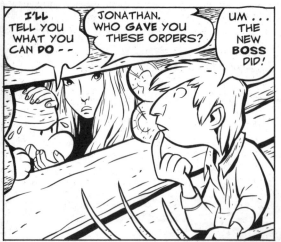

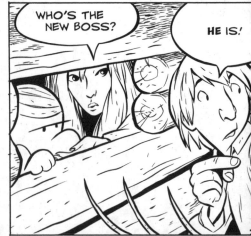

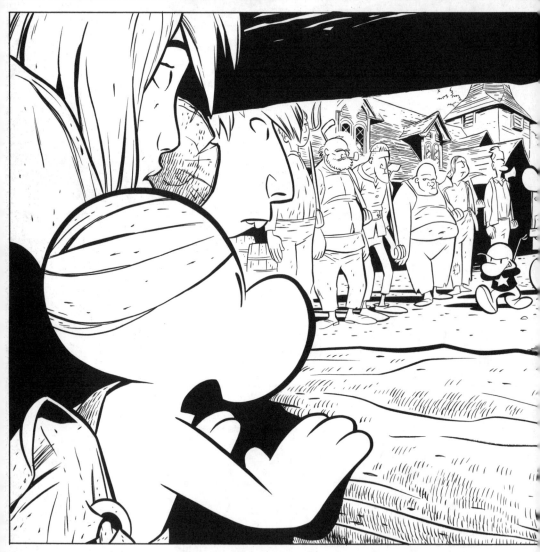

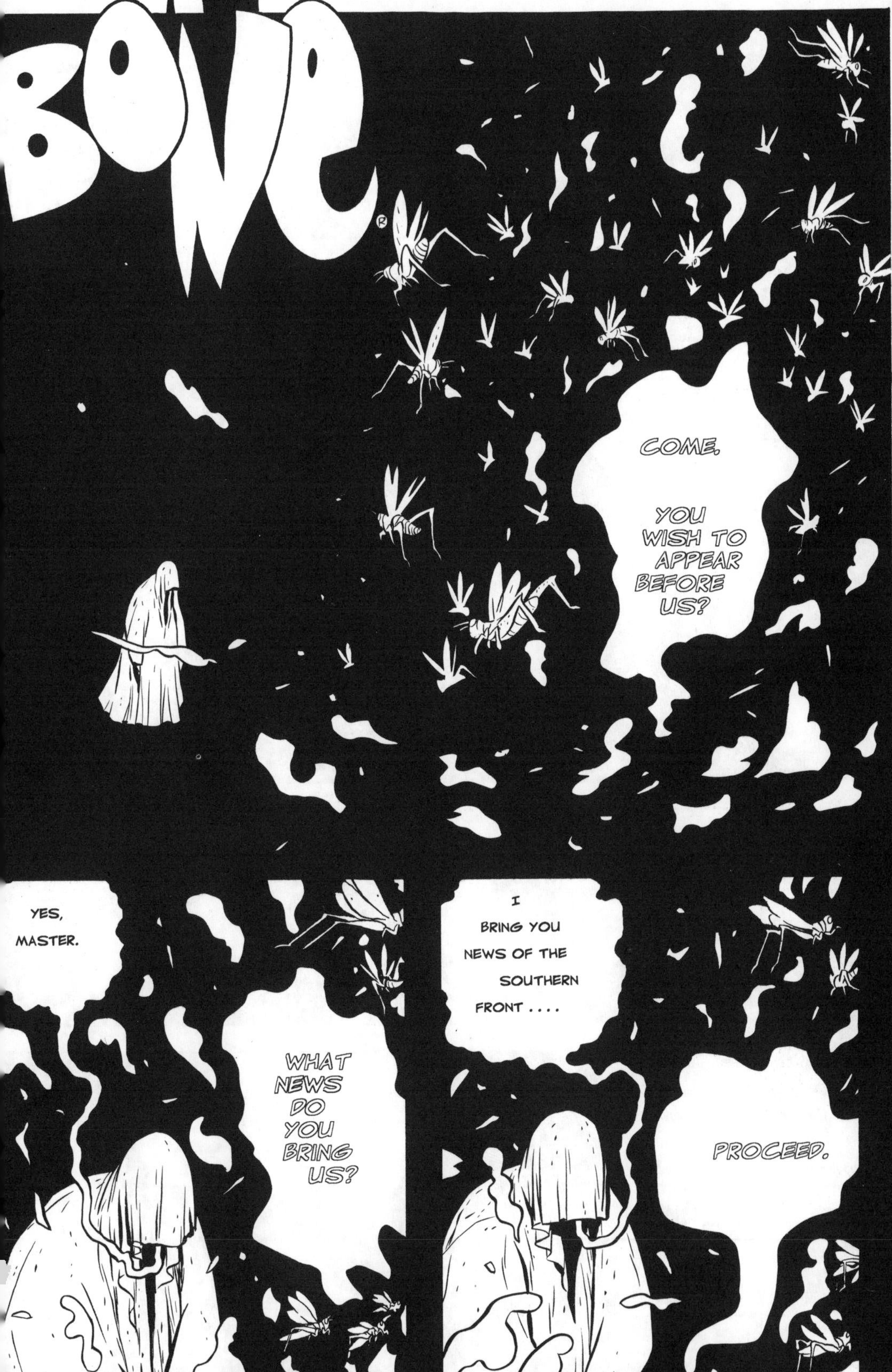
BONE®
COME.
YOU WISH TO APPEAR BEFORE US?
YES, MASTER.
WHAT NEWS DO YOU BRING US?
I BRING YOU NEWS OF THE SOUTHERN FRONT ....
PROCEED.

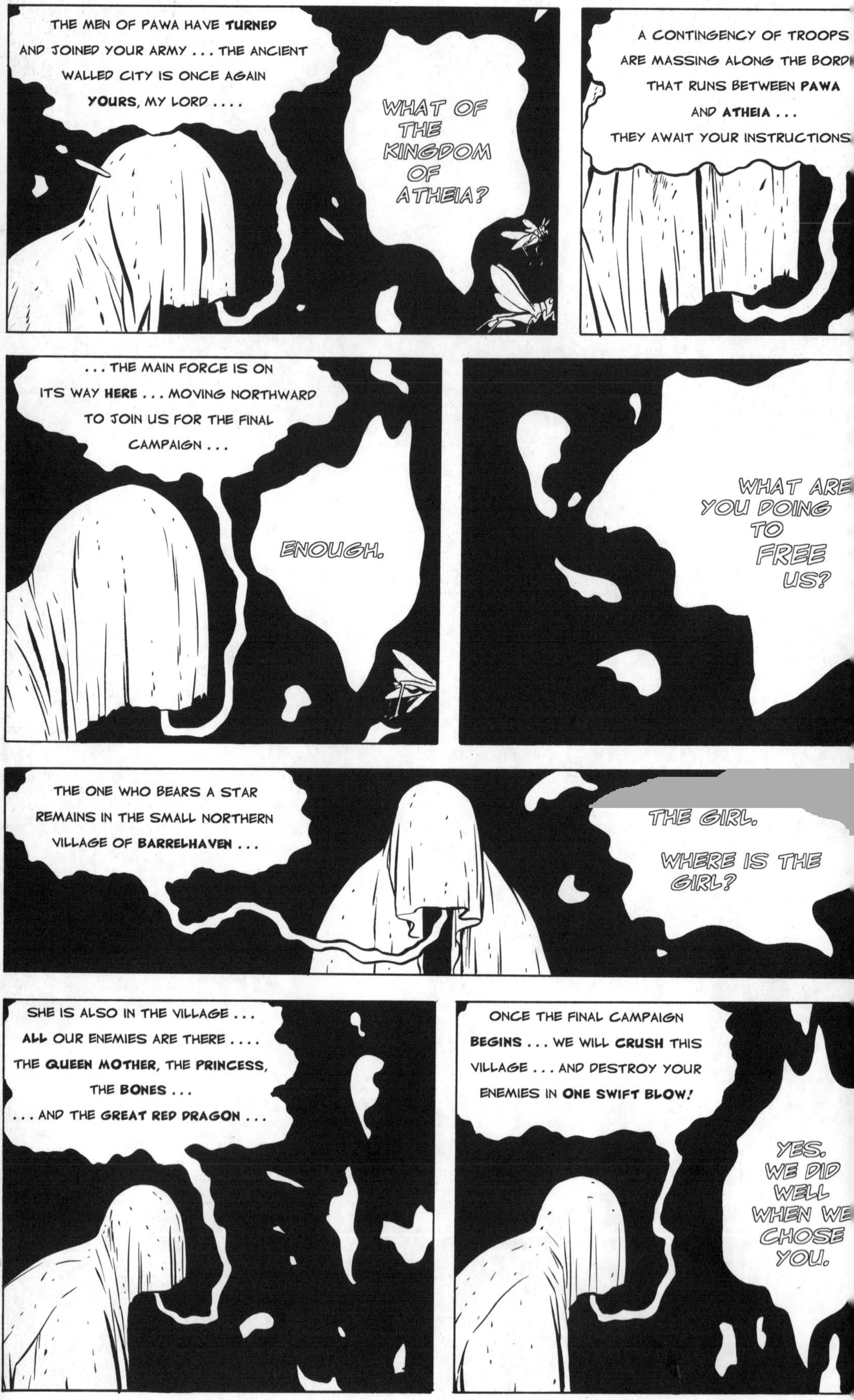
THE MEN OF PAWA HAVE TURNED AND JOINED YOUR ARMY . . . THE ANCIENT WALLED CITY IS ONCE AGAIN YOURS, MY LORD . . . .
WHAT OF THE KINGDOM OF ATHEIA?
A CONTINGENCY OF TROOPS ARE MASSING ALONG THE BORD THAT RUNS BETWEEN PAWA AND ATHEIA . . . THEY AWAIT YOUR INSTRUCTIONS
. . . THE MAIN FORCE IS ON ITS WAY HERE . . . MOVING NORTHWARD TO JOIN US FOR THE FINAL CAMPAIGN . . .
ENOUGH.
WHAT ARE YOU DOING TO FREE US?
THE ONE WHO BEARS A STAR REMAINS IN THE SMALL NORTHERN VILLAGE OF BARRELHAVEN . . .
THE GIRL.
WHERE IS THE GIRL?
SHE IS ALSO IN THE VILLAGE . . . ALL OUR ENEMIES ARE THERE . . . . THE QUEEN MOTHER, THE PRINCESS, THE BONES . . . . . . AND THE GREAT RED DRAGON . . .
ONCE THE FINAL CAMPAIGN BEGINS . . . WE WILL CRUSH THIS VILLAGE . . . AND DESTROY YOUR ENEMIES IN ONE SWIFT BLOW!
YES. WE DID WELL WHEN WE CHOSE YOU.

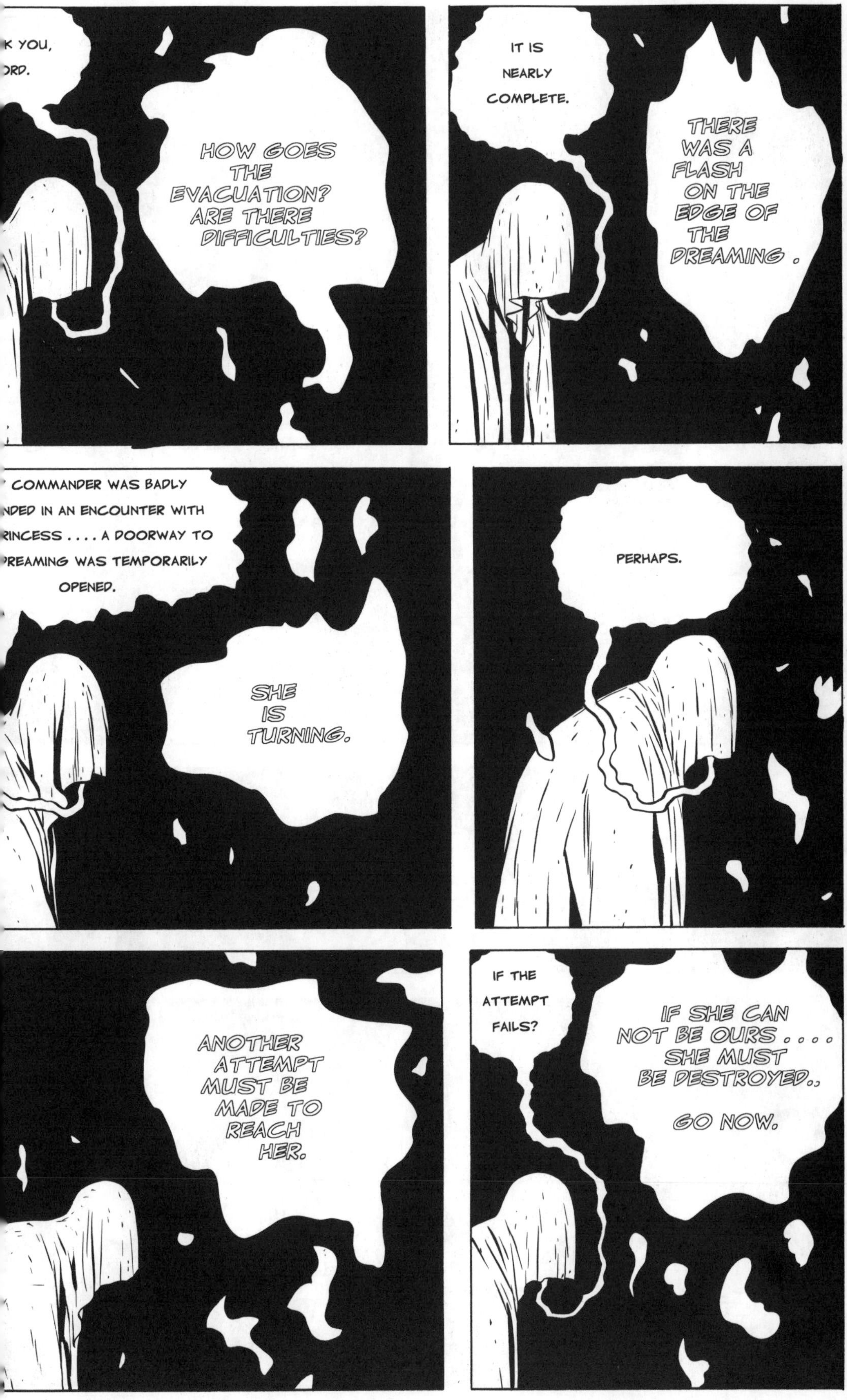
K YOU, ORD.
HOW GOES THE EVACUATION? ARE THERE DIFFICULTIES?
IT IS NEARLY COMPLETE.
THERE WAS A FLASH ON THE EDGE OF THE DREAMING .
COMMANDER WAS BADLY NDED IN AN ENCOUNTER WITH RINCESS . . . . A DOORWAY TO REAMING WAS TEMPORARILY OPENED.
SHE IS TURNING.
PERHAPS.
ANOTHER ATTEMPT MUST BE MADE TO REACH HER.
IF THE ATTEMPT FAILS?
IF SHE CAN NOT BE OURS . . . . SHE MUST BE DESTROYED.
GO NOW.

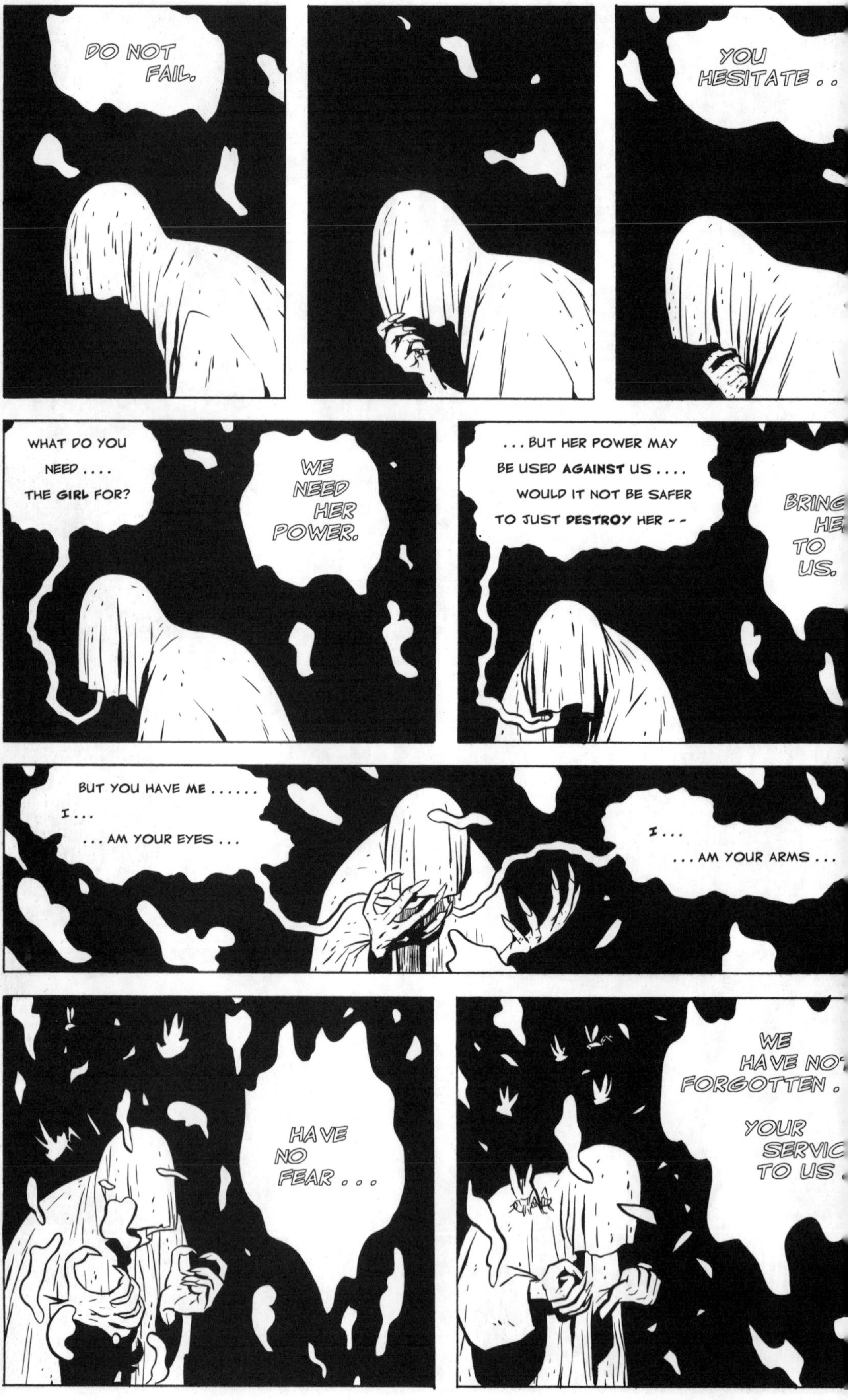
DO NOT FAIL.
YOU HESITATE . .
WHAT DO YOU NEED . . . . THE GIRL FOR?
WE NEED HER POWER.
. . . BUT HER POWER MAY BE USED AGAINST US . . . . WOULD IT NOT BE SAFER TO JUST DESTROY HER - -
BRING HE TO US.
BUT YOU HAVE ME . . . . . . I . . . . . . AM YOUR EYES . . .
I . . . . . . AM YOUR ARMS . . .
HAVE NO FEAR . . .
WE HAVE NO FORGOTTEN .
YOUR SERVIC TO US

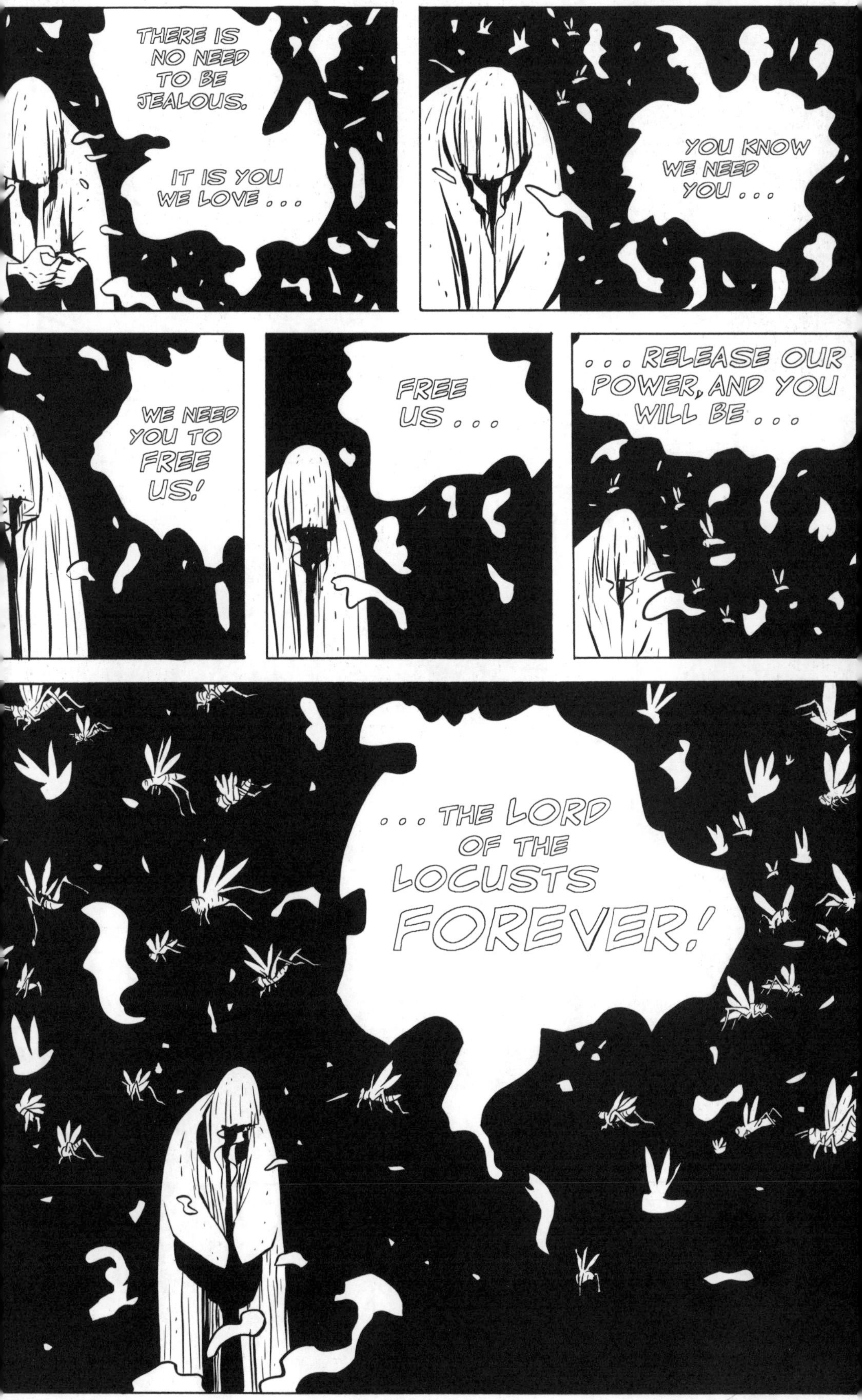
THERE IS NO NEED TO BE JEALOUS.
IT IS YOU WE LOVE . . .
YOU KNOW WE NEED YOU . . .
WE NEED YOU TO FREE US!
FREE US . . .
. . . RELEASE OUR POWER, AND YOU WILL BE . . .
. . . THE LORD OF THE LOCUSTS FOREVER!

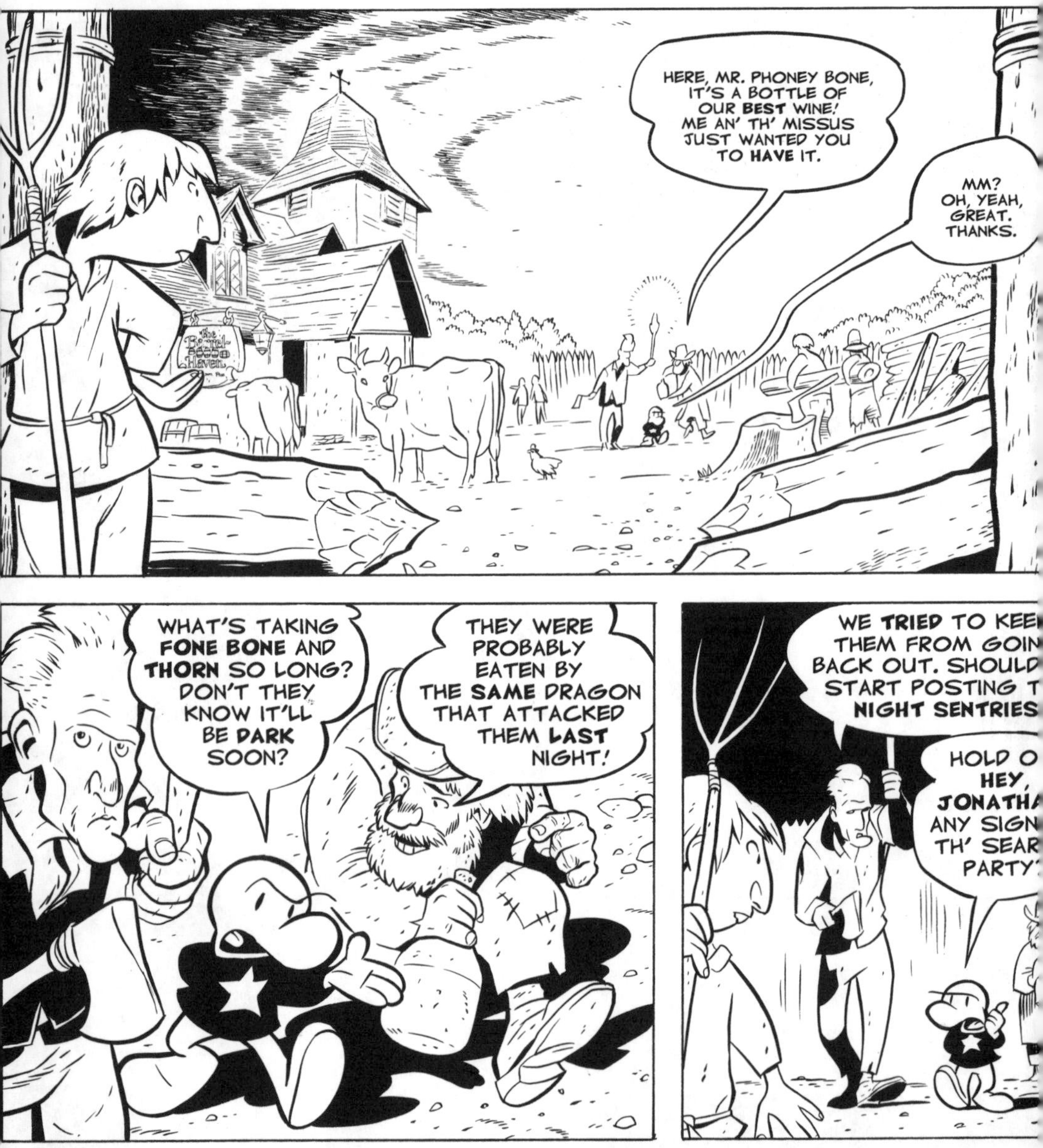
HERE, MR. PHONEY BONE, IT'S A BOTTLE OF OUR BEST WINE! ME AN' TH' MISSUS JUST WANTED YOU TO HAVE IT.
MM? OH, YEAH, GREAT. THANKS.
WHAT'S TAKING FONE BONE AND THORN SO LONG? DON'T THEY KNOW IT'LL BE DARK SOON?
THEY WERE PROBABLY EATEN BY THE SAME DRAGON THAT ATTACKED THEM LAST NIGHT!
WE TRIED TO KEE THEM FROM GOIN BACK OUT. SHOULD START POSTING T NIGHT SENTRIES
HOLD O HEY, JONATHA ANY SIGN TH' SEAR PARTY?
NOPE. NOT SINCE THEY WENT OUT THIS MORNING!
AN' LUCIUS ISN'T BACK YET, EITHER? WE'RE GONNA HAFTA PUT UP TH' GATES SOON.
HEY! HERE COMES SOMEBODY!
IT'S THEM!
DID YOU FIND GRAN'MA BEN?
NOTHING NOT A TRA OF GRAN'MA OR LUCIUS

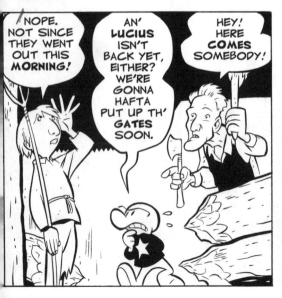

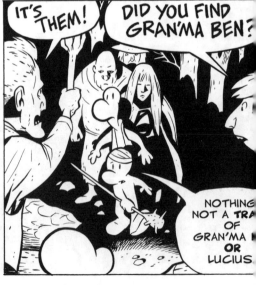

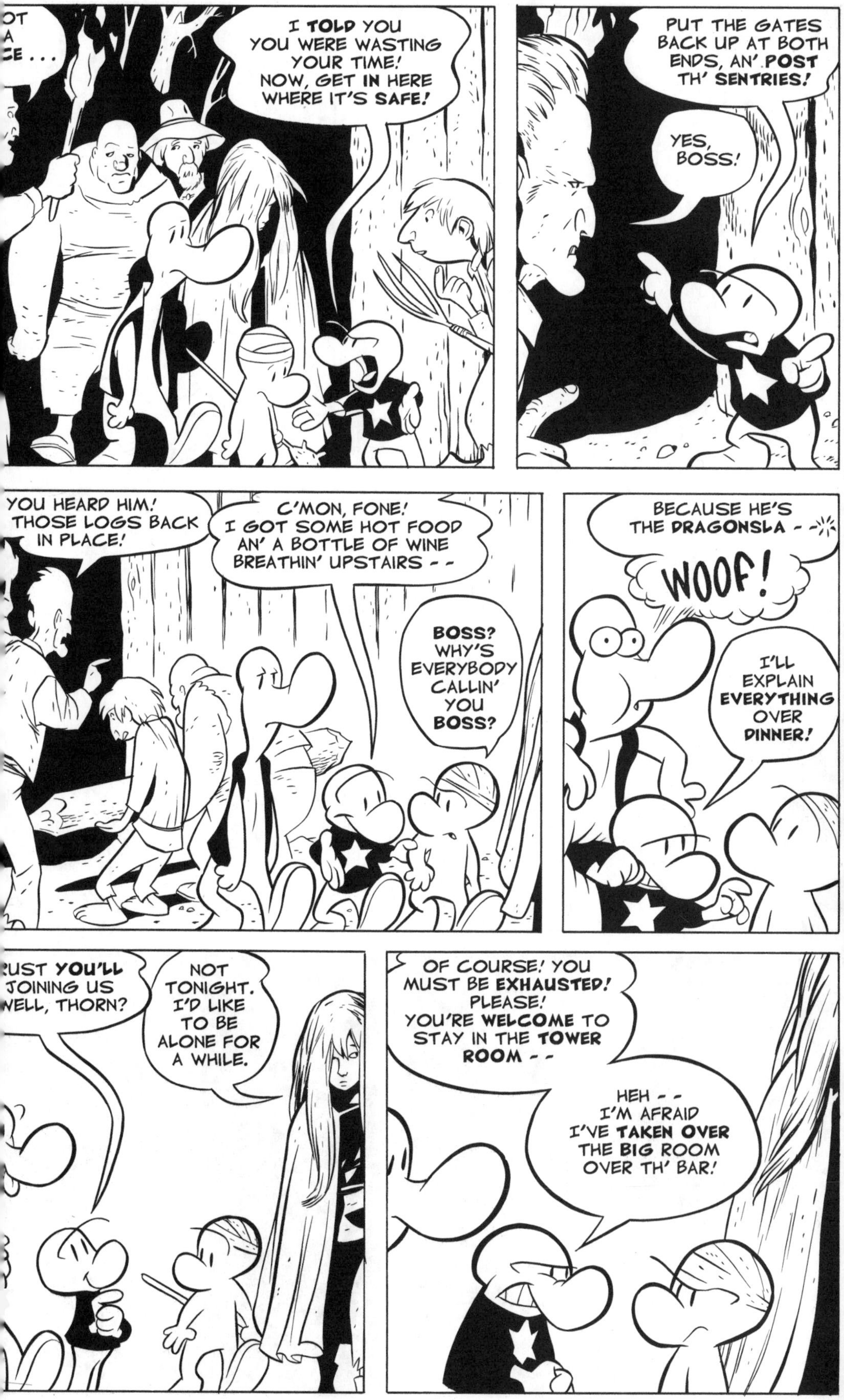

OT
A
CE . . .
I TOLD YOU YOU WERE WASTING YOUR TIME! NOW, GET IN HERE WHERE IT'S SAFE!
PUT THE GATES BACK UP AT BOTH ENDS, AN' POST TH' SENTRIES!
YES, BOSS!
YOU HEARD HIM! THOSE LOGS BACK IN PLACE!
C'MON, FONE! I GOT SOME HOT FOOD AN' A BOTTLE OF WINE BREATHIN' UPSTAIRS - -
BOSS? WHY'S EVERYBODY CALLIN' YOU BOSS?
BECAUSE HE'S THE DRAGONSLA - -
WOOF!
I'LL EXPLAIN EVERYTHING OVER DINNER!
RUST YOU'LL JOINING US WELL, THORN?
NOT TONIGHT. I'D LIKE TO BE ALONE FOR A WHILE.
OF COURSE! YOU MUST BE EXHAUSTED! PLEASE! YOU'RE WELCOME TO STAY IN THE TOWER ROOM - -
HEH - - I'M AFRAID I'VE TAKEN OVER THE BIG ROOM OVER TH' BAR!

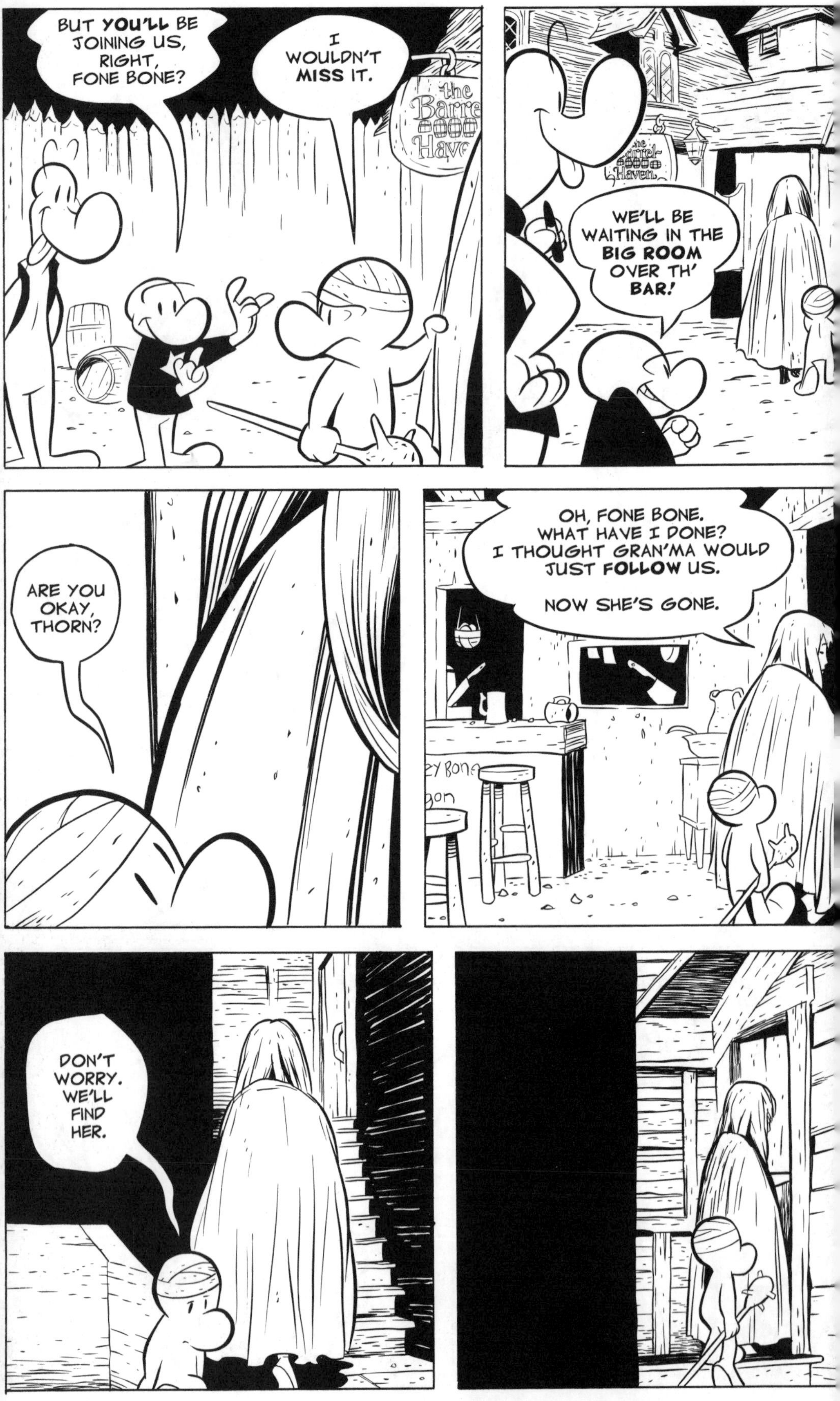
BUT YOU'LL BE JOINING US, RIGHT, FONE BONE?
I WOULDN'T MISS IT.
the Barrel Haven
WE'LL BE WAITING IN THE BIG ROOM OVER TH' BAR!
ARE YOU OKAY, THORN?
OH, FONE BONE. WHAT HAVE I DONE? I THOUGHT GRAN'MA WOULD JUST FOLLOW US.
NOW SHE'S GONE.
DON'T WORRY. WE'LL FIND HER.

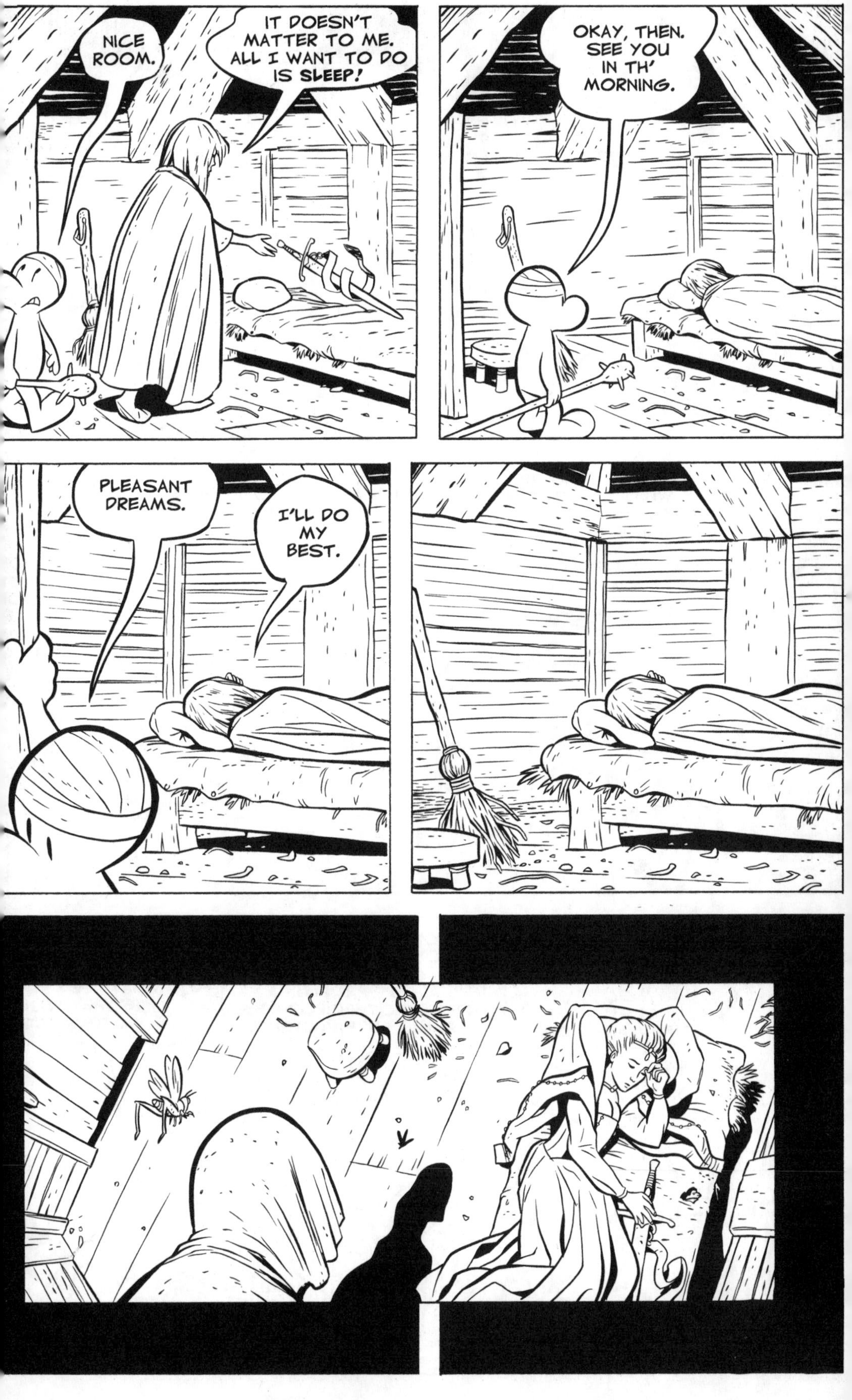
NICE ROOM.
IT DOESN'T MATTER TO ME. ALL I WANT TO DO IS SLEEP!
OKAY, THEN. SEE YOU IN TH' MORNING.
PLEASANT DREAMS.
I'LL DO MY BEST.

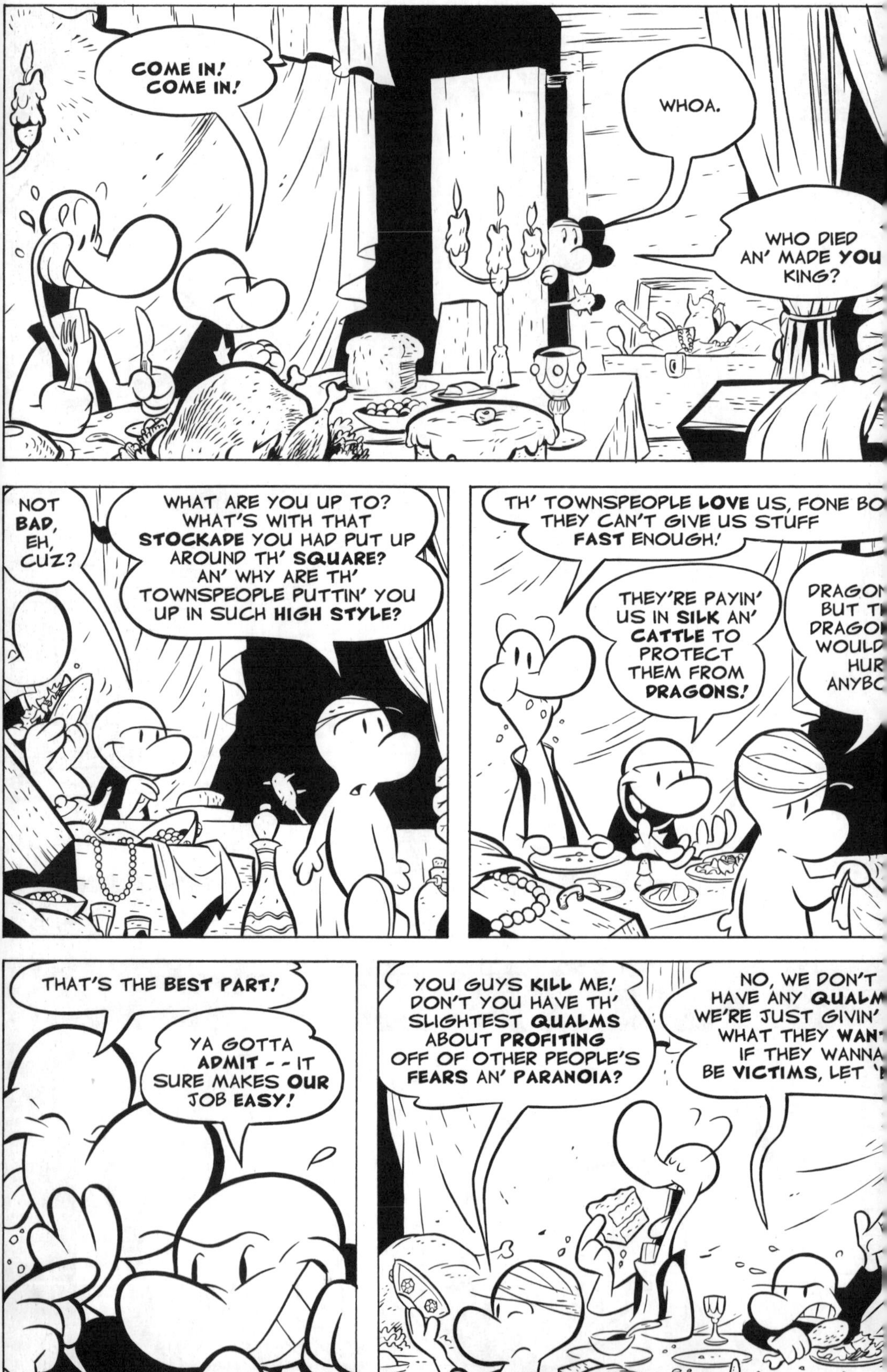
COME IN! COME IN!
WHOA.
WHO DIED AN' MADE YOU KING?
NOT BAD, EH, CUZ?
WHAT ARE YOU UP TO? WHAT'S WITH THAT STOCKADE YOU HAD PUT UP AROUND TH' SQUARE? AN' WHY ARE TH' TOWNSPEOPLE PUTTIN' YOU UP IN SUCH HIGH STYLE?
TH' TOWNSPEOPLE LOVE US, FONE BO
THEY CAN'T GIVE US STUFF FAST ENOUGH!
THEY'RE PAYIN' US IN SILK AN' CATTLE TO PROTECT THEM FROM DRAGONS!
DRAGON BUT T DRAGO WOULD HUR ANYBC
THAT'S THE BEST PART!
YA GOTTA ADMIT - - IT SURE MAKES OUR JOB EASY!
YOU GUYS KILL ME! DON'T YOU HAVE TH' SLIGHTEST QUALMS ABOUT PROFITING OFF OF OTHER PEOPLE'S FEARS AN' PARANOIA?
NO, WE DON'T HAVE ANY QUALM WE'RE JUST GIVIN' WHAT THEY WAN IF THEY WANNA BE VICTIMS, LET

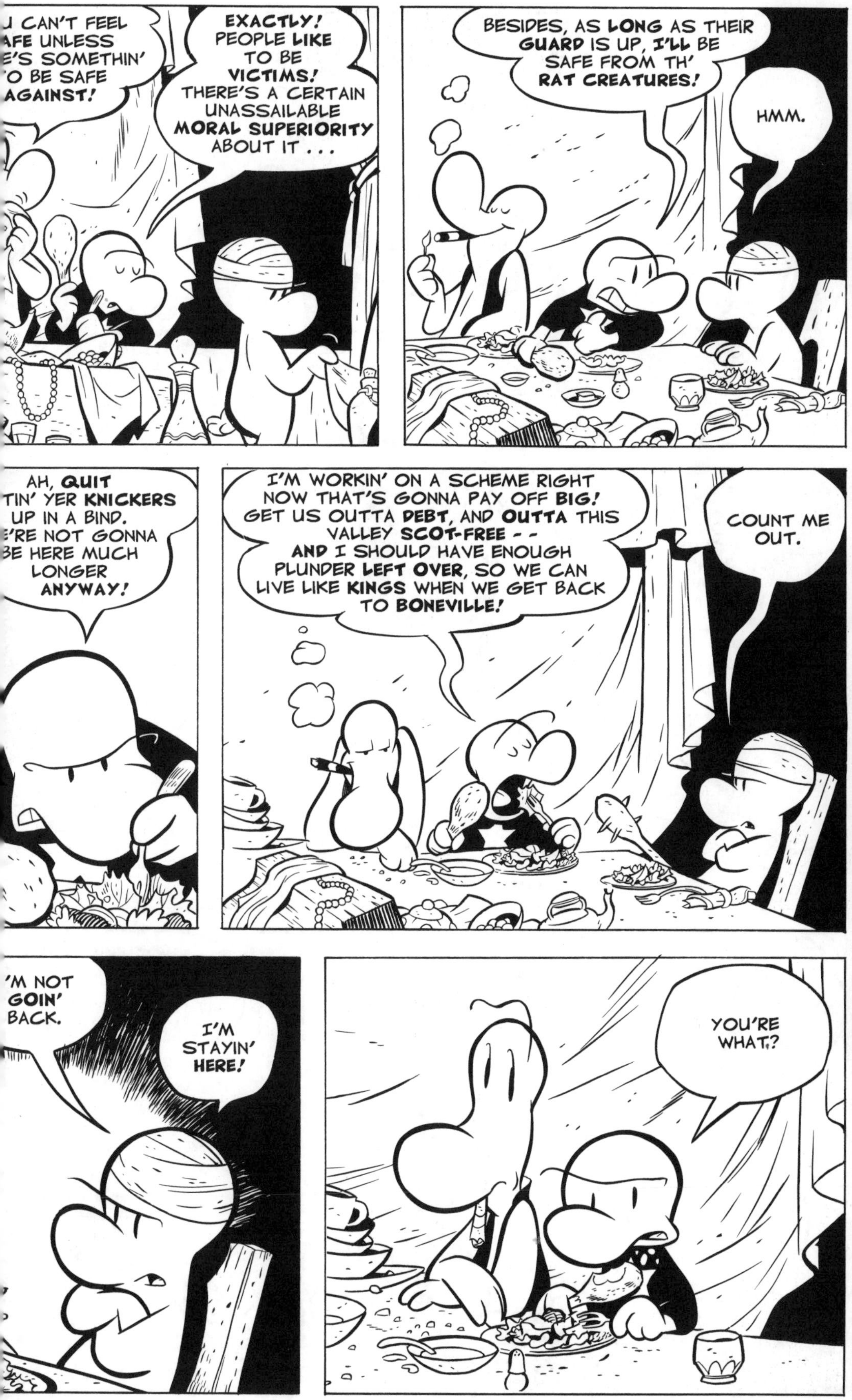

U CAN'T FEEL AFE UNLESS E'S SOMETHIN' 'O BE SAFE AGAINST!
EXACTLY! PEOPLE LIKE TO BE VICTIMS! THERE'S A CERTAIN UNASSAILABLE MORAL SUPERIORITY ABOUT IT . . .
BESIDES, AS LONG AS THEIR GUARD IS UP, I'LL BE SAFE FROM TH' RAT CREATURES!
HMM.
AH, QUIT TIN' YER KNICKERS UP IN A BIND. 'RE NOT GONNA BE HERE MUCH LONGER ANYWAY!
I'M WORKIN' ON A SCHEME RIGHT NOW THAT'S GONNA PAY OFF BIG! GET US OUTTA DEBT, AND OUTTA THIS VALLEY SCOT-FREE - - AND I SHOULD HAVE ENOUGH PLUNDER LEFT OVER, SO WE CAN LIVE LIKE KINGS WHEN WE GET BACK TO BONEVILLE!
COUNT ME OUT.
'M NOT GOIN' BACK.
I'M STAYIN' HERE!
YOU'RE WHAT?

YOU'RE JUST **KIDDIN'**, RIGHT, FONE BONE?

NO, I'M **SERIOUS!** I'M **STAYIN' HERE.** THERE'S TOO MUCH UNFINISHED BUSINESS.

BUT, **FONE**, YOU **GOTTA** COME BACK! WE CAN'T LEAVE WITHOUT YOU!

HOLD IT -- THIS IS ABOUT **THORN**, ISN'T IT?

YE:

FONE BONE, FONE BONE . . . COUSIN -- **OLD PAL**, WHEN ARE YOU GONNA GET A **CLUE?** YOU DON'T HAVE A **CHANCE** WITH THORN!

THAT'S NOT WHAT I'M TALKING ABOUT!

GET **OVER** HER, MAN! YOU'RE NOT HER **TYPE!**

HEY, LISTEN -

I'M JUST **SAYING**, THAT IF I WERE **YOU**, I'D START LOOKIN' FOR ANOTHER GIRLFRIEND!

SHE'S NOT MY **GIRLFRIEND**, AND THAT'S **NOT** WHAT I'M **TALKING** ABOUT!

YEAH, YEAH.

I'M TALKIN' ABOUT ALL THE **TROUBLE** THAT GOIN' ON IN TH' **VALLE** WITH TH' **DRAGON** AND **RAT CREATURES!**

WE'RE MIXED **UP** IN ALL THIS!

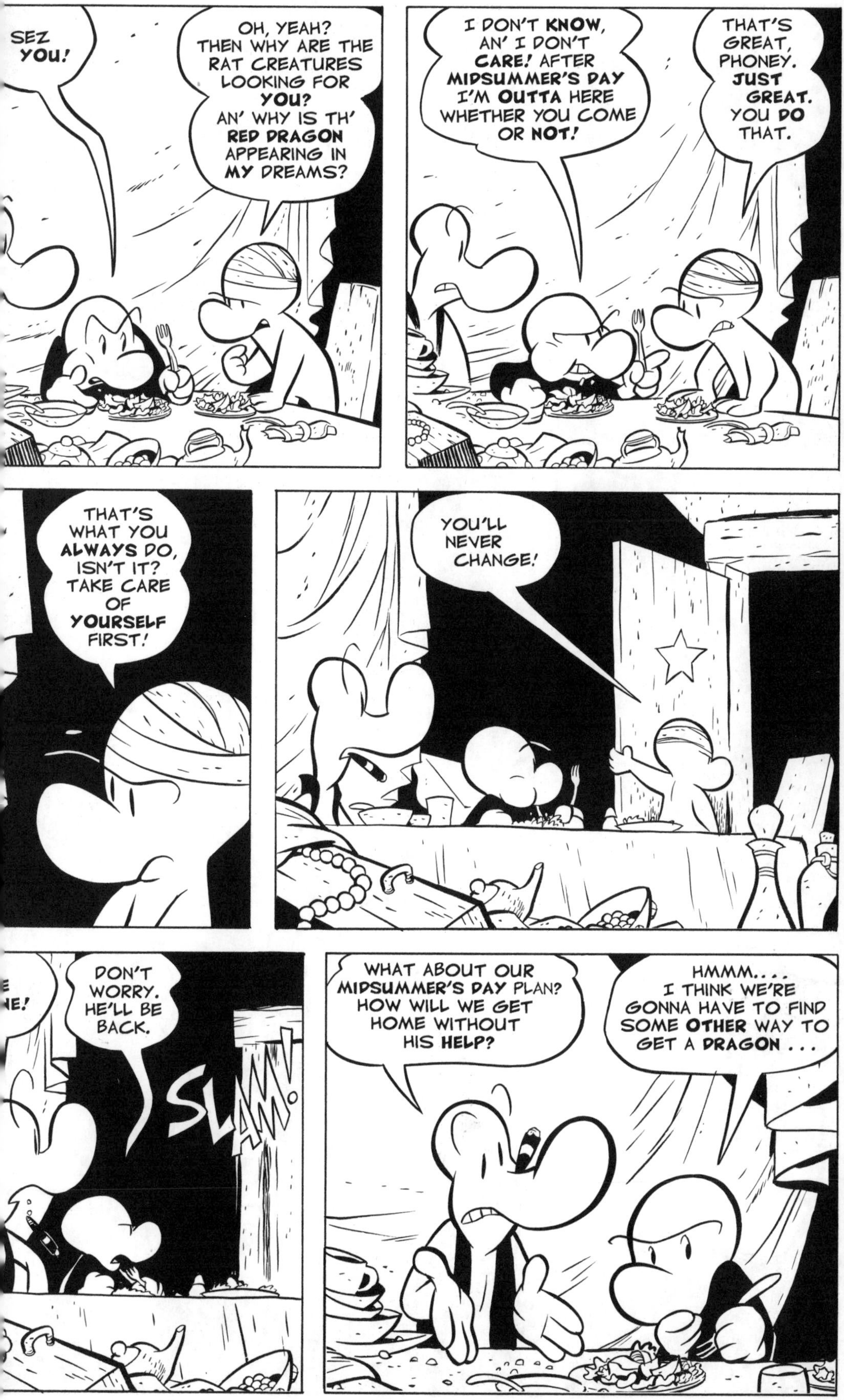
SEZ YOU!
OH, YEAH? THEN WHY ARE THE RAT CREATURES LOOKING FOR YOU? AN' WHY IS TH' RED DRAGON APPEARING IN MY DREAMS?
I DON'T KNOW, AN' I DON'T CARE! AFTER MIDSUMMER'S DAY I'M OUTTA HERE WHETHER YOU COME OR NOT!
THAT'S GREAT, PHONEY. JUST GREAT. YOU DO THAT.
THAT'S WHAT YOU ALWAYS DO, ISN'T IT? TAKE CARE OF YOURSELF FIRST!
YOU'LL NEVER CHANGE!
DON'T WORRY. HE'LL BE BACK.
SLAM!
WHAT ABOUT OUR MIDSUMMER'S DAY PLAN? HOW WILL WE GET HOME WITHOUT HIS HELP?
HMMM.... I THINK WE'RE GONNA HAVE TO FIND SOME OTHER WAY TO GET A DRAGON . . .

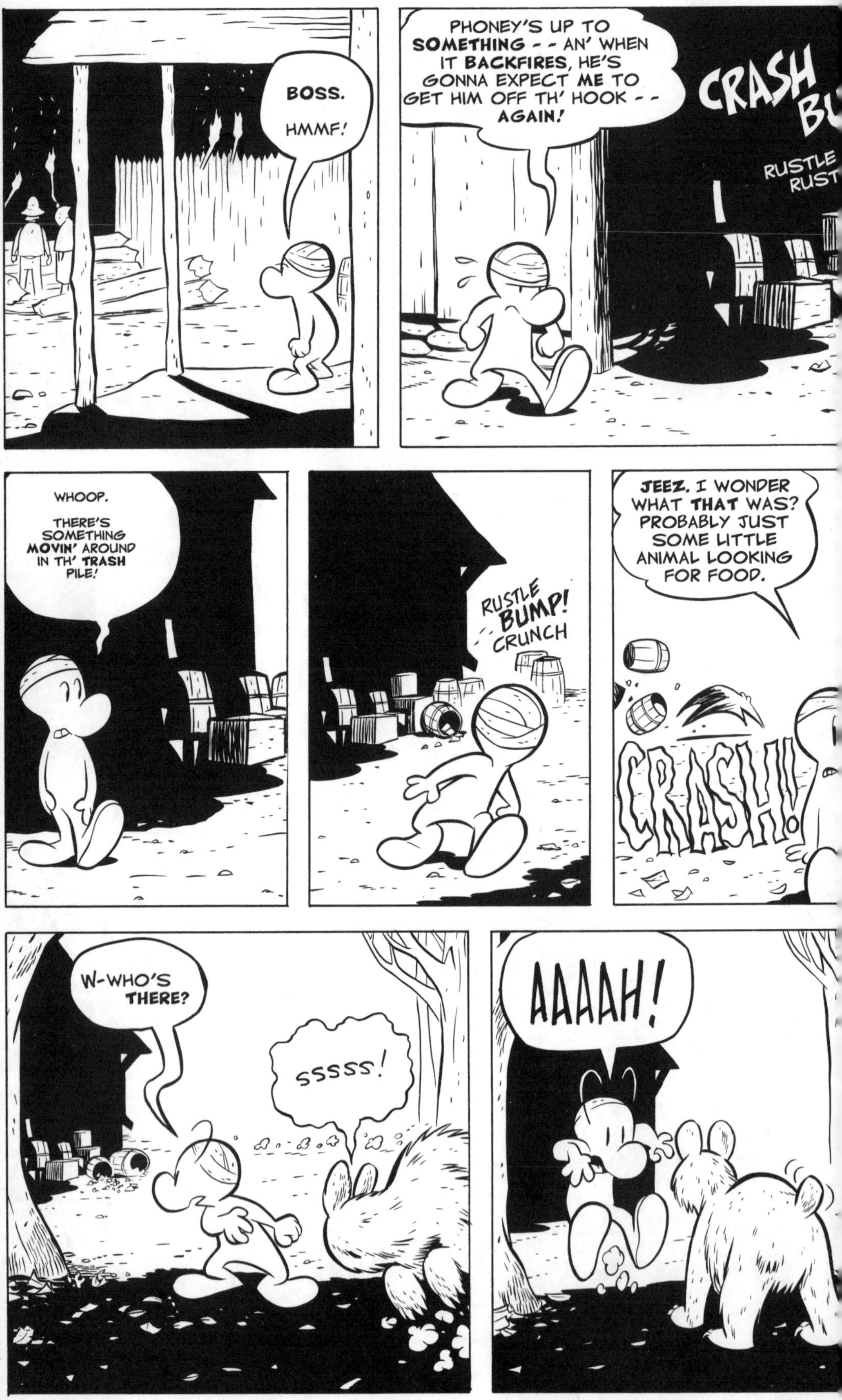

BOSS.
HMMF!
PHONEY'S UP TO SOMETHING - - AN' WHEN IT BACKFIRES, HE'S GONNA EXPECT ME TO GET HIM OFF TH' HOOK - - AGAIN!
CRASH
RUSTLE
WHOOP. THERE'S SOMETHING MOVIN' AROUND IN TH' TRASH PILE!
RUSTLE BUMP! CRUNCH
JEEZ. I WONDER WHAT THAT WAS? PROBABLY JUST SOME LITTLE ANIMAL LOOKING FOR FOOD.
CRASH!
W-WHO'S THERE?
SSSSS!
AAAAH!

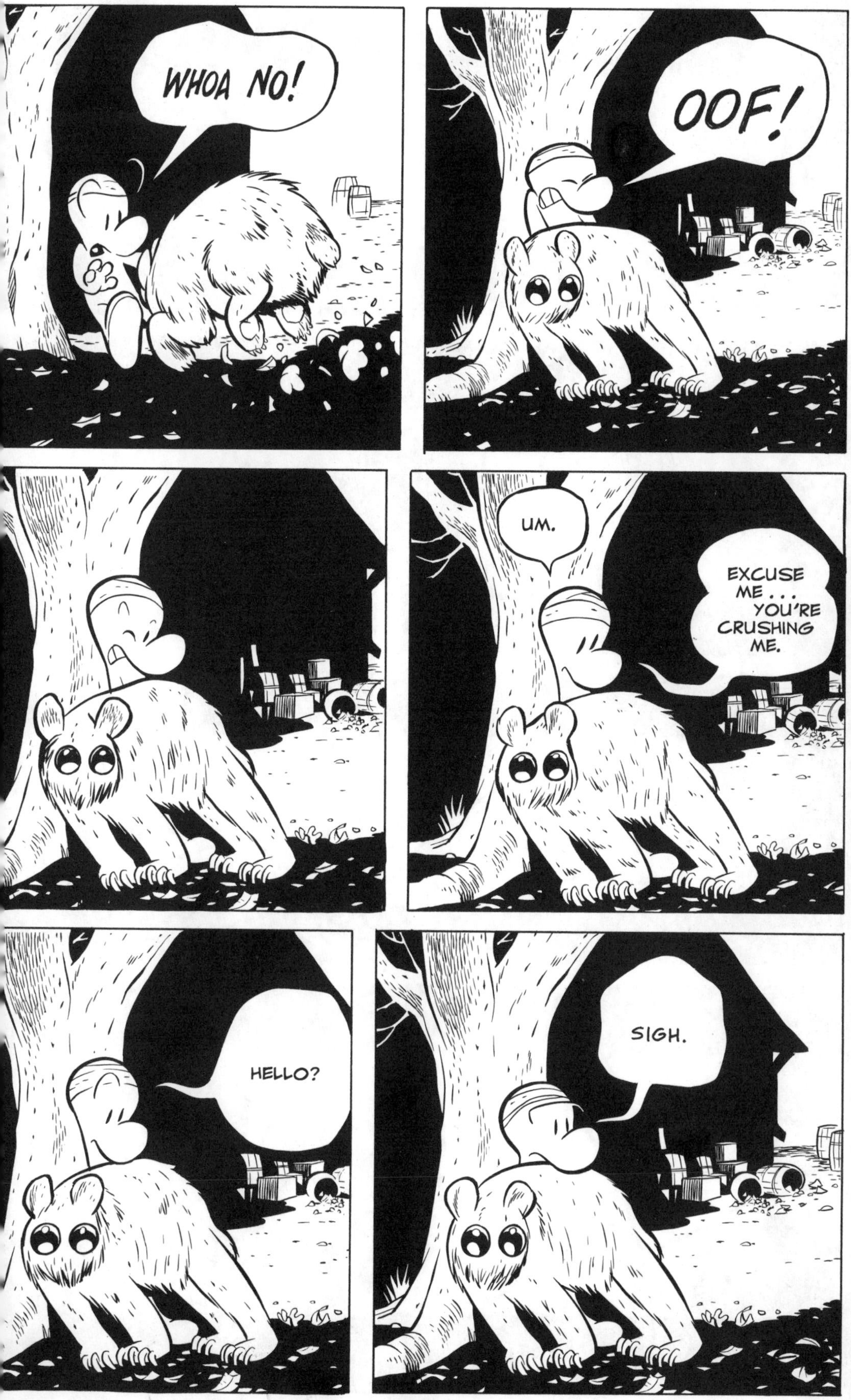
WHOA NO!
OOF!
UM.
EXCUSE ME . . . YOU'RE CRUSHING ME.
HELLO?
SIGH.

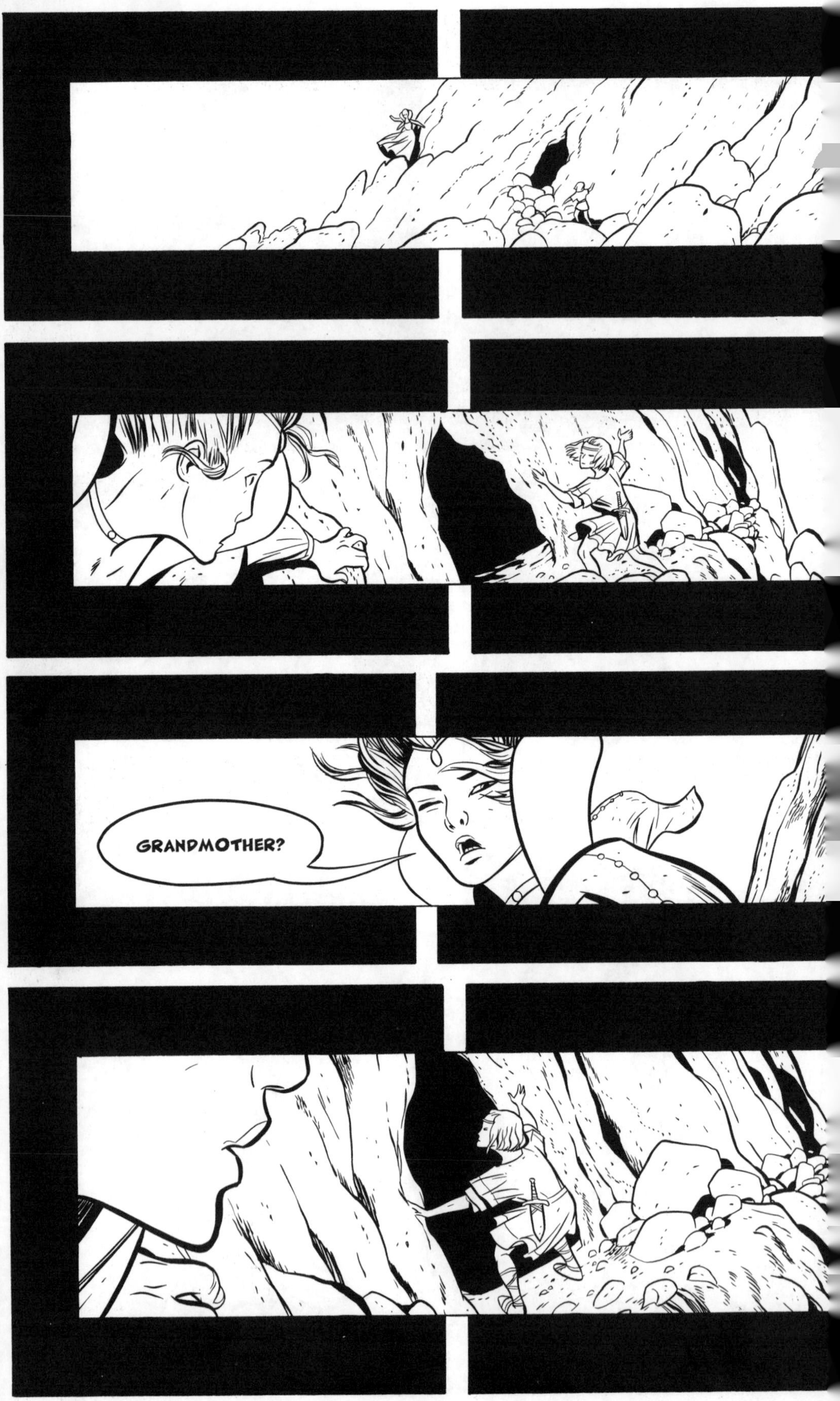
GRANDMOTHER?

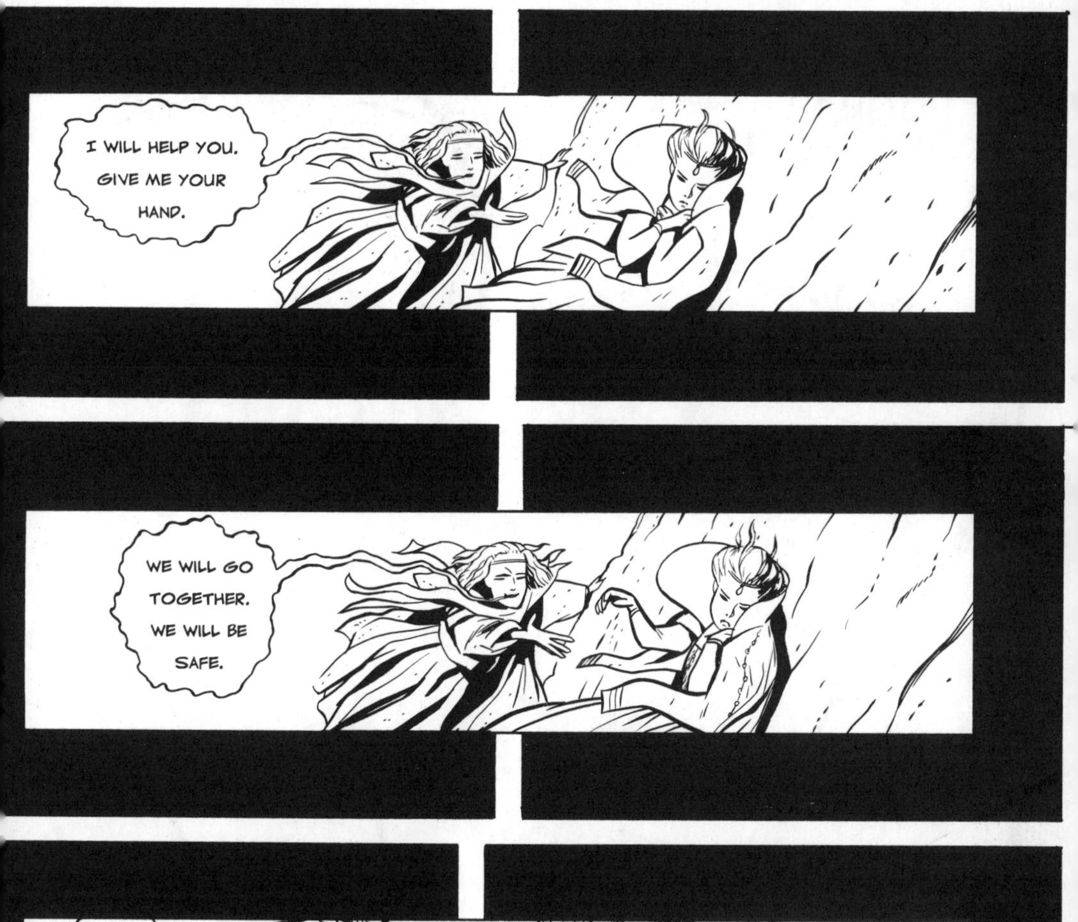
I WILL HELP YOU. GIVE ME YOUR HAND.
WE WILL GO TOGETHER. WE WILL BE SAFE.
THAT IS GOOD. YOU ARE A GOOD --
NO!
WAKE UP!
NO!

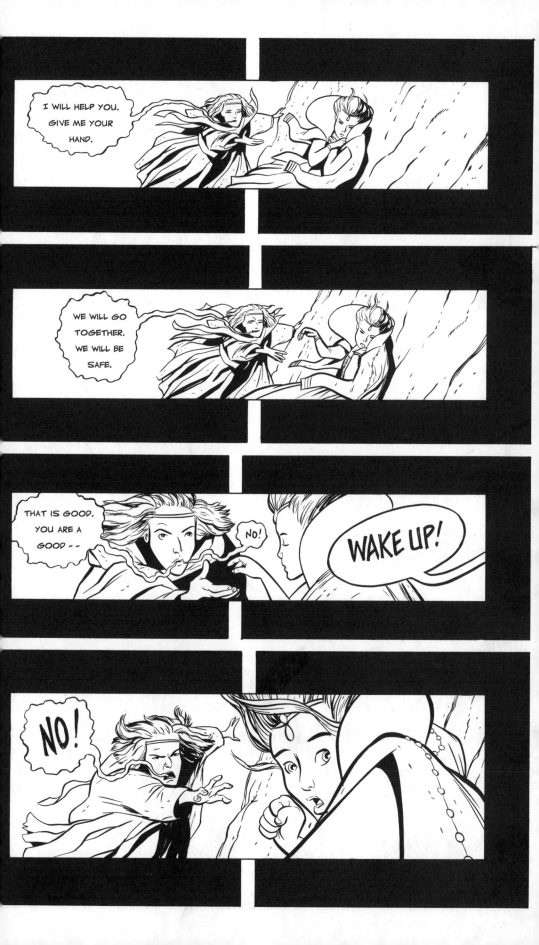

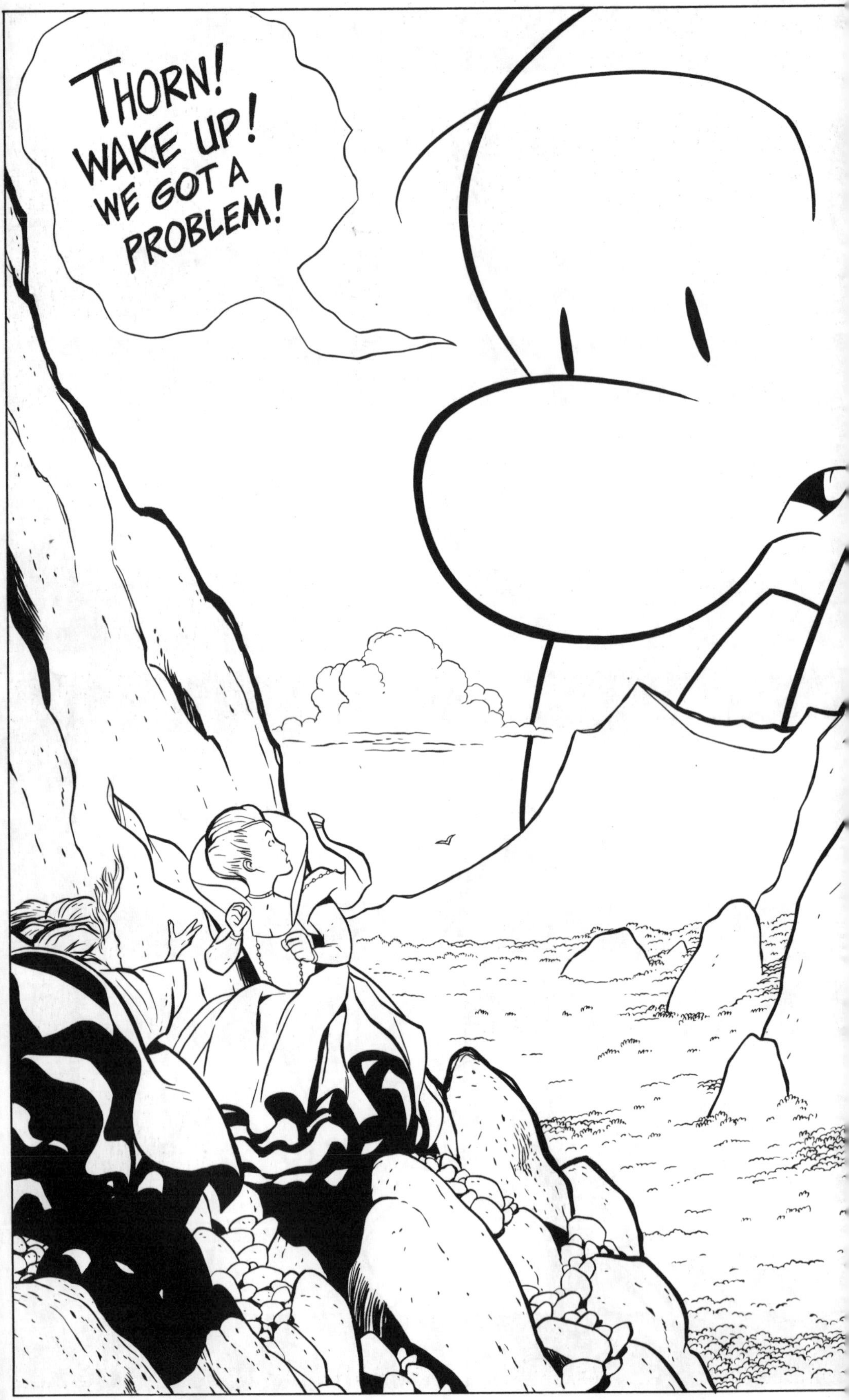
THORN! WAKE UP! WE GOT A PROBLEM!

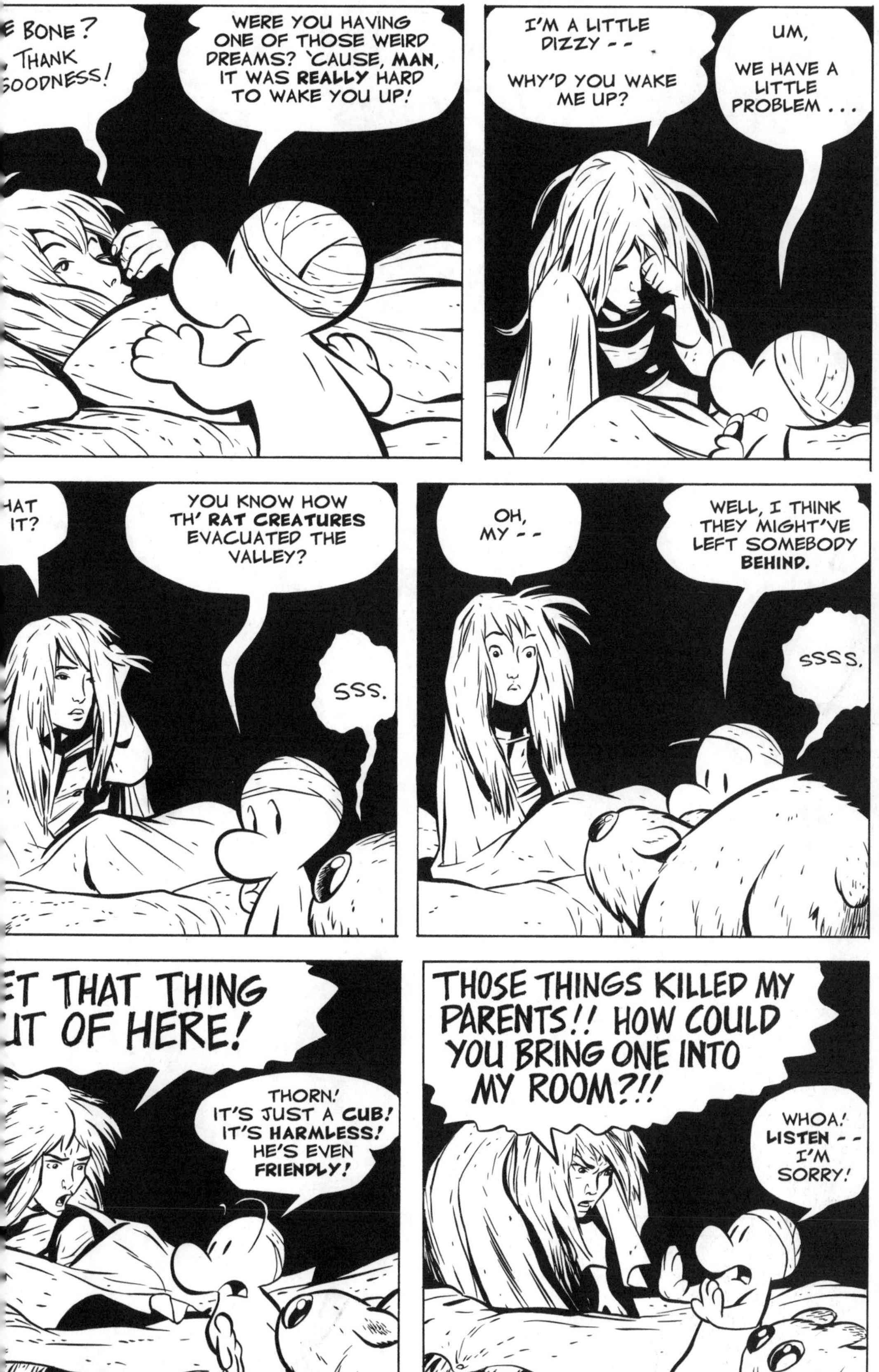

E BONE? THANK GOODNESS!
WERE YOU HAVING ONE OF THOSE WEIRD DREAMS? 'CAUSE, MAN, IT WAS REALLY HARD TO WAKE YOU UP!
I'M A LITTLE DIZZY - - WHY'D YOU WAKE ME UP?
UM, WE HAVE A LITTLE PROBLEM . . .
HAT IT?
YOU KNOW HOW TH' RAT CREATURES EVACUATED THE VALLEY?
SSS.
OH, MY - -
WELL, I THINK THEY MIGHT'VE LEFT SOMEBODY BEHIND.
SSSS.
ET THAT THING UT OF HERE!
THORN! IT'S JUST A CUB! IT'S HARMLESS! HE'S EVEN FRIENDLY!
THOSE THINGS KILLED MY PARENTS!! HOW COULD YOU BRING ONE INTO MY ROOM?!!
WHOA! LISTEN - - I'M SORRY!

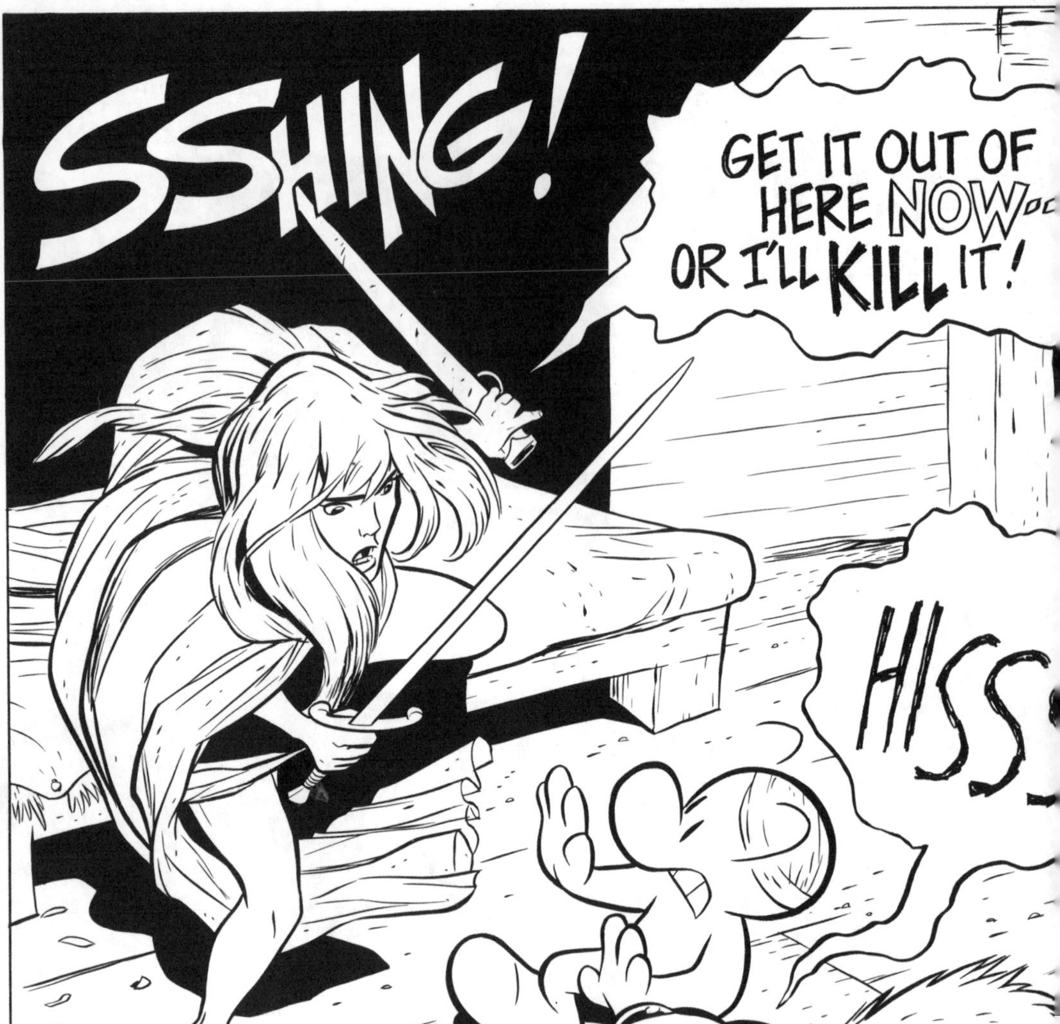
SSHING!
GET IT OUT OF HERE NOW.. OR I'LL KILL IT!
HISS

NEXT: WAR

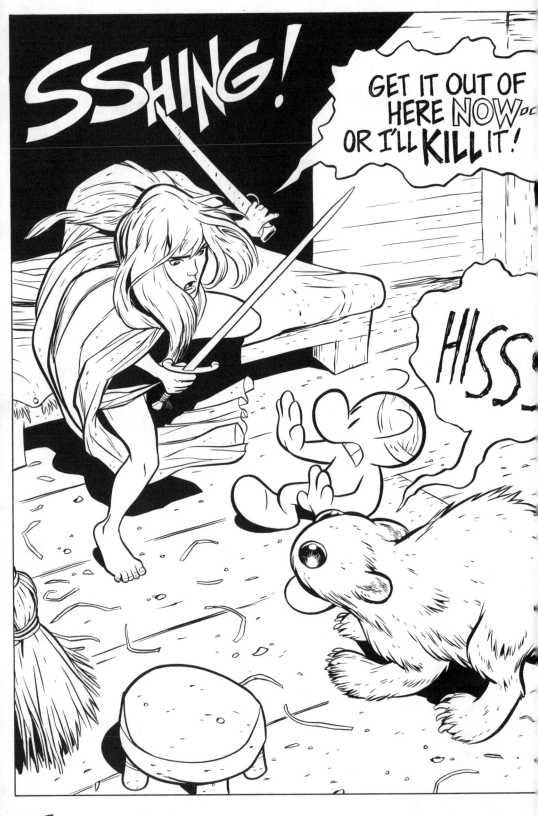

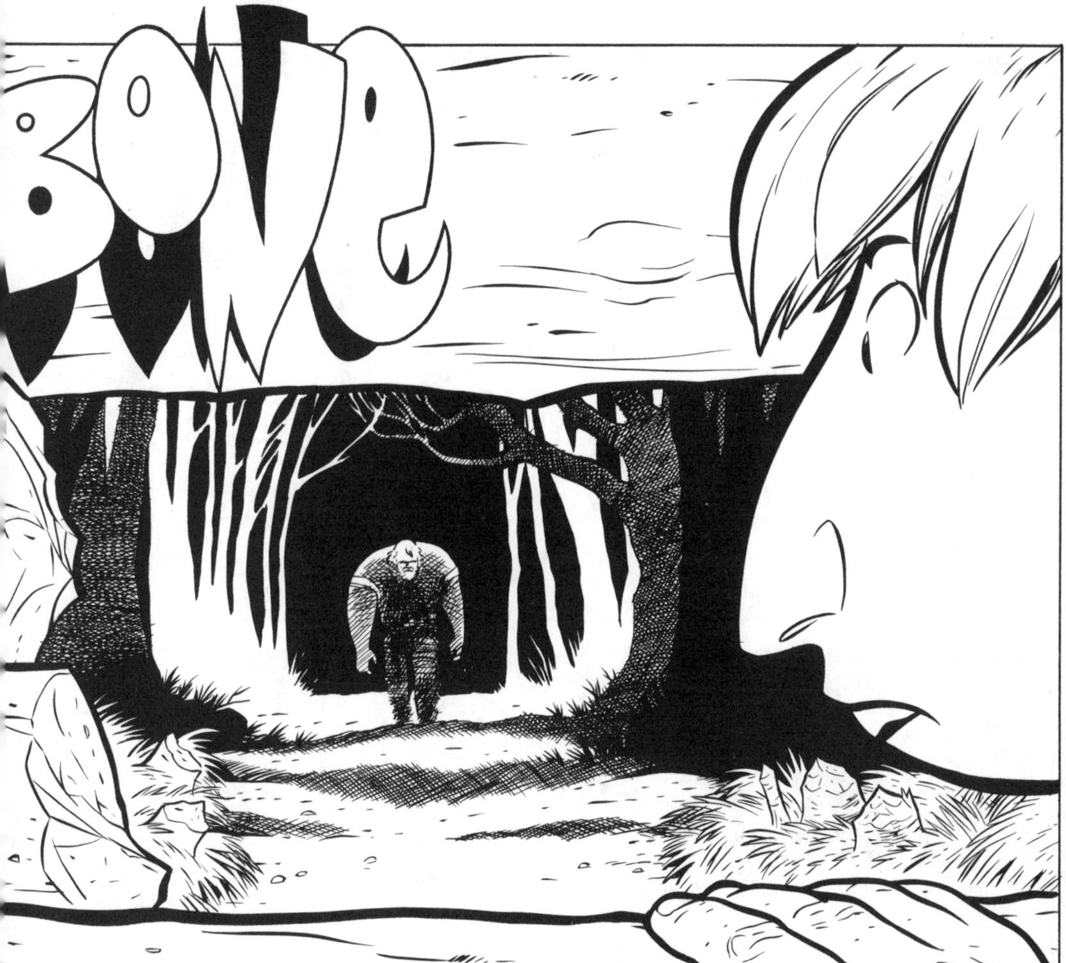
BONE
BAM! BAM! BAM!
SORRY TO WAKE YOU, SIR, BUT IT'S LUCIUS! HE'S BACK AND HE'S APPROACHING TH' GATE!
WHAT? WHAT IS IT?
HOLY--!
OKAY... LET HIM IN! ND GIVE HIM ANYTHING HE WANTS! I'LL BE RIGHT OUT!
GOT IT!
SMILEY! GET DRESSED AN' GO ROUND UP TH' MILITIA!
AYE, AYE, CAP'N!

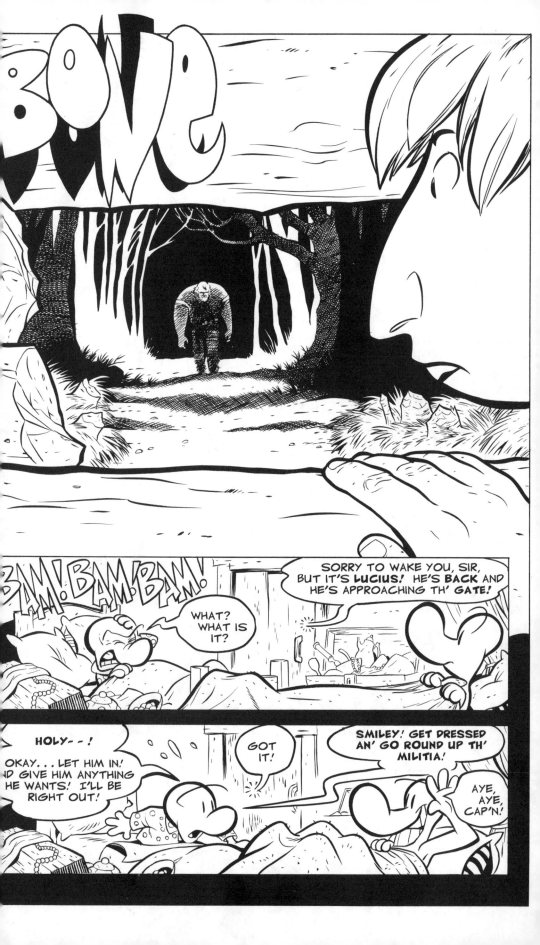

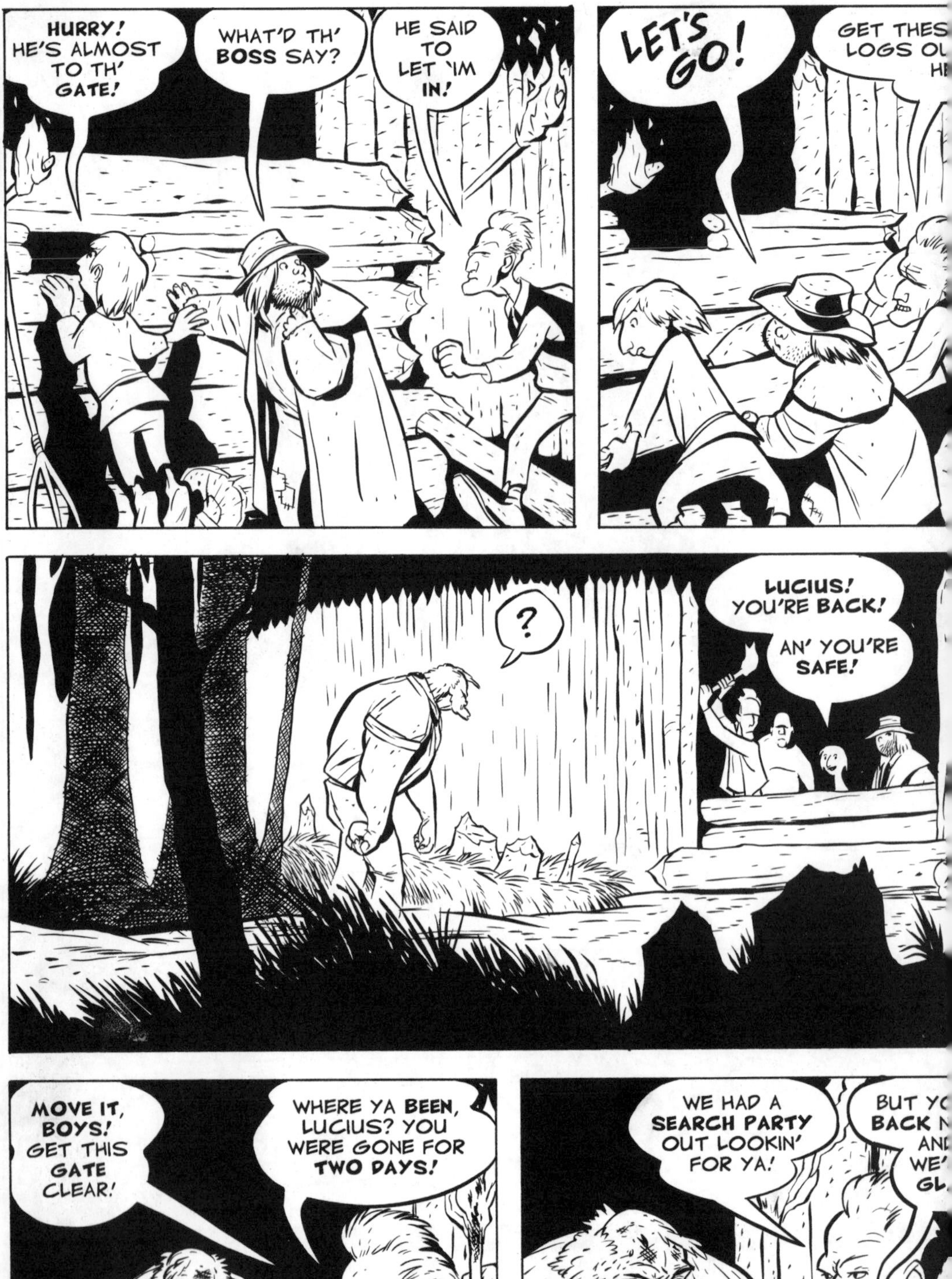

HURRY! HE'S ALMOST TO TH' GATE!
WHAT'D TH' BOSS SAY?
HE SAID TO LET 'IM IN!
LET'S GO!
GET THES LOGS OU H
?
LUCIUS! YOU'RE BACK!
AN' YOU'RE SAFE!
MOVE IT, BOYS! GET THIS GATE CLEAR!
WHERE YA BEEN, LUCIUS? YOU WERE GONE FOR TWO DAYS!
WE HAD A SEARCH PARTY OUT LOOKIN' FOR YA!
BUT Y BACK AN WE' GL
C'M WE ORD T LET IN G

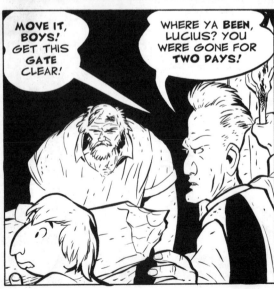

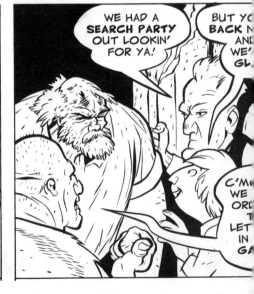

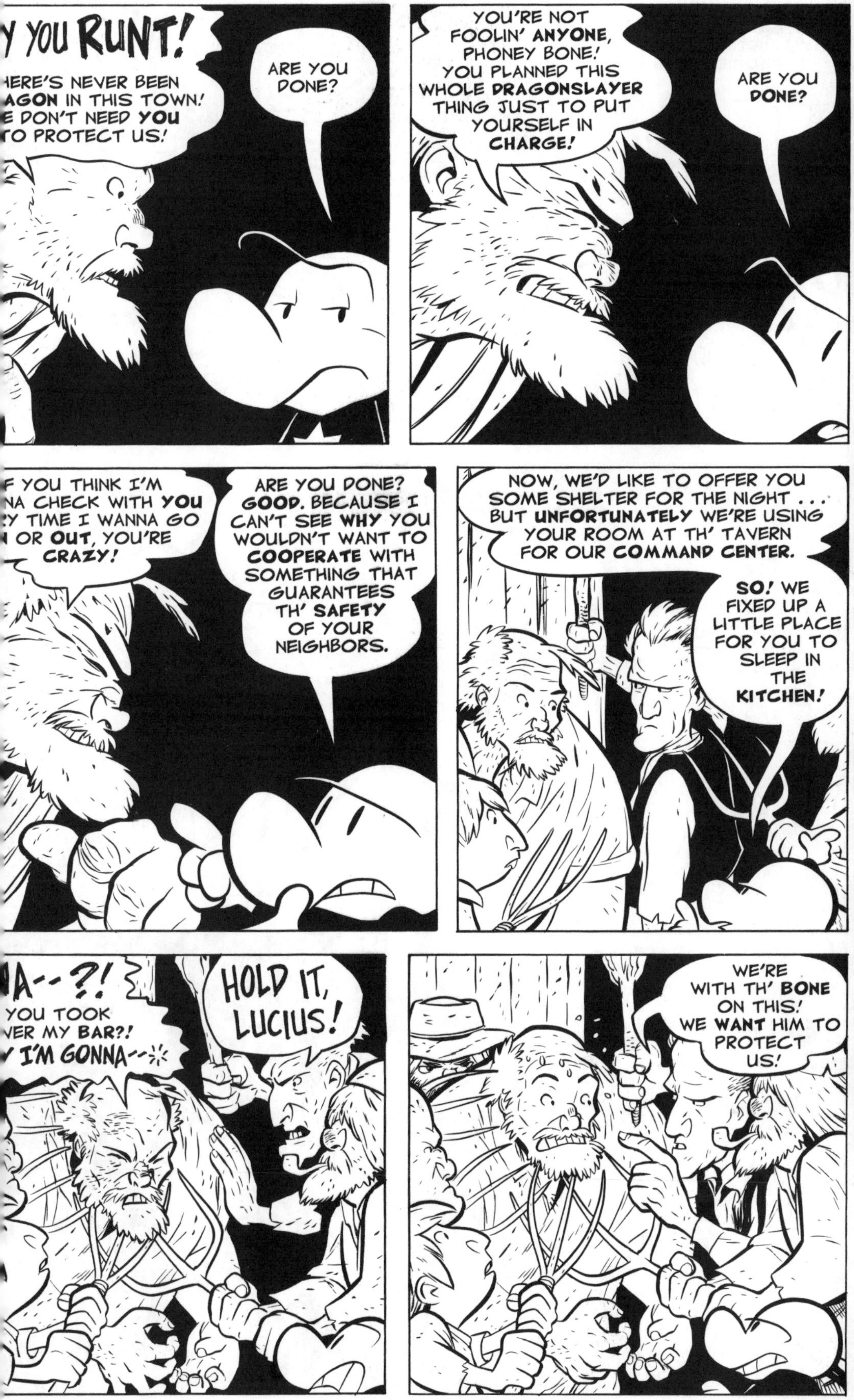

Y YOU RUNT!
HERE'S NEVER BEEN
AGON IN THIS TOWN!
E DON'T NEED YOU
TO PROTECT US!
ARE YOU DONE?
YOU'RE NOT FOOLIN' ANYONE, PHONEY BONE! YOU PLANNED THIS WHOLE DRAGONSLAYER THING JUST TO PUT YOURSELF IN CHARGE!
ARE YOU DONE?
F YOU THINK I'M
NA CHECK WITH YOU
Y TIME I WANNA GO
OR OUT, YOU'RE CRAZY!
ARE YOU DONE? GOOD. BECAUSE I CAN'T SEE WHY YOU WOULDN'T WANT TO COOPERATE WITH SOMETHING THAT GUARANTEES TH' SAFETY OF YOUR NEIGHBORS.
NOW, WE'D LIKE TO OFFER YOU SOME SHELTER FOR THE NIGHT . . . BUT UNFORTUNATELY WE'RE USING YOUR ROOM AT TH' TAVERN FOR OUR COMMAND CENTER.
SO! WE FIXED UP A LITTLE PLACE FOR YOU TO SLEEP IN THE KITCHEN!
HA--?!
YOU TOOK
VER MY BAR?!
I'M GONNA--
HOLD IT, LUCIUS!
WE'RE WITH TH' BONE ON THIS! WE WANT HIM TO PROTECT US!

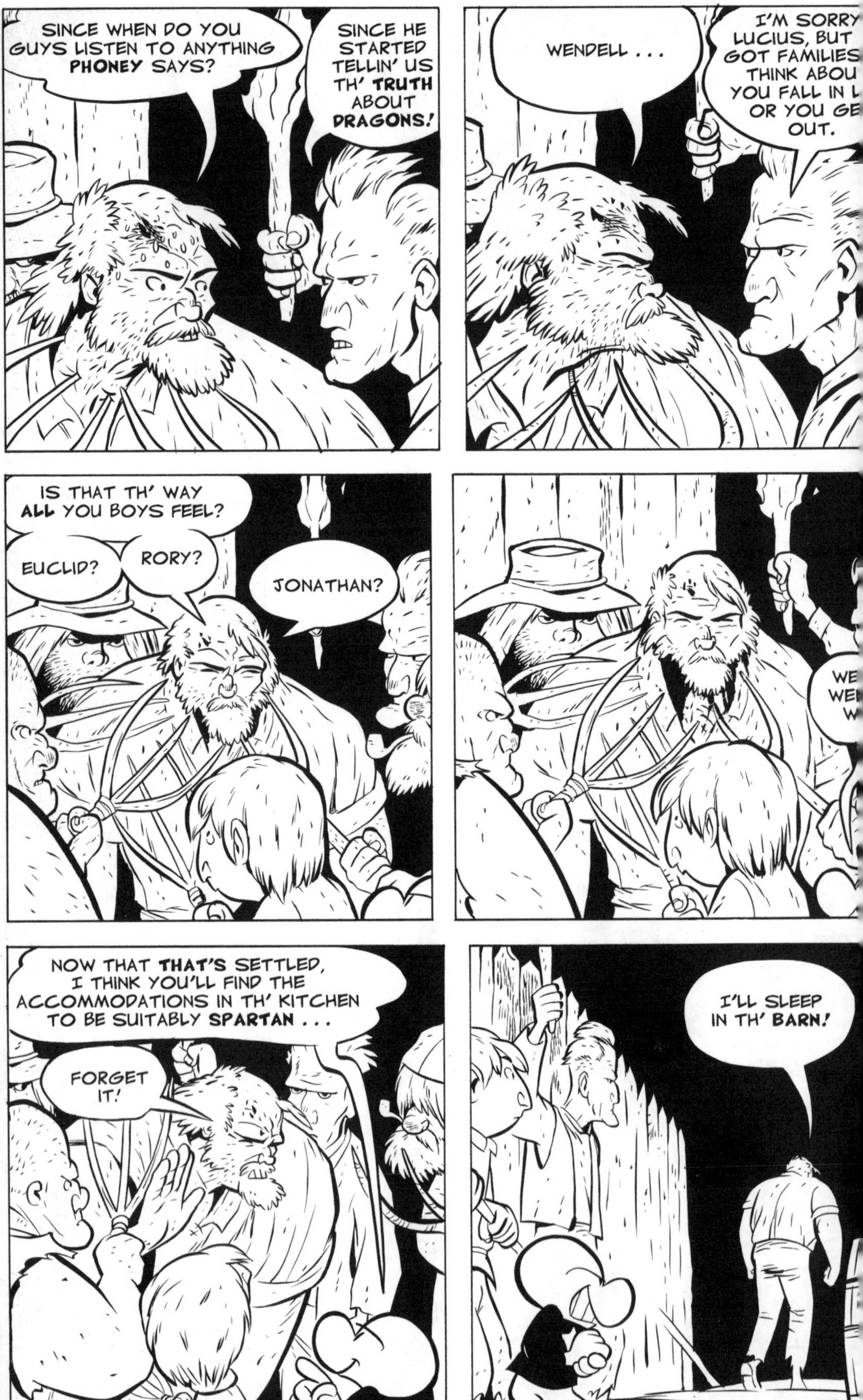
SINCE WHEN DO YOU GUYS LISTEN TO ANYTHING **PHONEY** SAYS?
SINCE HE STARTED TELLIN' US TH' **TRUTH** ABOUT **DRAGONS!**
WENDELL . . .
I'M SORRY LUCIUS, BUT GOT FAMILIES THINK ABOU YOU FALL IN L OR YOU GE OUT.
IS THAT TH' WAY **ALL** YOU BOYS FEEL?
EUCLID?
RORY?
JONATHAN?
NOW THAT **THAT'S** SETTLED, I THINK YOU'LL FIND THE ACCOMMODATIONS IN TH' KITCHEN TO BE SUITABLY **SPARTAN** . . .
FORGET IT!
I'LL SLEEP IN TH' **BARN!**

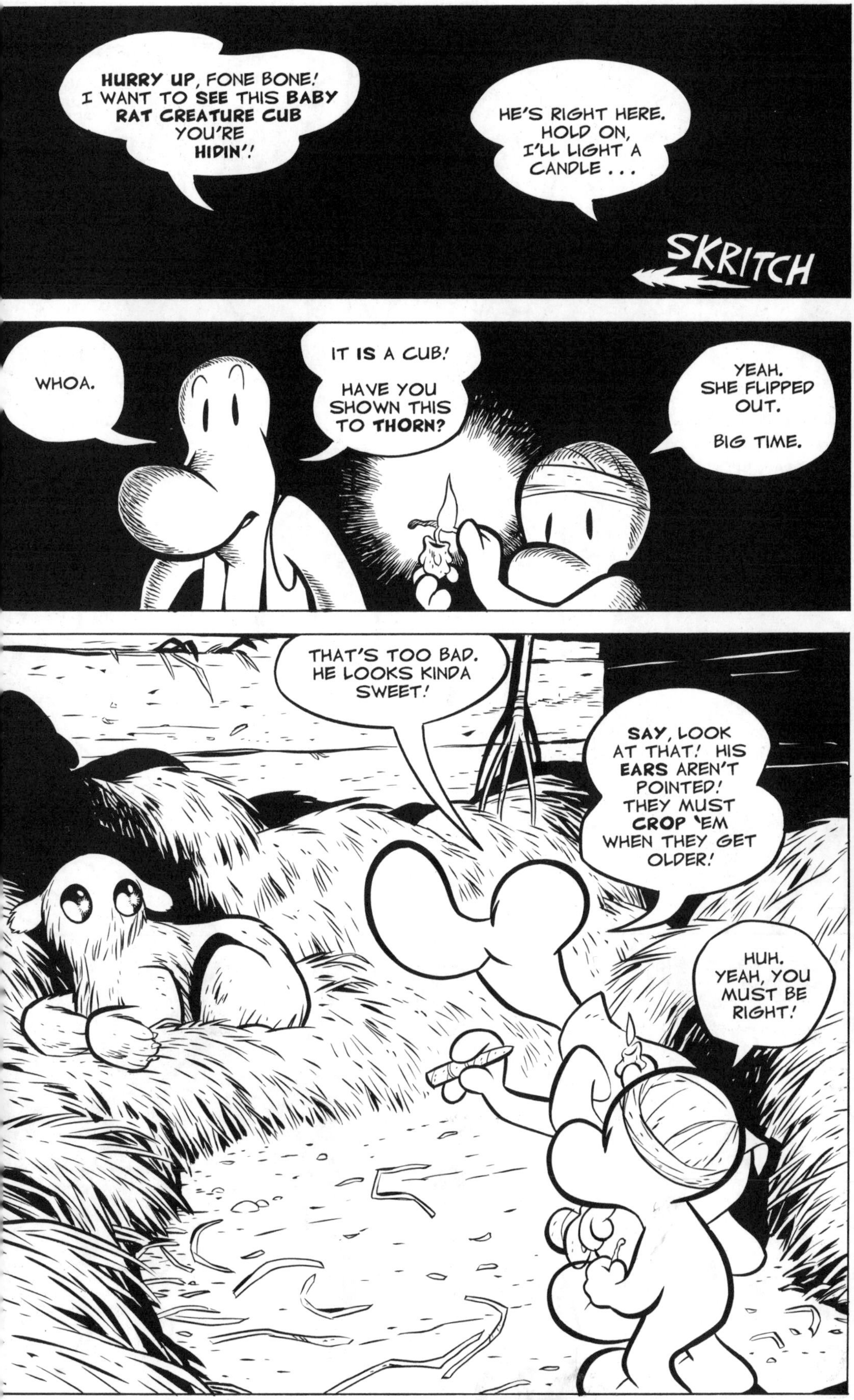
HURRY UP, FONE BONE! I WANT TO SEE THIS BABY RAT CREATURE CUB YOU'RE HIDIN'!
HE'S RIGHT HERE. HOLD ON, I'LL LIGHT A CANDLE . . .
SKRITCH
WHOA.
IT IS A CUB! HAVE YOU SHOWN THIS TO THORN?
YEAH. SHE FLIPPED OUT. BIG TIME.
THAT'S TOO BAD. HE LOOKS KINDA SWEET!
SAY, LOOK AT THAT! HIS EARS AREN'T POINTED! THEY MUST CROP 'EM WHEN THEY GET OLDER!
HUH. YEAH, YOU MUST BE RIGHT!

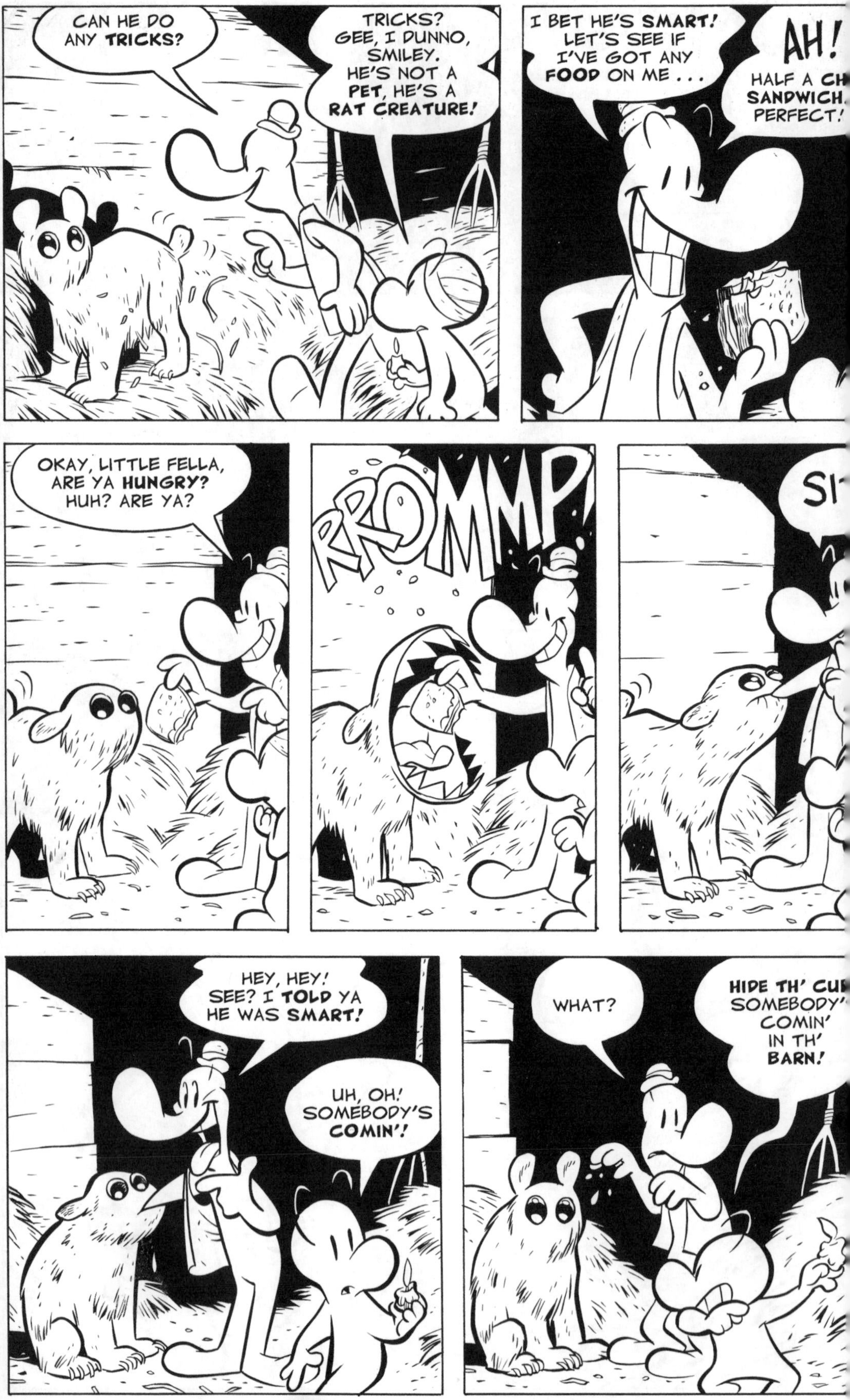
CAN HE DO ANY **TRICKS?**
TRICKS? GEE, I DUNNO, SMILEY. HE'S NOT A **PET**, HE'S A **RAT CREATURE!**
I BET HE'S **SMART!** LET'S SEE IF I'VE GOT ANY **FOOD** ON ME . . .
AH!
HALF A CH SANDWICH. PERFECT!
OKAY, LITTLE FELLA, ARE YA **HUNGRY?** HUH? ARE YA?
RROMMMP!
SI
HEY, HEY! SEE? I **TOLD** YA HE WAS **SMART!**
UH, OH! SOMEBODY'S **COMIN'!**
WHAT?
HIDE TH' CU SOMEBODY' COMIN' IN TH' **BARN!**

WHO'S IN THERE?

SPEAK UP! WHO'S THERE?

IT'S US, MR. DOWN! FONE BONE AND SMILEY BONE!

ONE BONE! WHERE'S ROSE? WHERE'S THORN? HAS ANYTHING 'PENED TO THEM?

THORN IS SAFE -- SHE'S SLEEPING AT THE TAVERN! I DON'T KNOW WHERE GRAN'MA IS!

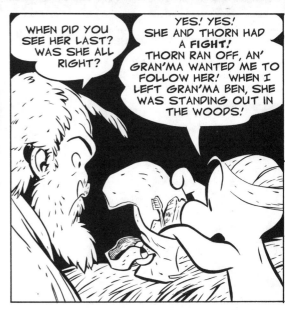

WHEN DID YOU SEE HER LAST? WAS SHE ALL RIGHT?

YES! YES! SHE AND THORN HAD A FIGHT! THORN RAN OFF, AN' GRAN'MA WANTED ME TO FOLLOW HER! WHEN I LEFT GRAN'MA BEN, SHE WAS STANDING OUT IN THE WOODS!

BUT BEFORE I WENT SHE HANDED ME THIS!

YOU GOT THIS FROM GRAN'MA BEN?

YES. SHE WANTED ME TO TELL YOU THAT THE RAT CREATURES HAVE EVACUATED TH' VALLEY!

MMMM...
EVACUATED THE VALLEY...

IT'S THE **NIGHTS OF LIGHTNING** ALL OVER AGAIN...

THE NIGHTS OF LIGHTNING!

WHAT'S A NIGHT OF LIGHTNING?

IT'S A **SNEAK ATTACK** BY THE **RAT CREATURES!!**

ROSE MUST THINK THE RAT CREATURES ARE GOING TO BREAK TH' **TREATY**

GULP!

W͟ TH C͟ HE

THIS IS TH' **TREATY ZONE.**

DID ROSE TELL YOU ANYTHING ELSE? DID SHE SAY WHERE SHE WAS GOING?

NO...

BUT SHE **DID** TELL US THE TRUTH ABO͟ HER BEING THE **QUEEN OF ATHEIA,** AN' THAT **THORN** IS THE **HEIR TO THE THRONE!**

HEL-LO͟.

SHE **DID?**

YEAH! AND SHE SAID THORN'S GREATEST **ENEMY** WAS THE **LORD OF THE LOCUSTS!**

DOES THAT MEAN THORN'S A **PRINCESS?**

THAT'S ODD. THE LORD OF THE LOCUSTS WAS AN ANCIENT ENEMY OF THE **DRAGONS!** I THOUGHT HE GOT TURNED INTO **STONE** OR SOMETHING BACK WHEN THE **DRAGONS** STILL RULED THE EARTH.

HAV͟ IDEA͟ GRA͟ W PRE͟ UP͟ AB͟ IT͟

SACRÉ BLEU!

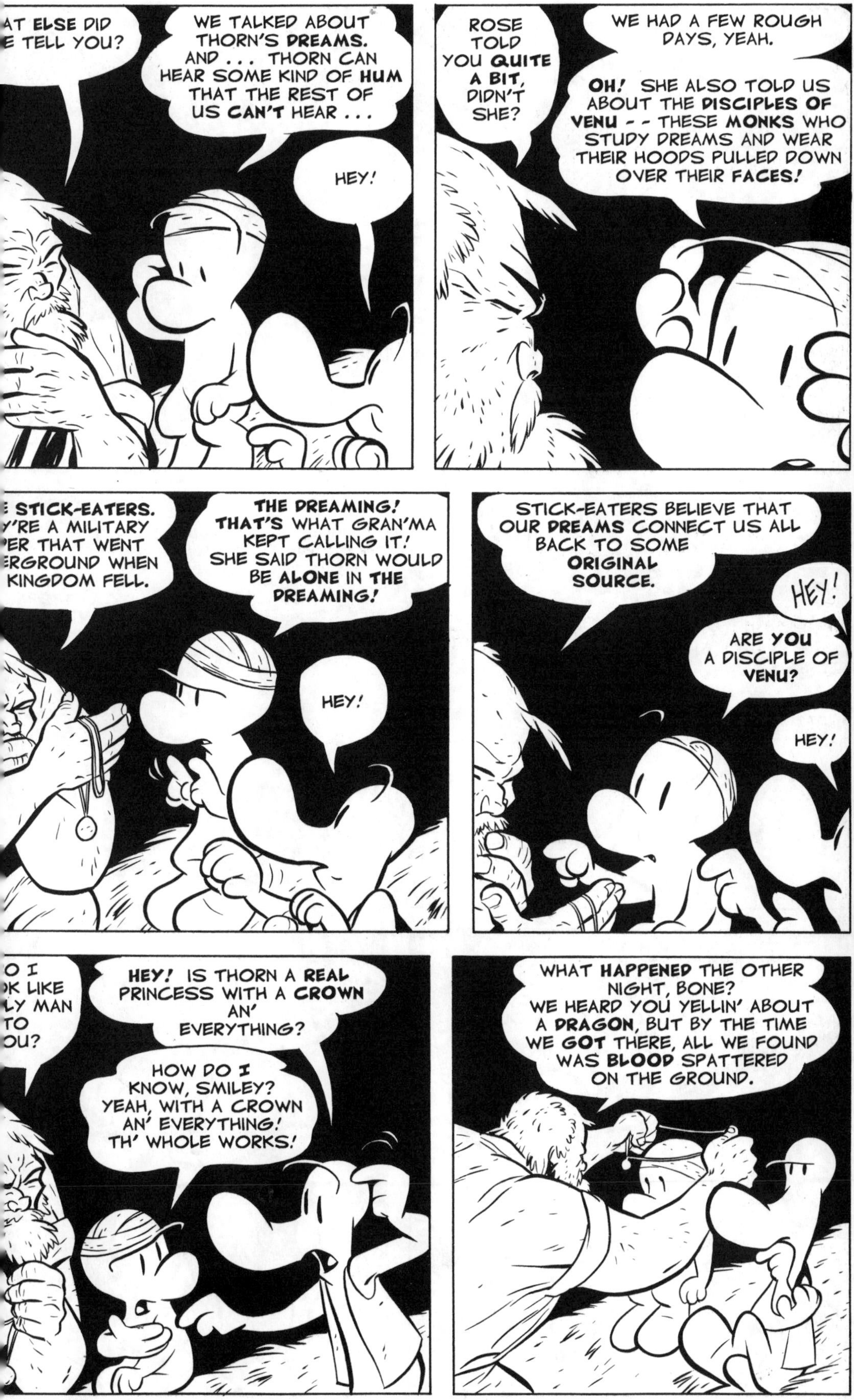
AT ELSE DID
E TELL YOU?
WE TALKED ABOUT THORN'S DREAMS. AND . . . THORN CAN HEAR SOME KIND OF HUM THAT THE REST OF US CAN'T HEAR . . .
HEY!
ROSE TOLD YOU QUITE A BIT, DIDN'T SHE?
WE HAD A FEW ROUGH DAYS, YEAH.
OH! SHE ALSO TOLD US ABOUT THE DISCIPLES OF VENU - - THESE MONKS WHO STUDY DREAMS AND WEAR THEIR HOODS PULLED DOWN OVER THEIR FACES!
STICK-EATERS. Y'RE A MILITARY ER THAT WENT ERGROUND WHEN KINGDOM FELL.
THE DREAMING! THAT'S WHAT GRAN'MA KEPT CALLING IT! SHE SAID THORN WOULD BE ALONE IN THE DREAMING!
HEY!
STICK-EATERS BELIEVE THAT OUR DREAMS CONNECT US ALL BACK TO SOME ORIGINAL SOURCE.
HEY!
ARE YOU A DISCIPLE OF VENU?
HEY!
O I
K LIKE
LY MAN
TO
OU?
HEY! IS THORN A REAL PRINCESS WITH A CROWN AN' EVERYTHING?
HOW DO I KNOW, SMILEY? YEAH, WITH A CROWN AN' EVERYTHING! TH' WHOLE WORKS!
WHAT HAPPENED THE OTHER NIGHT, BONE? WE HEARD YOU YELLIN' ABOUT A DRAGON, BUT BY THE TIME WE GOT THERE, ALL WE FOUND WAS BLOOD SPATTERED ON THE GROUND.

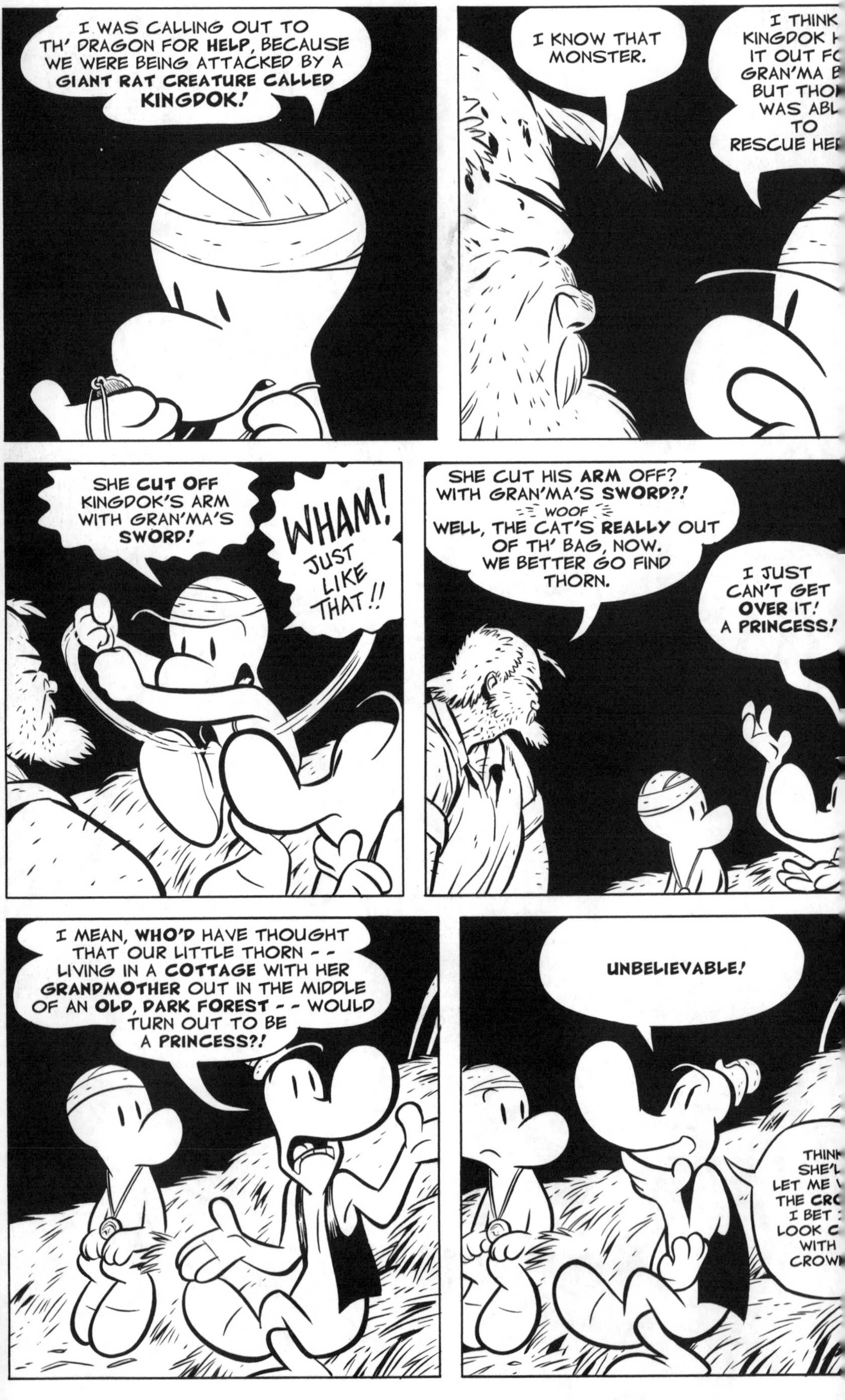

I WAS CALLING OUT TO TH' DRAGON FOR **HELP**, BECAUSE WE WERE BEING ATTACKED BY A **GIANT RAT CREATURE CALLED KINGDOK!**
I KNOW THAT MONSTER.
I THINK KINGDOK H IT OUT FO GRAN'MA B BUT THO WAS ABL TO RESCUE HE
SHE **CUT OFF** KINGDOK'S ARM WITH GRAN'MA'S **SWORD!**
WHAM! JUST LIKE THAT!!
SHE CUT HIS **ARM** OFF? WITH GRAN'MA'S **SWORD?!**
WOOF
WELL, THE CAT'S **REALLY** OUT OF TH' BAG, NOW. WE BETTER GO FIND THORN.
I JUST CAN'T GET **OVER** IT! A **PRINCESS!**
I MEAN, **WHO'D** HAVE THOUGHT THAT OUR LITTLE THORN - - LIVING IN A **COTTAGE** WITH HER **GRANDMOTHER** OUT IN THE MIDDLE OF AN **OLD, DARK FOREST** - - WOULD TURN OUT TO BE A **PRINCESS?!**
UNBELIEVABLE!
THINK SHE'L LET ME THE CRO I BET LOOK C WITH CROW

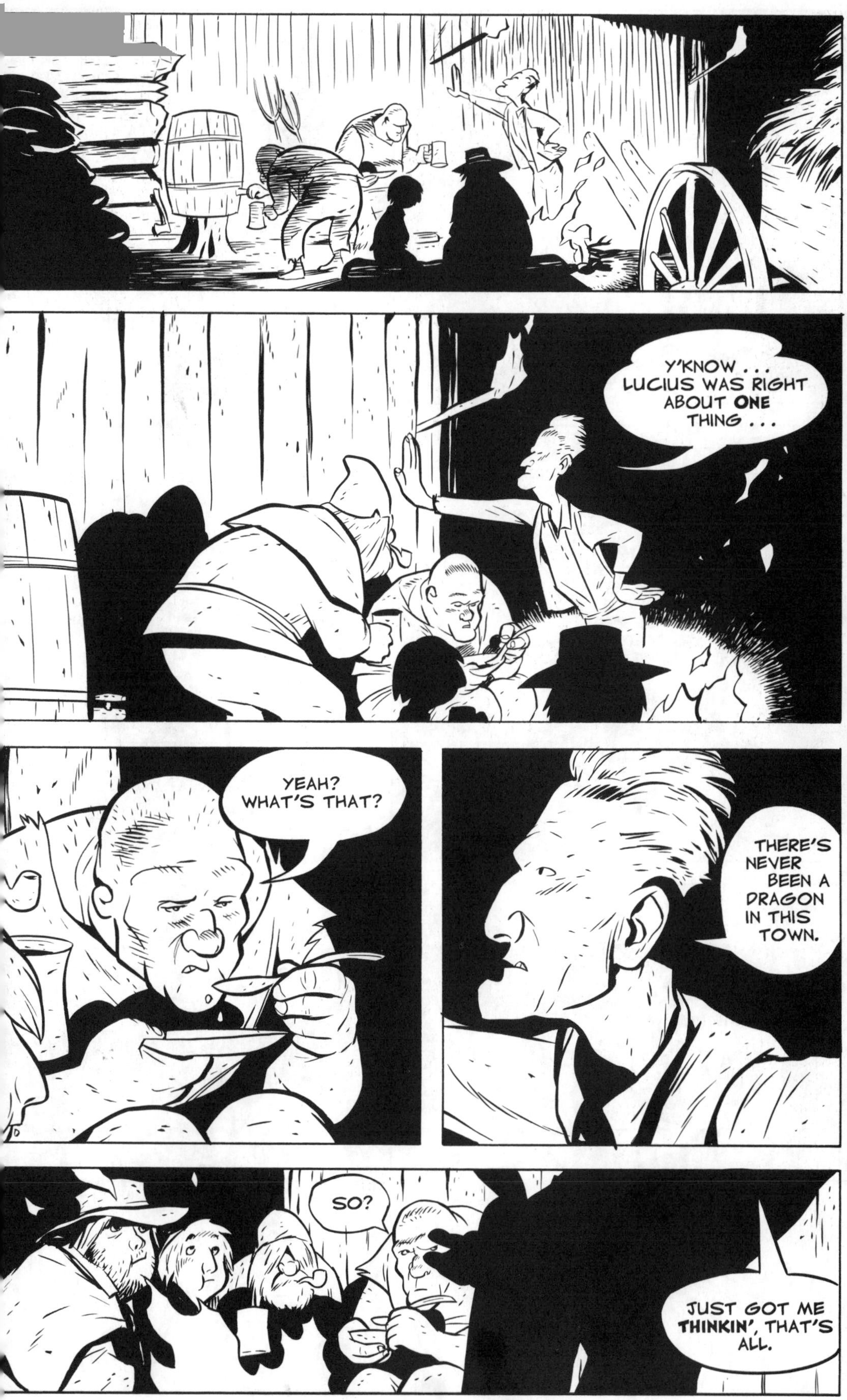
Y'KNOW . . . LUCIUS WAS RIGHT ABOUT ONE THING . . .
YEAH? WHAT'S THAT?
THERE'S NEVER BEEN A DRAGON IN THIS TOWN.
SO?
JUST GOT ME THINKIN', THAT'S ALL.

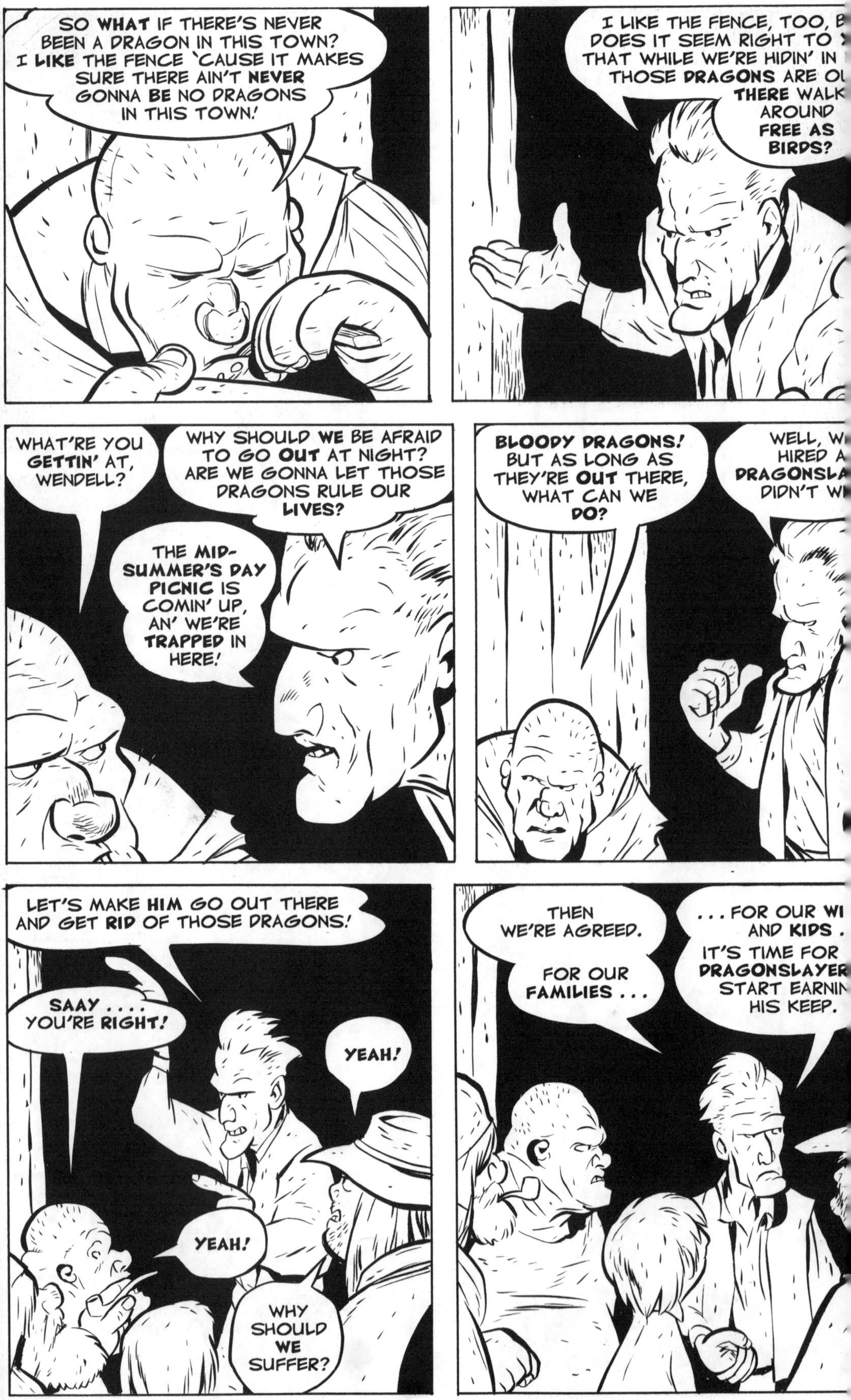
SO WHAT IF THERE'S NEVER BEEN A DRAGON IN THIS TOWN? I LIKE THE FENCE 'CAUSE IT MAKES SURE THERE AIN'T NEVER GONNA BE NO DRAGONS IN THIS TOWN!
I LIKE THE FENCE, TOO, B DOES IT SEEM RIGHT TO THAT WHILE WE'RE HIDIN' IN THOSE DRAGONS ARE O THERE WALK AROUND FREE AS BIRDS?
WHAT'RE YOU GETTIN' AT, WENDELL?
WHY SHOULD WE BE AFRAID TO GO OUT AT NIGHT? ARE WE GONNA LET THOSE DRAGONS RULE OUR LIVES?
THE MID-SUMMER'S DAY PICNIC IS COMIN' UP, AN' WE'RE TRAPPED IN HERE!
BLOODY DRAGONS! BUT AS LONG AS THEY'RE OUT THERE, WHAT CAN WE DO?
WELL, W HIRED A DRAGONSLA DIDN'T W
LET'S MAKE HIM GO OUT THERE AND GET RID OF THOSE DRAGONS!
SAAY . . . . YOU'RE RIGHT!
YEAH!
YEAH!
WHY SHOULD WE SUFFER?
THEN WE'RE AGREED.
FOR OUR FAMILIES . . .
. . . FOR OUR WI AND KIDS .
IT'S TIME FOR DRAGONSLAYER START EARNIN HIS KEEP.

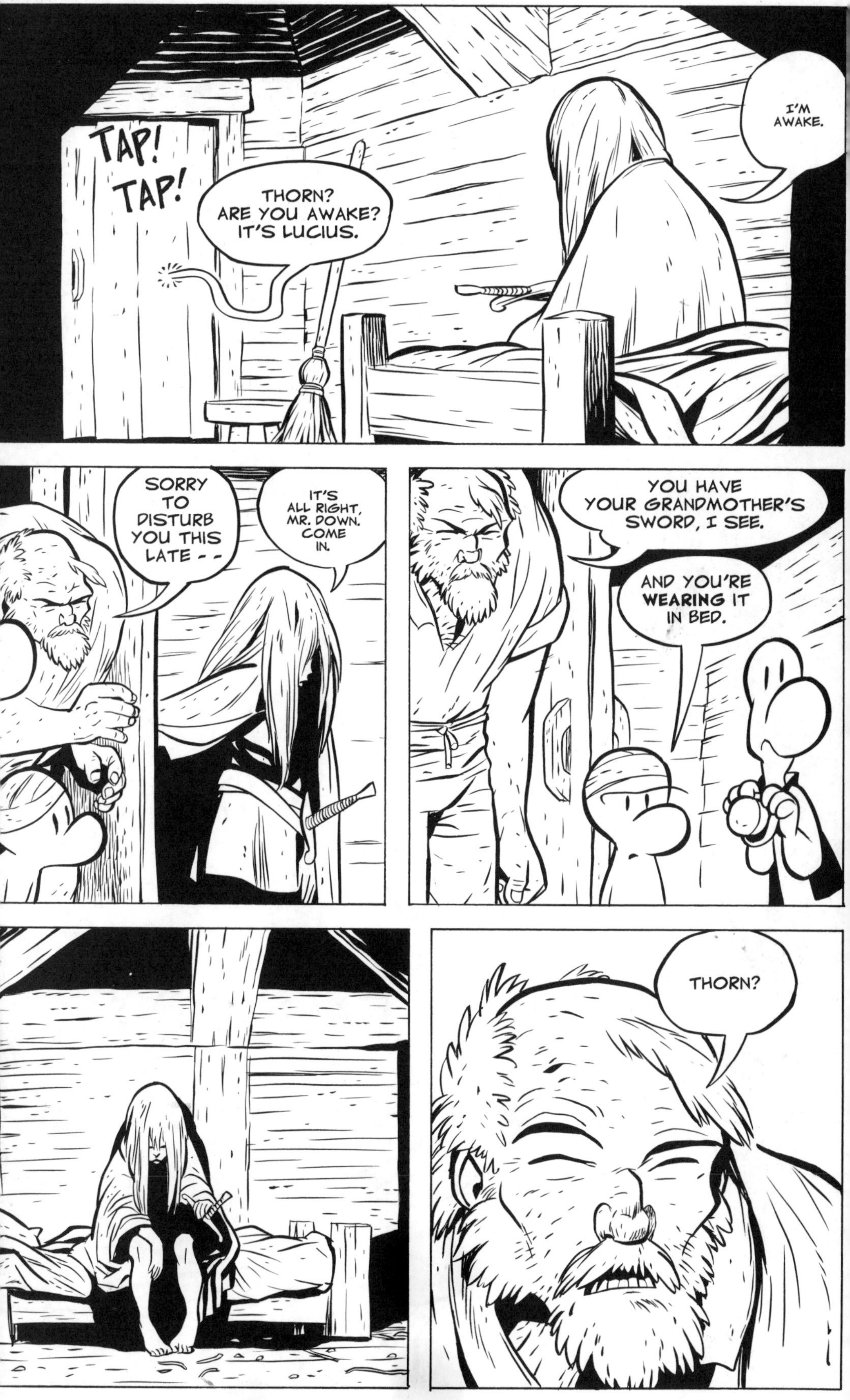
TAP! TAP!
THORN? ARE YOU AWAKE? IT'S LUCIUS.
I'M AWAKE.
SORRY TO DISTURB YOU THIS LATE - -
IT'S ALL RIGHT, MR. DOWN. COME IN.
YOU HAVE YOUR GRANDMOTHER'S SWORD, I SEE.
AND YOU'RE WEARING IT IN BED.
THORN?

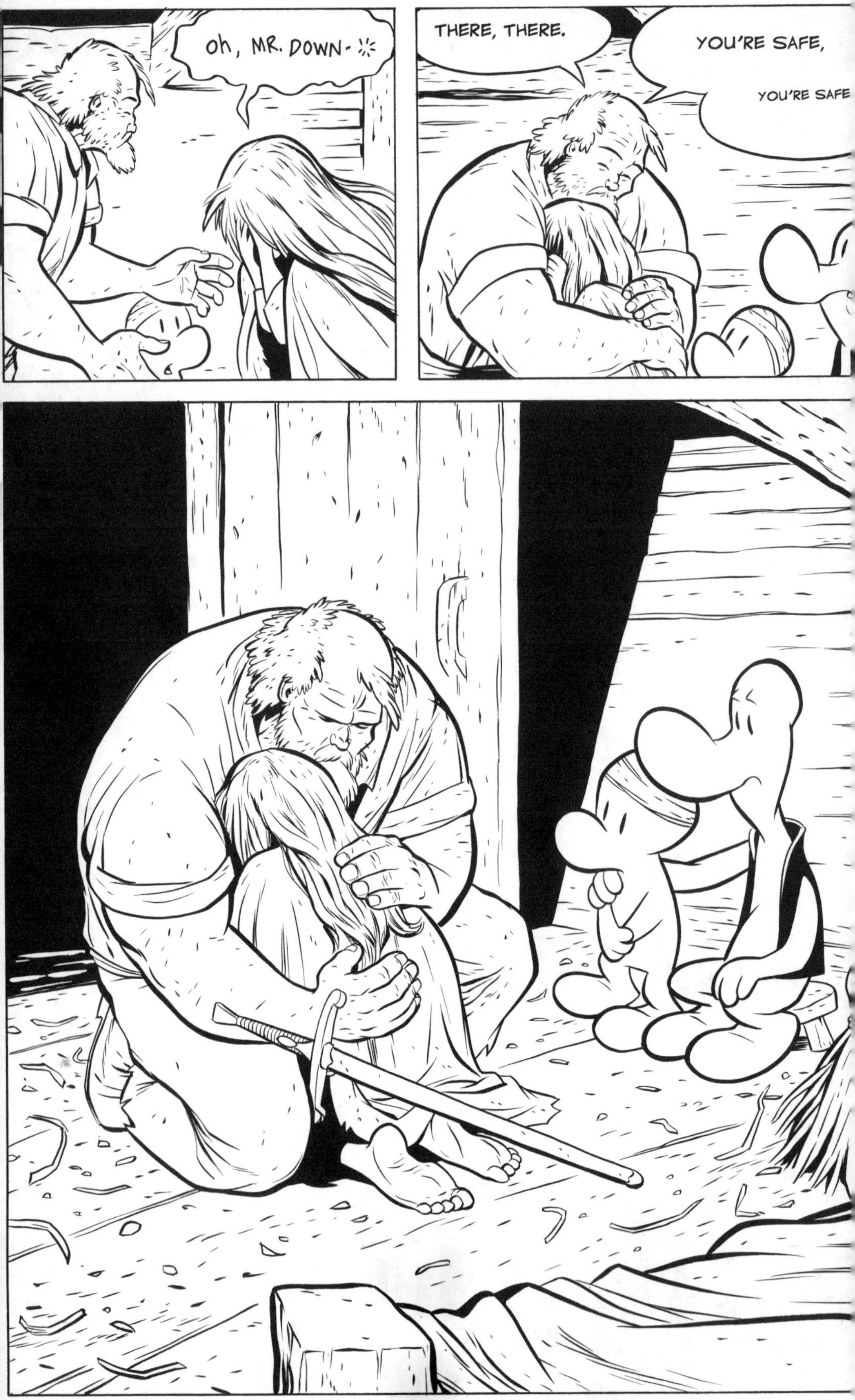

oh, MR. DOWN-
THERE, THERE.
YOU'RE SAFE,
YOU'RE SAFE

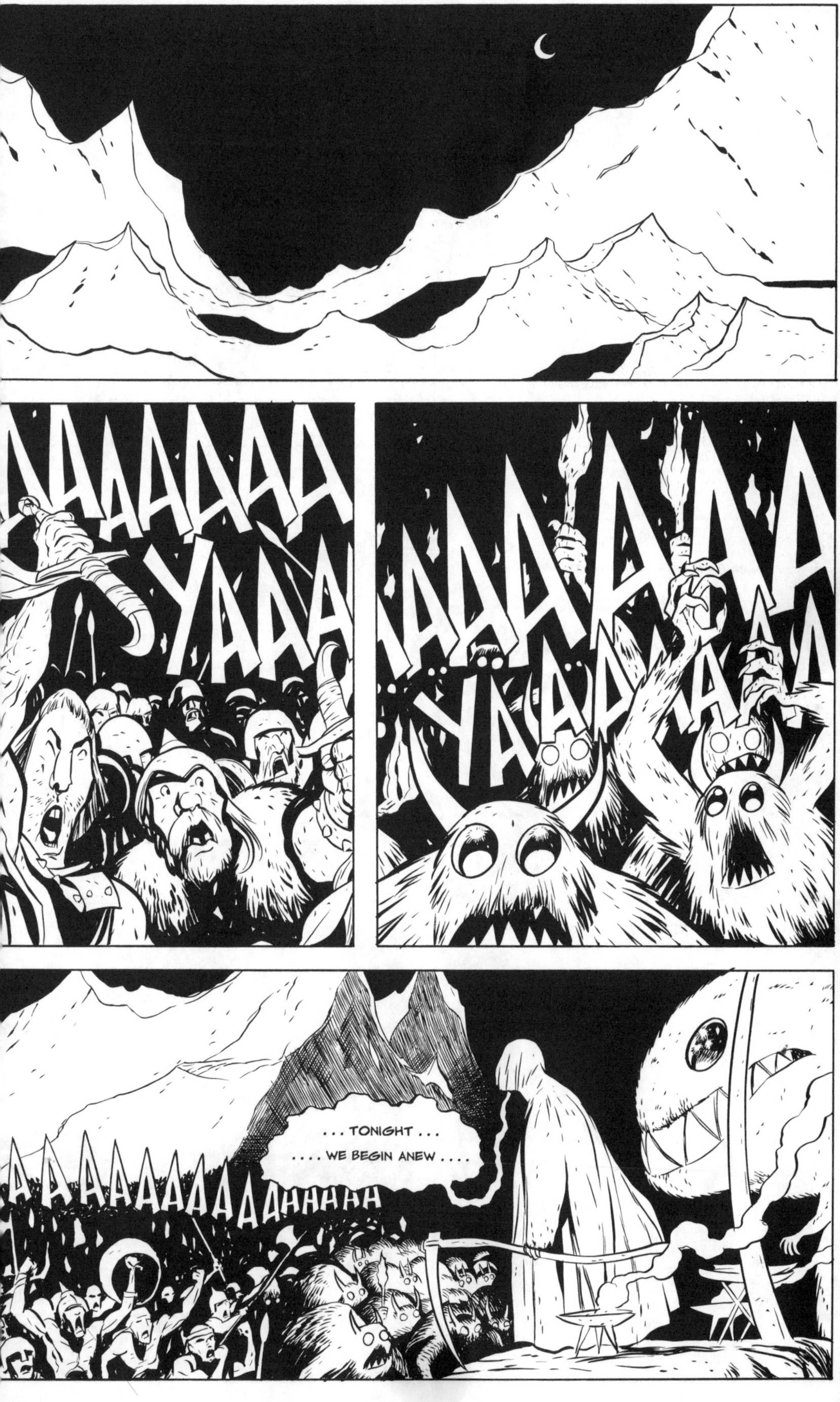
. . . TONIGHT . . .
. . . . WE BEGIN ANEW . . . .

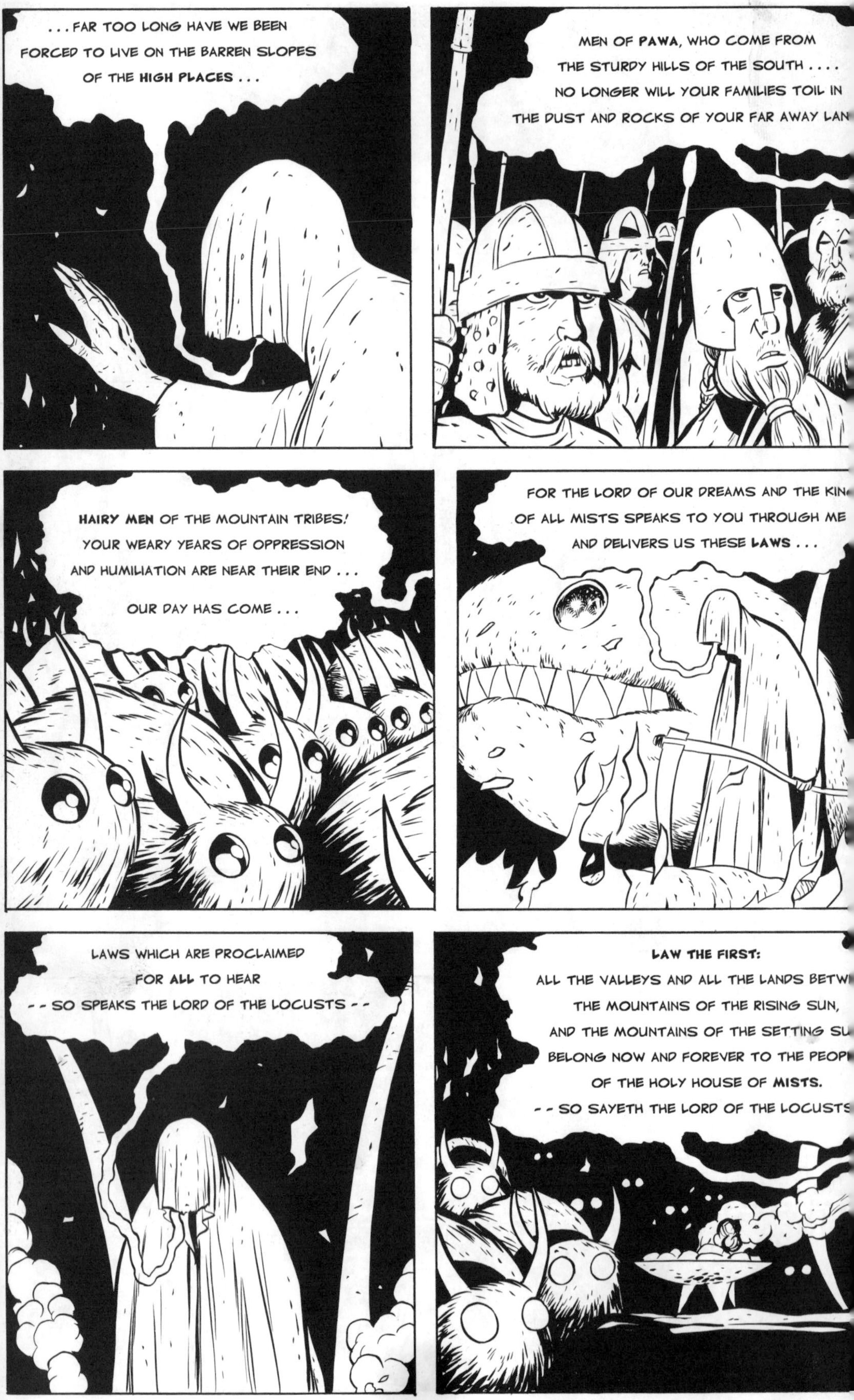
. . . FAR TOO LONG HAVE WE BEEN FORCED TO LIVE ON THE BARREN SLOPES OF THE HIGH PLACES . . .
MEN OF PAWA, WHO COME FROM THE STURDY HILLS OF THE SOUTH . . . . NO LONGER WILL YOUR FAMILIES TOIL IN THE DUST AND ROCKS OF YOUR FAR AWAY LAN
HAIRY MEN OF THE MOUNTAIN TRIBES! YOUR WEARY YEARS OF OPPRESSION AND HUMILIATION ARE NEAR THEIR END . . .
OUR DAY HAS COME . . .
FOR THE LORD OF OUR DREAMS AND THE KIN OF ALL MISTS SPEAKS TO YOU THROUGH ME AND DELIVERS US THESE LAWS . . .
LAWS WHICH ARE PROCLAIMED FOR ALL TO HEAR - - SO SPEAKS THE LORD OF THE LOCUSTS - -
LAW THE FIRST:
ALL THE VALLEYS AND ALL THE LANDS BETW THE MOUNTAINS OF THE RISING SUN, AND THE MOUNTAINS OF THE SETTING SU BELONG NOW AND FOREVER TO THE PEOP OF THE HOLY HOUSE OF MISTS.
- - SO SAYETH THE LORD OF THE LOCUSTS

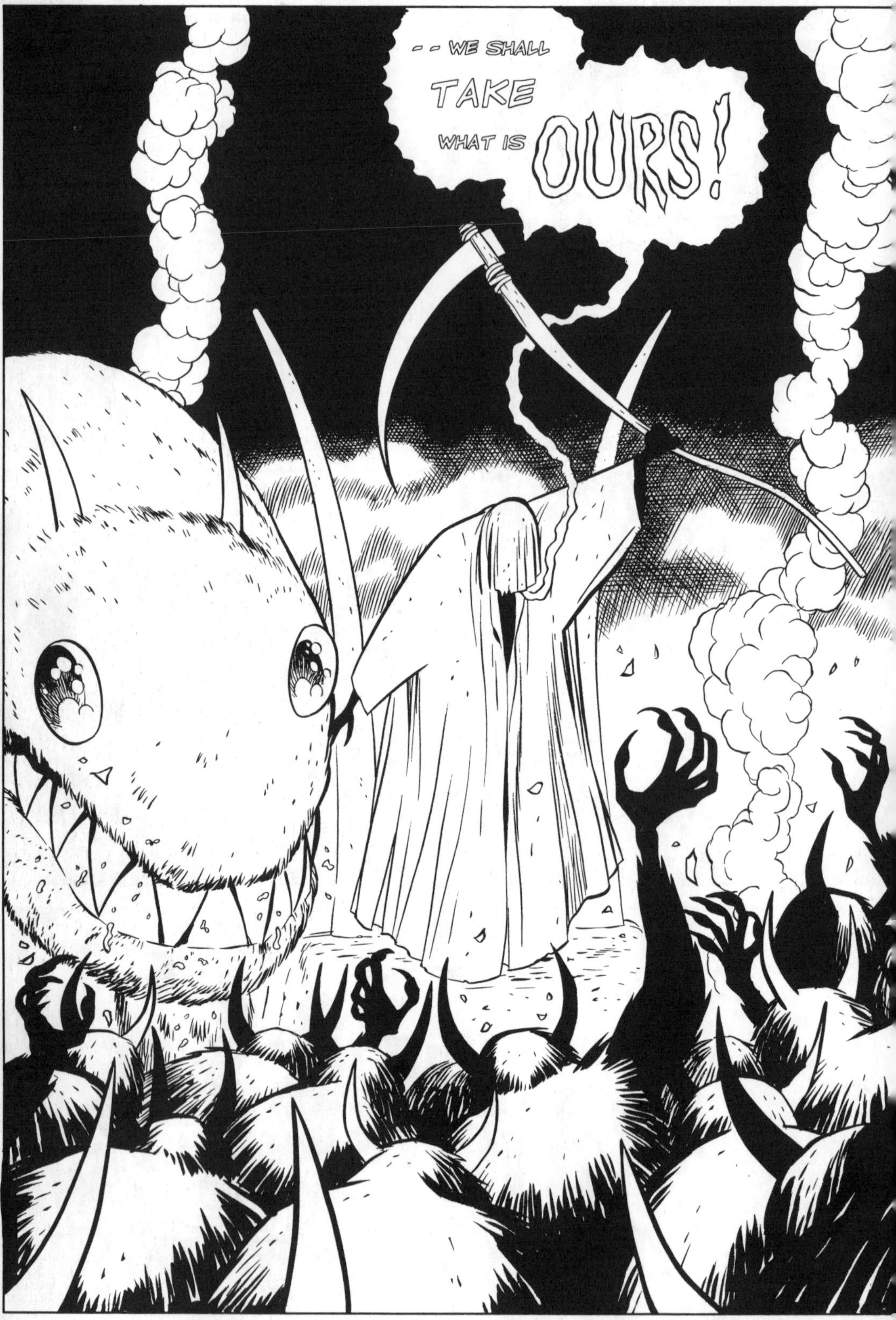
-- WE SHALL TAKE WHAT IS OURS!

NEXT: THE MID SUMMER'S DAY PLA

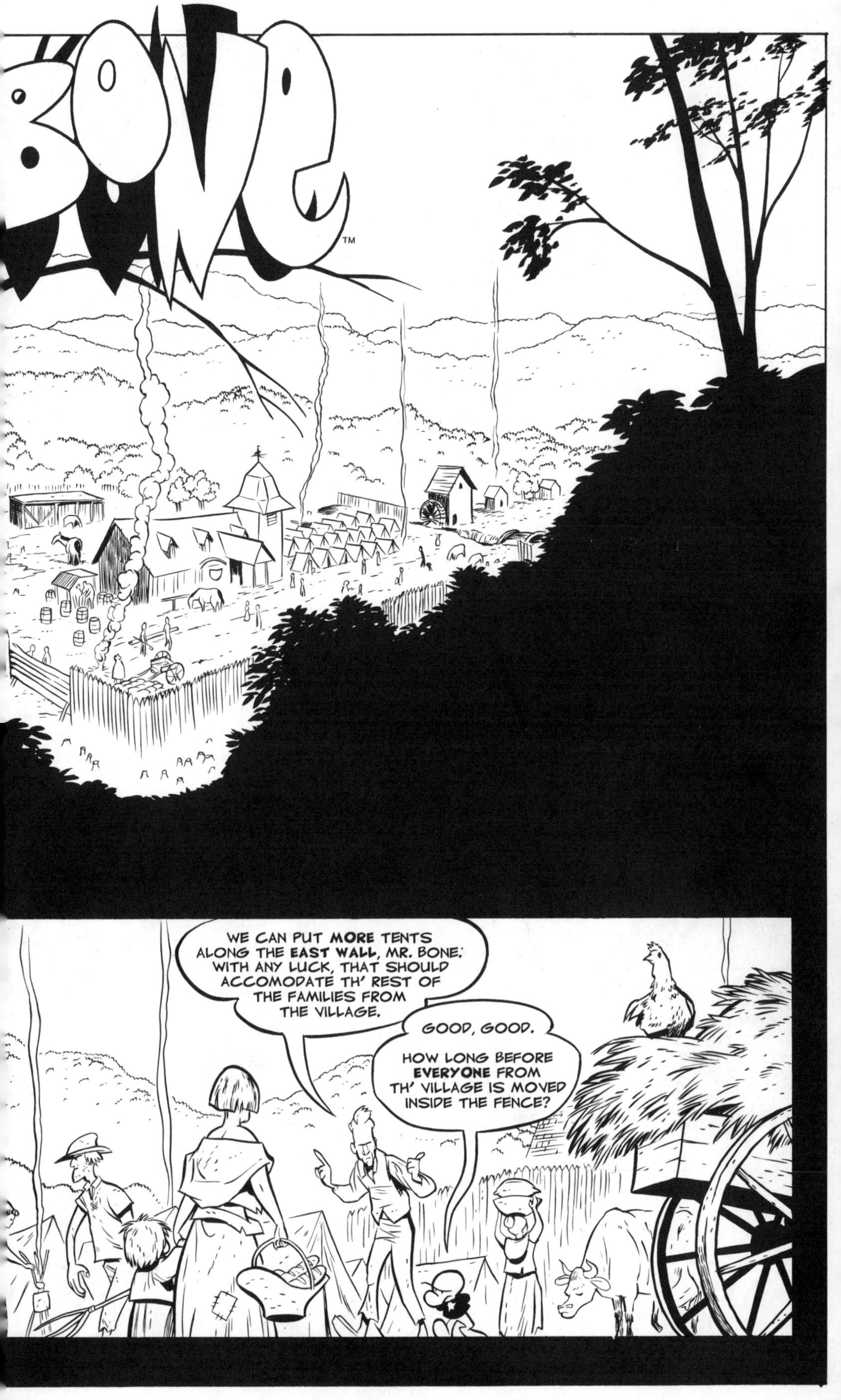
BONE™
WE CAN PUT MORE TENTS ALONG THE EAST WALL, MR. BONE. WITH ANY LUCK, THAT SHOULD ACCOMODATE TH' REST OF THE FAMILIES FROM THE VILLAGE.
GOOD, GOOD.
HOW LONG BEFORE EVERYONE FROM TH' VILLAGE IS MOVED INSIDE THE FENCE?

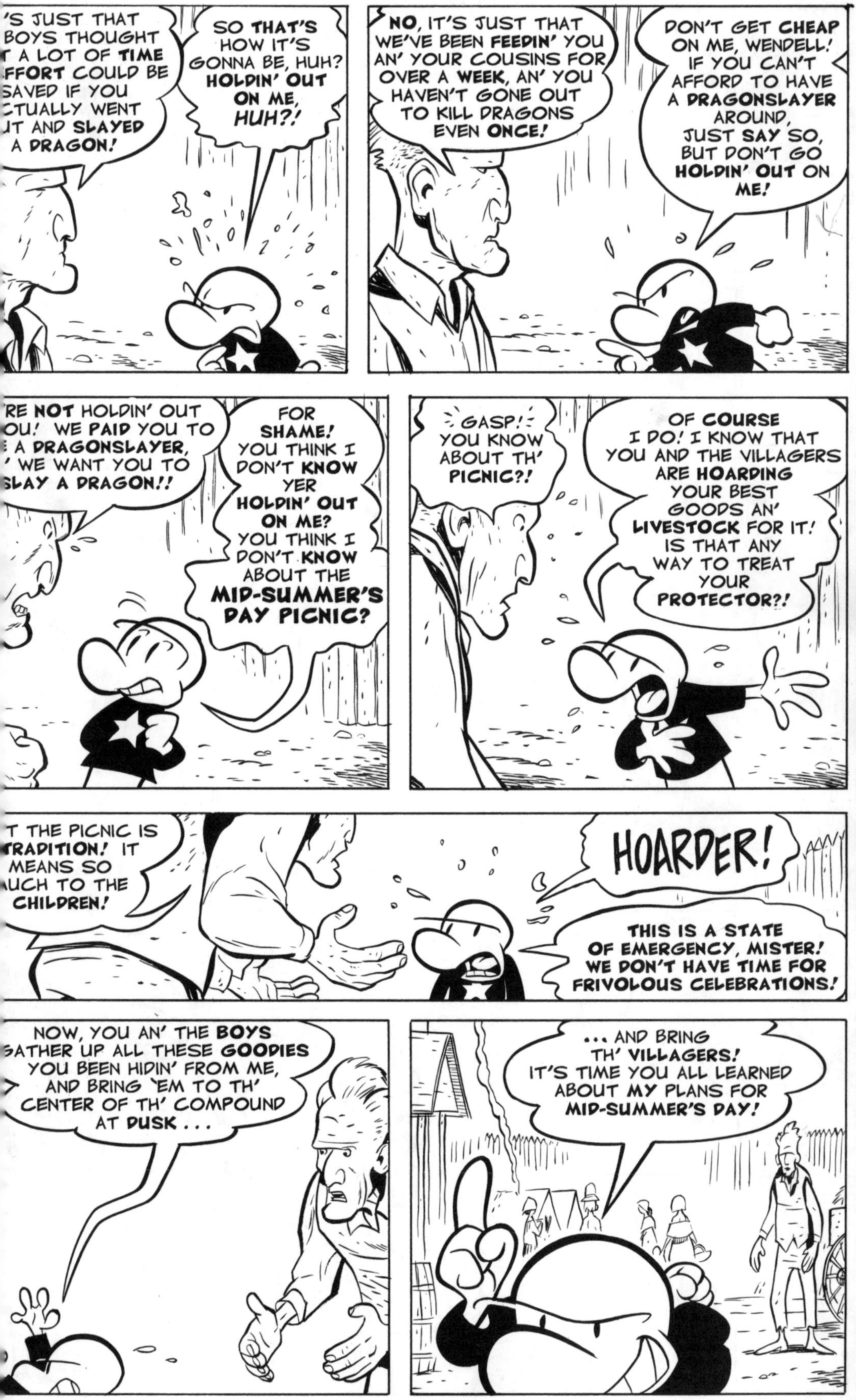

'S JUST THAT BOYS THOUGHT T A LOT OF TIME FFORT COULD BE SAVED IF YOU CTUALLY WENT JT AND SLAYED A DRAGON!
SO THAT'S HOW IT'S GONNA BE, HUH? HOLDIN' OUT ON ME, HUH?!
NO, IT'S JUST THAT WE'VE BEEN FEEDIN' YOU AN' YOUR COUSINS FOR OVER A WEEK, AN' YOU HAVEN'T GONE OUT TO KILL DRAGONS EVEN ONCE!
DON'T GET CHEAP ON ME, WENDELL! IF YOU CAN'T AFFORD TO HAVE A DRAGONSLAYER AROUND, JUST SAY SO, BUT DON'T GO HOLDIN' OUT ON ME!
'RE NOT HOLDIN' OUT OU! WE PAID YOU TO E A DRAGONSLAYER, ' WE WANT YOU TO SLAY A DRAGON!!
FOR SHAME! YOU THINK I DON'T KNOW YER HOLDIN' OUT ON ME? YOU THINK I DON'T KNOW ABOUT THE MID-SUMMER'S DAY PICNIC?
GASP! YOU KNOW ABOUT TH' PICNIC?!
OF COURSE I DO! I KNOW THAT YOU AND THE VILLAGERS ARE HOARDING YOUR BEST GOODS AN' LIVESTOCK FOR IT! IS THAT ANY WAY TO TREAT YOUR PROTECTOR?!
T THE PICNIC IS TRADITION! IT MEANS SO UCH TO THE CHILDREN!
HOARDER!
THIS IS A STATE OF EMERGENCY, MISTER! WE DON'T HAVE TIME FOR FRIVOLOUS CELEBRATIONS!
NOW, YOU AN' THE BOYS GATHER UP ALL THESE GOODIES YOU BEEN HIDIN' FROM ME, AND BRING 'EM TO TH' CENTER OF TH' COMPOUND AT DUSK...
...AND BRING TH' VILLAGERS! IT'S TIME YOU ALL LEARNED ABOUT MY PLANS FOR MID-SUMMER'S DAY!

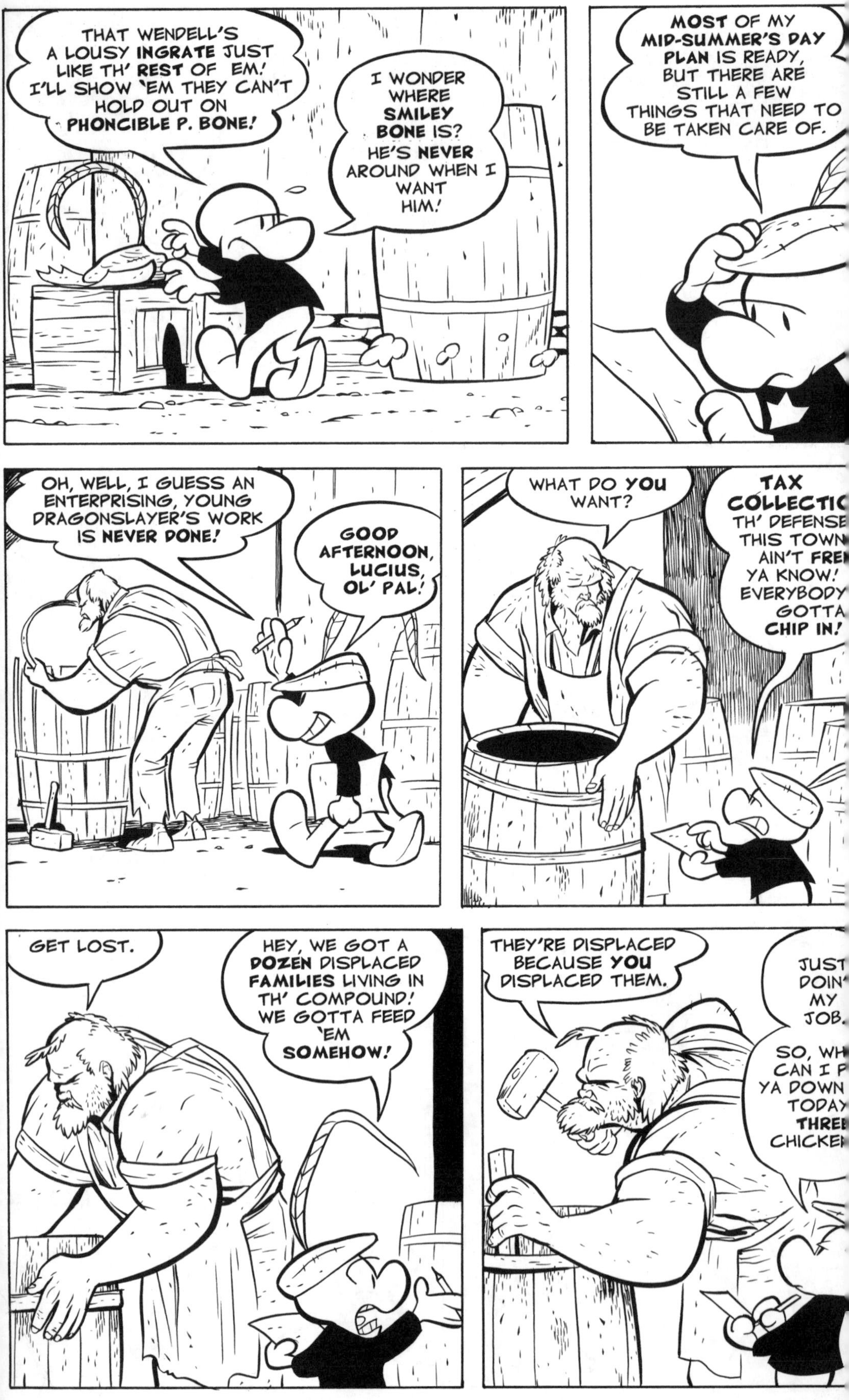
THAT WENDELL'S A LOUSY **INGRATE** JUST LIKE TH' **REST** OF EM! I'LL SHOW 'EM THEY CAN'T HOLD OUT ON **PHONCIBLE P. BONE!**
I WONDER WHERE **SMILEY BONE** IS? HE'S **NEVER** AROUND WHEN I WANT HIM!
MOST OF MY **MID-SUMMER'S DAY PLAN** IS READY, BUT THERE ARE STILL A FEW THINGS THAT NEED TO BE TAKEN CARE OF.
OH, WELL, I GUESS AN ENTERPRISING, YOUNG DRAGONSLAYER'S WORK IS **NEVER DONE!**
GOOD AFTERNOON, LUCIUS, OL' PAL!
WHAT DO **YOU** WANT?
TAX COLLECTI
TH' DEFENSE
THIS TOWN
AIN'T **FRE**
YA KNOW!
EVERYBODY
GOTTA
CHIP IN!
GET LOST.
HEY, WE GOT A **DOZEN** DISPLACED **FAMILIES** LIVING IN TH' COMPOUND! WE GOTTA FEED 'EM **SOMEHOW!**
THEY'RE DISPLACED BECAUSE **YOU** DISPLACED THEM.
JUST
DOIN'
MY
JOB.
SO, WH
CAN I P
YA DOWN
TODAY
THRE
CHICKE

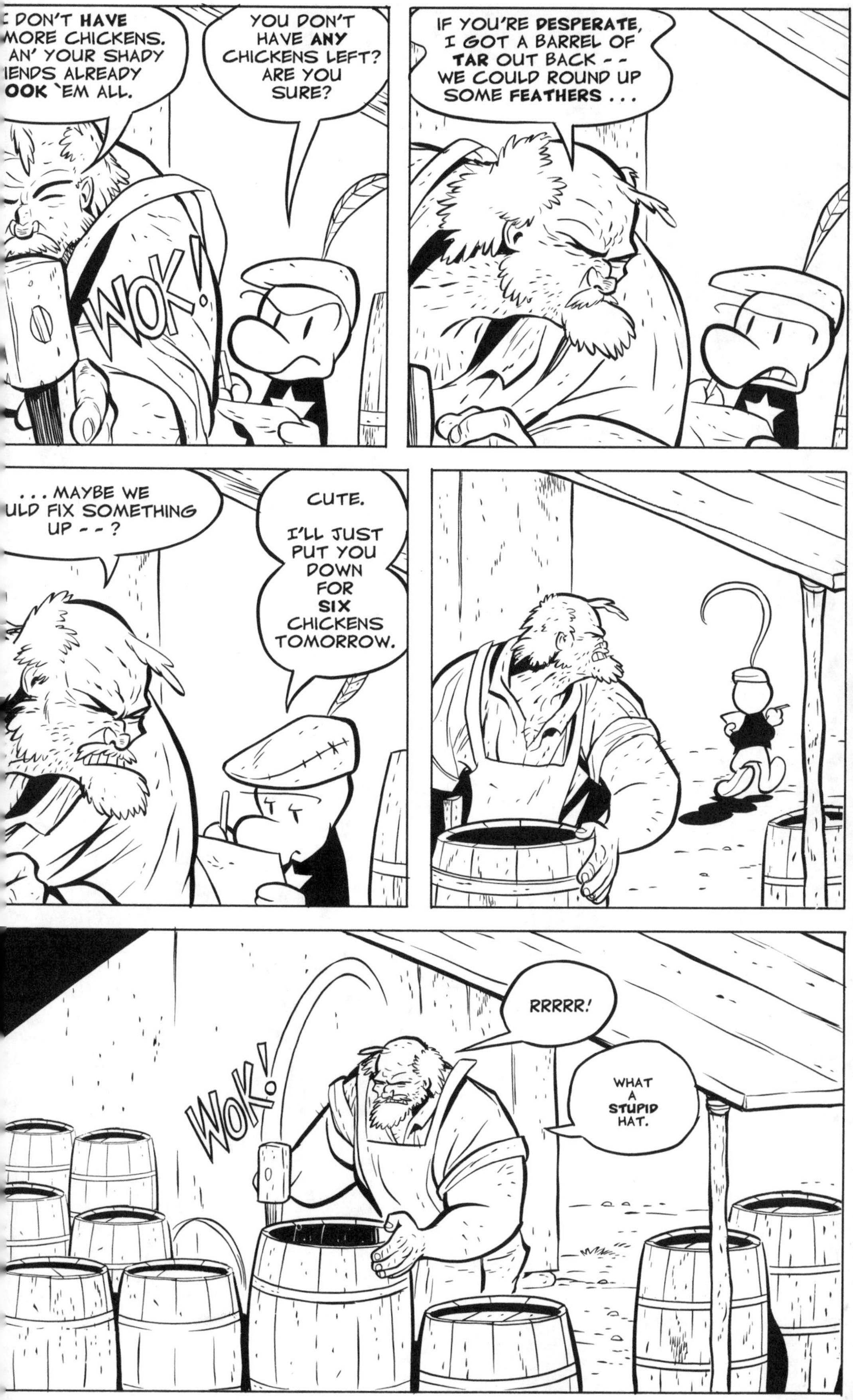
I DON'T HAVE MORE CHICKENS. AN' YOUR SHADY FRIENDS ALREADY TOOK `EM ALL.
WOK!
YOU DON'T HAVE ANY CHICKENS LEFT? ARE YOU SURE?
IF YOU'RE DESPERATE, I GOT A BARREL OF TAR OUT BACK - - WE COULD ROUND UP SOME FEATHERS . . .
. . . MAYBE WE COULD FIX SOMETHING UP - - ?
CUTE.
I'LL JUST PUT YOU DOWN FOR SIX CHICKENS TOMORROW.
RRRRR!
WOK!
WHAT A STUPID HAT.

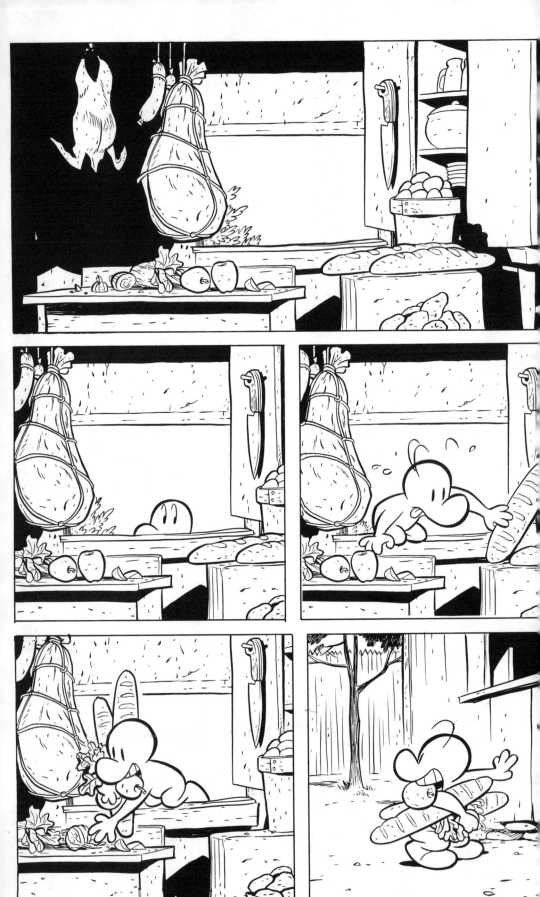

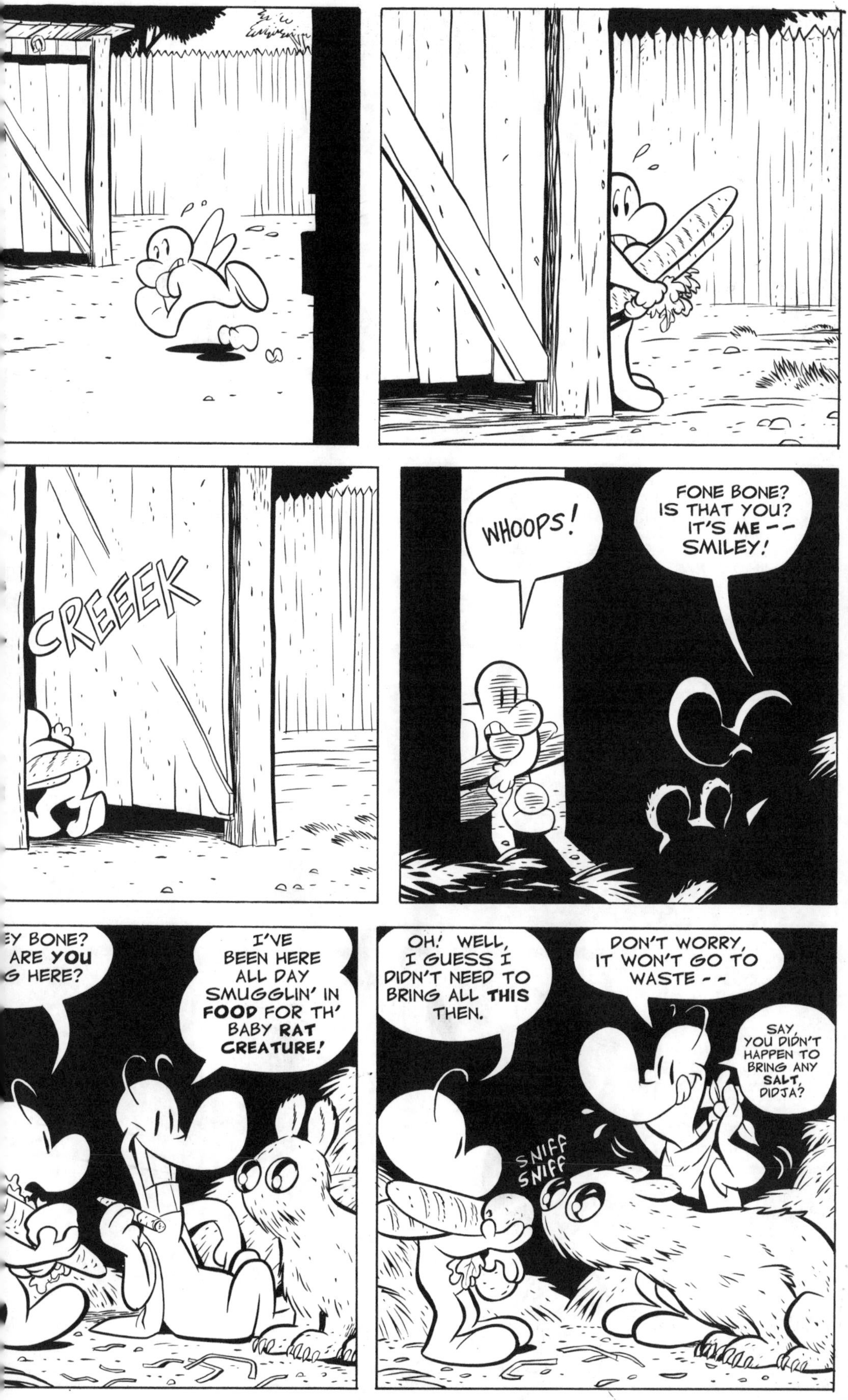
CREEEK
WHOOPS!
FONE BONE? IS THAT YOU? IT'S **ME** -- SMILEY!
EY BONE? ARE **YOU** G HERE?
I'VE BEEN HERE ALL DAY SMUGGLIN' IN **FOOD** FOR TH' BABY **RAT CREATURE**!
OH! WELL, I GUESS I DIDN'T NEED TO BRING ALL **THIS** THEN.
DON'T WORRY, IT WON'T GO TO WASTE --
SAY, YOU DIDN'T HAPPEN TO BRING ANY **SALT**, DIDJA?
SNIFF SNIFF

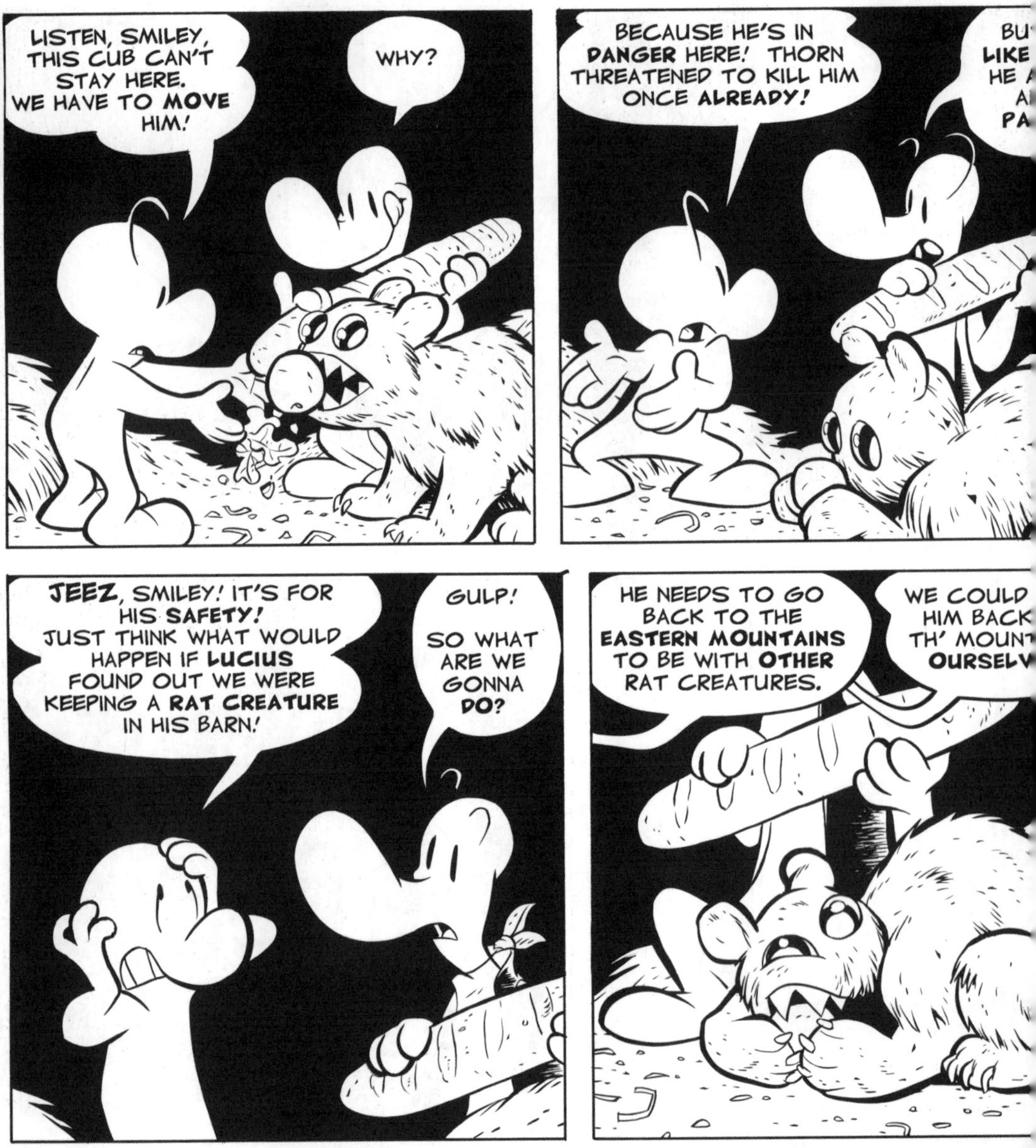
LISTEN, SMILEY, THIS CUB CAN'T STAY HERE. WE HAVE TO MOVE HIM!
WHY?
BECAUSE HE'S IN DANGER HERE! THORN THREATENED TO KILL HIM ONCE ALREADY!
BU LIKE HE A A PA
JEEZ, SMILEY! IT'S FOR HIS SAFETY! JUST THINK WHAT WOULD HAPPEN IF LUCIUS FOUND OUT WE WERE KEEPING A RAT CREATURE IN HIS BARN!
GULP!
SO WHAT ARE WE GONNA DO?
HE NEEDS TO GO BACK TO THE EASTERN MOUNTAINS TO BE WITH OTHER RAT CREATURES.
WE COULD HIM BACK TH' MOUNT OURSELV
THAT'S NOT EXACTLY WHAT I HAD IN MIND; I FIGURED IT WOULD BE GOOD ENOUGH IF WE COULD JUST GET HIM OUT OF THE COMPOUND!
HISS!
SOME-BODY'S COMIN'!
YOU HIDE TH' CUB -- I'LL HIDE TH' FOOD!
C'MON, BUDDY!

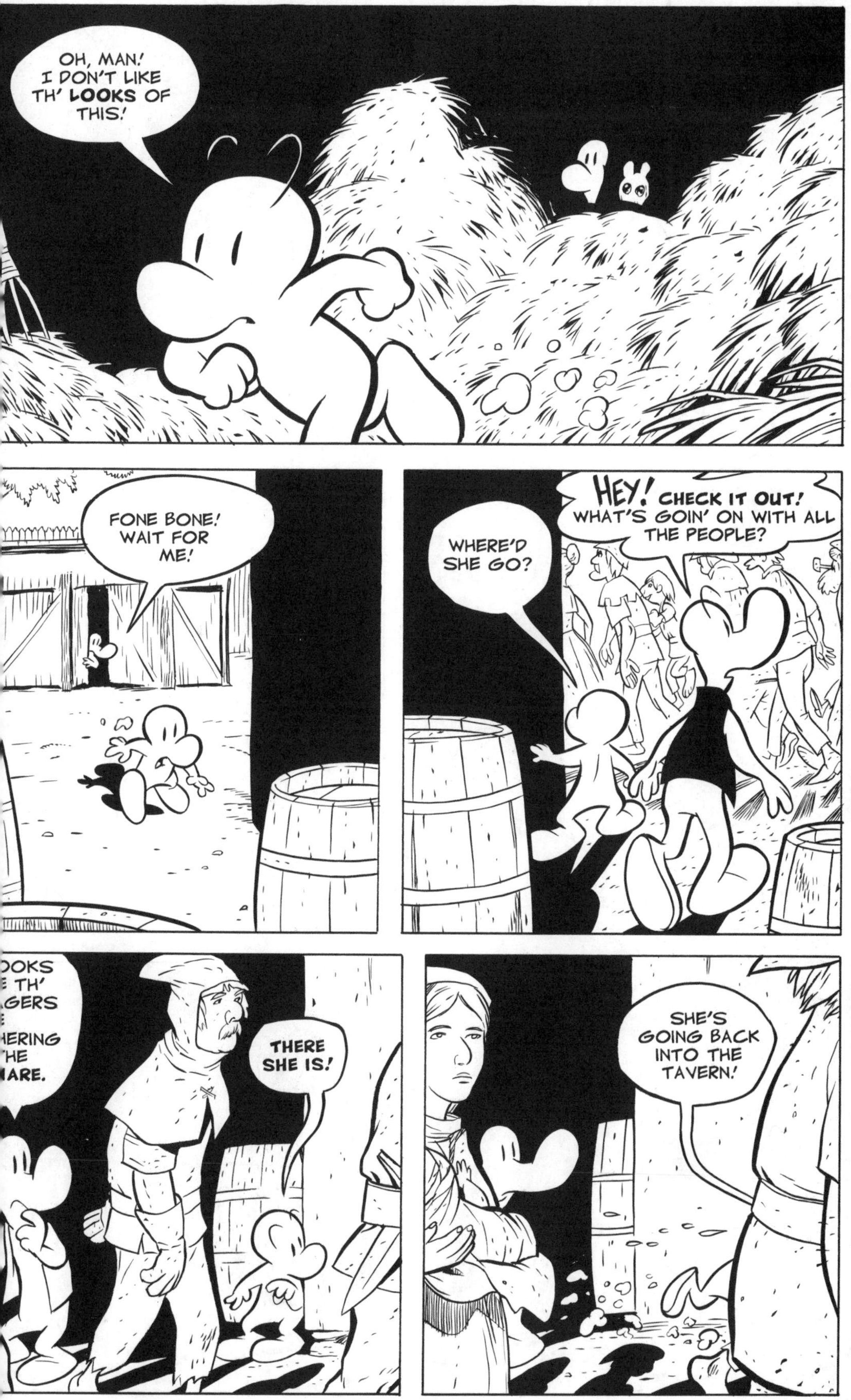

OH, MAN! I DON'T LIKE TH' **LOOKS** OF THIS!
FONE BONE! WAIT FOR ME!
WHERE'D SHE GO?
HEY! CHECK IT OUT! WHAT'S GOIN' ON WITH ALL THE PEOPLE?
OOKS E TH' GERS E HERING HE ARE.
THERE SHE IS!
SHE'S GOING BACK INTO THE TAVERN!

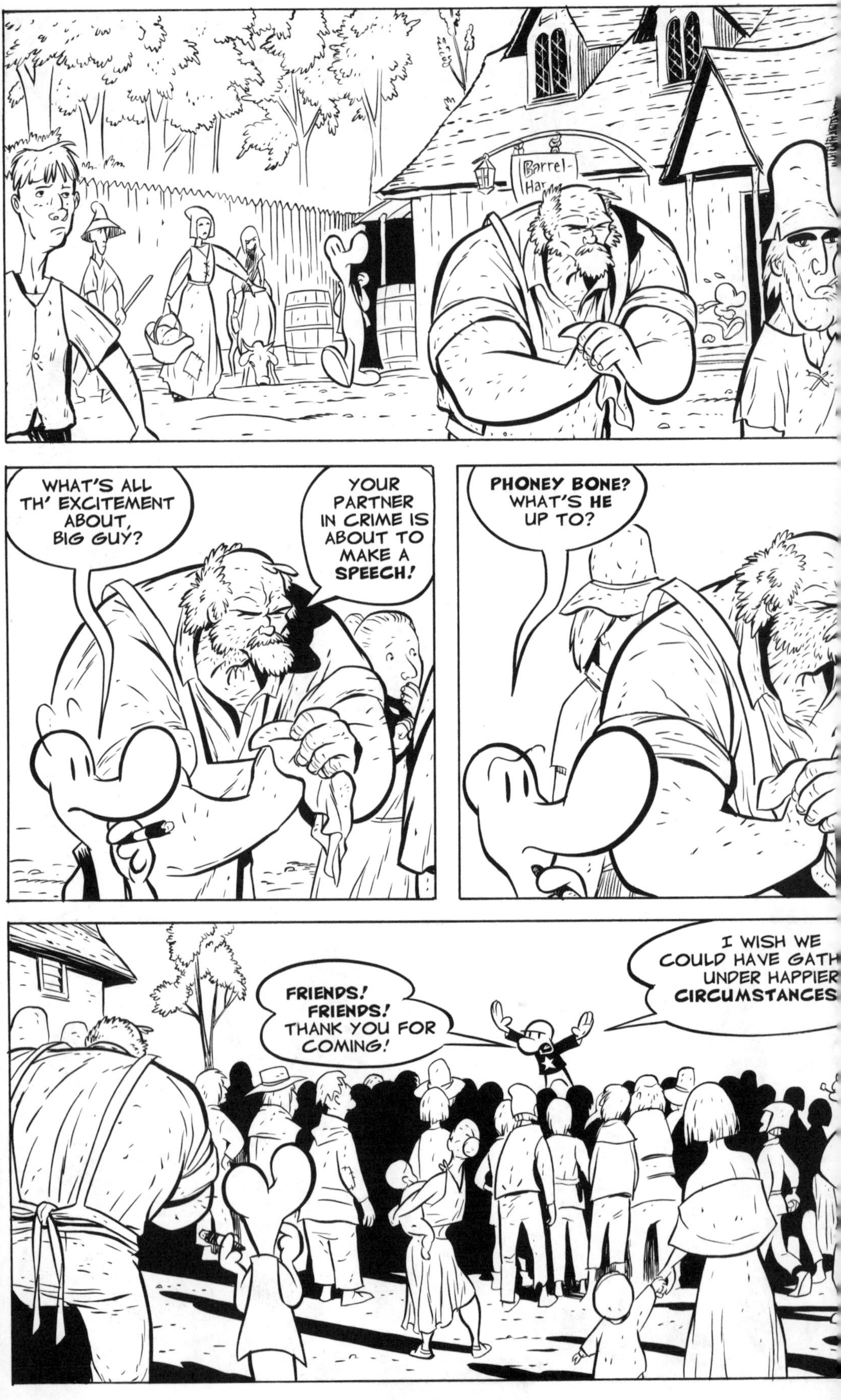
Barrel-Hav
WHAT'S ALL TH' EXCITEMENT ABOUT, BIG GUY?
YOUR PARTNER IN CRIME IS ABOUT TO MAKE A SPEECH!
PHONEY BONE? WHAT'S HE UP TO?
FRIENDS! FRIENDS! THANK YOU FOR COMING!
I WISH WE COULD HAVE GATH UNDER HAPPIER CIRCUMSTANCES

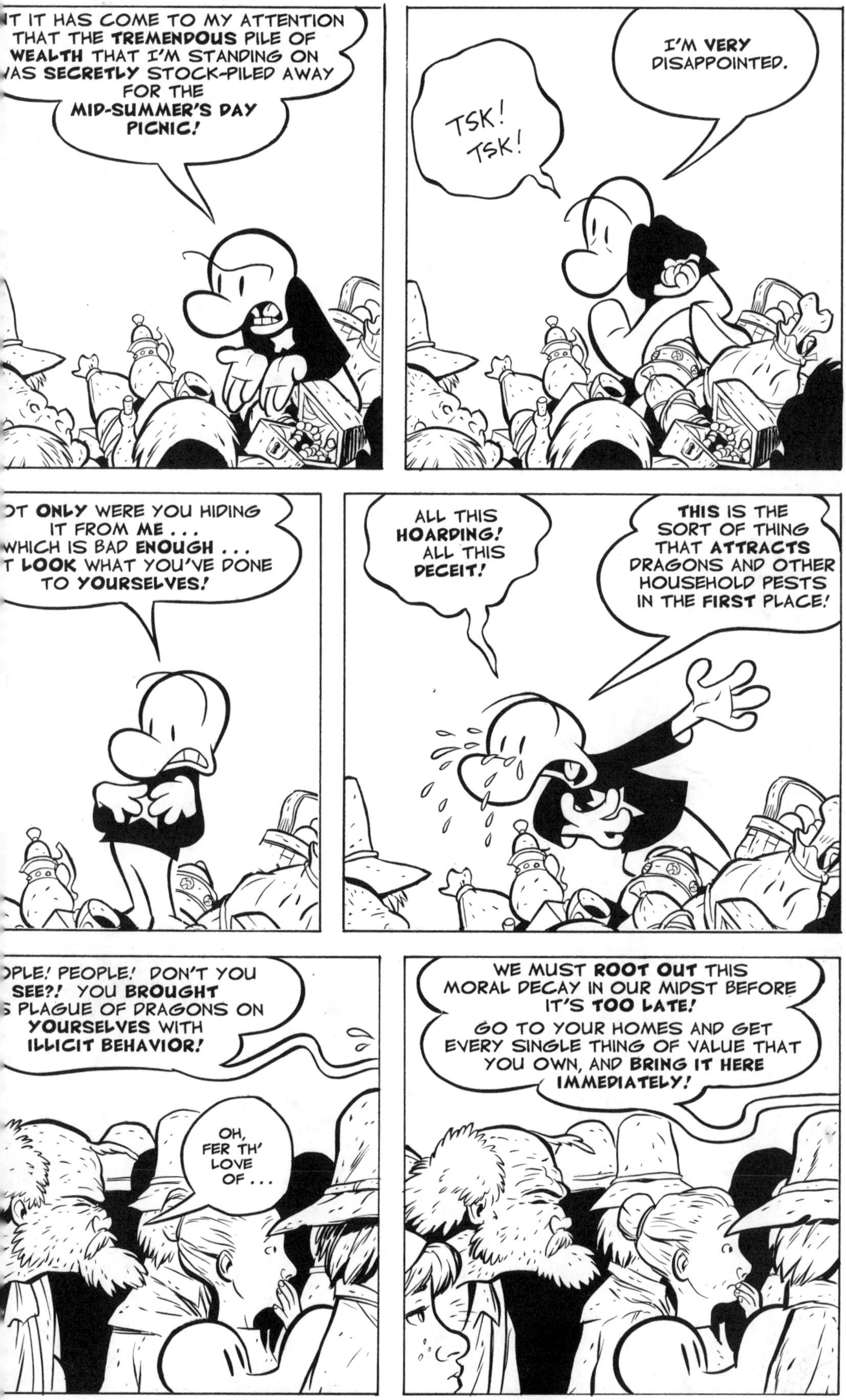
...T IT HAS COME TO MY ATTENTION THAT THE TREMENDOUS PILE OF WEALTH THAT I'M STANDING ON ...AS SECRETLY STOCK-PILED AWAY FOR THE MID-SUMMER'S DAY PICNIC!
TSK! TSK!
I'M VERY DISAPPOINTED.
...OT ONLY WERE YOU HIDING IT FROM ME ... WHICH IS BAD ENOUGH ... ...T LOOK WHAT YOU'VE DONE TO YOURSELVES!
ALL THIS HOARDING! ALL THIS DECEIT!
THIS IS THE SORT OF THING THAT ATTRACTS DRAGONS AND OTHER HOUSEHOLD PESTS IN THE FIRST PLACE!
...OPLE! PEOPLE! DON'T YOU SEE?! YOU BROUGHT ...S PLAGUE OF DRAGONS ON YOURSELVES WITH ILLICIT BEHAVIOR!
OH, FER TH' LOVE OF ...
WE MUST ROOT OUT THIS MORAL DECAY IN OUR MIDST BEFORE IT'S TOO LATE!
GO TO YOUR HOMES AND GET EVERY SINGLE THING OF VALUE THAT YOU OWN, AND BRING IT HERE IMMEDIATELY!

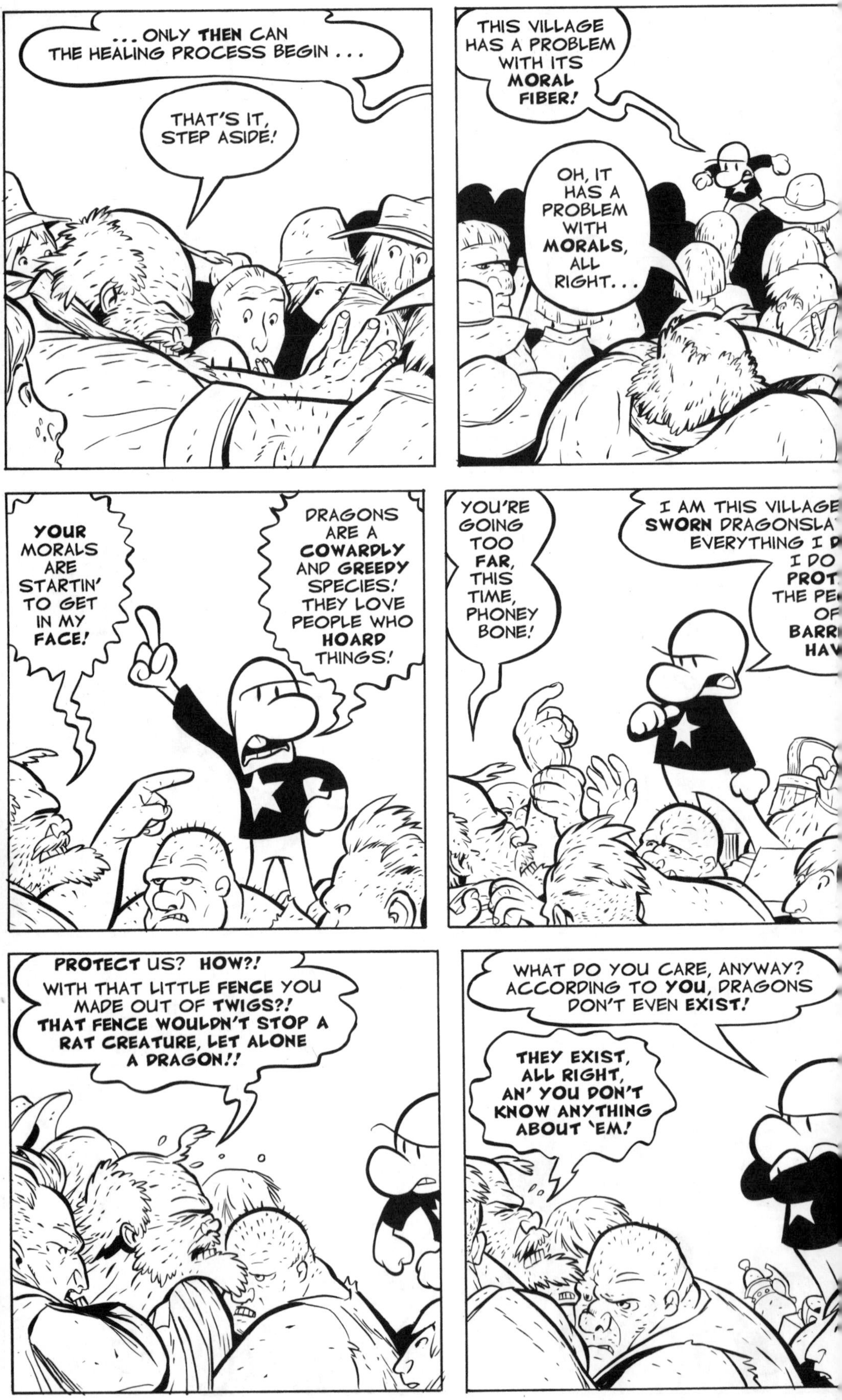
...ONLY THEN CAN THE HEALING PROCESS BEGIN...
THAT'S IT, STEP ASIDE!
THIS VILLAGE HAS A PROBLEM WITH ITS MORAL FIBER!
OH, IT HAS A PROBLEM WITH MORALS, ALL RIGHT...
DRAGONS ARE A COWARDLY AND GREEDY SPECIES! THEY LOVE PEOPLE WHO HOARD THINGS!
YOUR MORALS ARE STARTIN' TO GET IN MY FACE!
I AM THIS VILLAGE SWORN DRAGONSLA EVERYTHING I D I DO PROT THE PE OF BARR HAV
YOU'RE GOING TOO FAR, THIS TIME, PHONEY BONE!
PROTECT US? HOW?! WITH THAT LITTLE FENCE YOU MADE OUT OF TWIGS?! THAT FENCE WOULDN'T STOP A RAT CREATURE, LET ALONE A DRAGON!!
WHAT DO YOU CARE, ANYWAY? ACCORDING TO YOU, DRAGONS DON'T EVEN EXIST!
THEY EXIST, ALL RIGHT, AN' YOU DON'T KNOW ANYTHING ABOUT 'EM!

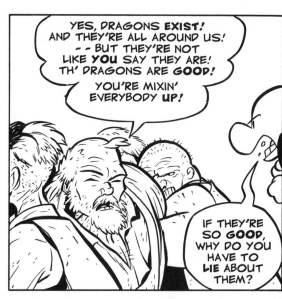

SO! YOU FINALLY ADMIT THAT DRAGONS DO EXIST! YOU ADMIT THAT IT'S ME WHO'S TELLING THE TRUTH!

YES, DRAGONS EXIST! AND THEY'RE ALL AROUND US! --BUT THEY'RE NOT LIKE YOU SAY THEY ARE! TH' DRAGONS ARE GOOD! YOU'RE MIXIN' EVERYBODY UP!

IF THEY'RE SO GOOD, WHY DO YOU HAVE TO LIE ABOUT THEM?

I DON'T HAVE TO--

IT'S NOT LIKE THAT--

JUST TELL ME ONE THING, LUCIUS--JUST ONE THING-- IF YOU KNEW DRAGONS WERE REAL ALL ALONG, WHY DID YOU TELL EVERYONE THEY WERE MAKE-BELIEVE?

HUH? WHY?!

WHAT'S THE MATTER, LUCIUS? CAT GOT YER TONGUE?

OR MAYBE THE REAL QUESTION IS: DOES A DRAGON HAVE YOUR TONGUE?

...HMM. I THOUGHT AS MUCH.

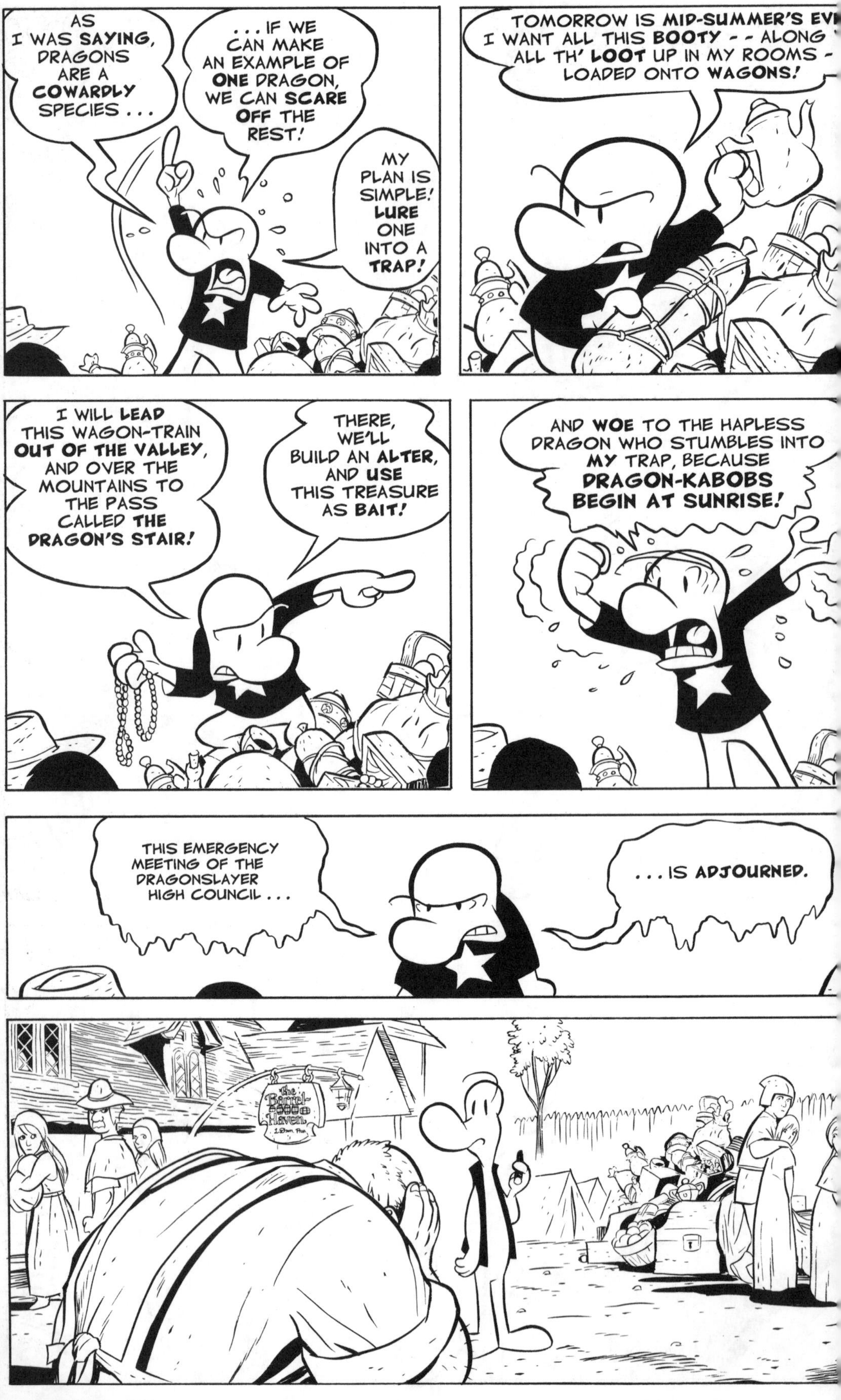
AS I WAS SAYING, DRAGONS ARE A COWARDLY SPECIES . . .
. . . IF WE CAN MAKE AN EXAMPLE OF ONE DRAGON, WE CAN SCARE OFF THE REST!
MY PLAN IS SIMPLE! LURE ONE INTO A TRAP!
TOMORROW IS MID-SUMMER'S EVE! I WANT ALL THIS BOOTY - - ALONG WITH ALL TH' LOOT UP IN MY ROOMS - - LOADED ONTO WAGONS!
I WILL LEAD THIS WAGON-TRAIN OUT OF THE VALLEY, AND OVER THE MOUNTAINS TO THE PASS CALLED THE DRAGON'S STAIR!
THERE, WE'LL BUILD AN ALTER, AND USE THIS TREASURE AS BAIT!
AND WOE TO THE HAPLESS DRAGON WHO STUMBLES INTO MY TRAP, BECAUSE DRAGON-KABOBS BEGIN AT SUNRISE!
THIS EMERGENCY MEETING OF THE DRAGONSLAYER HIGH COUNCIL . . .
. . . IS ADJOURNED.
The Barrel Haven

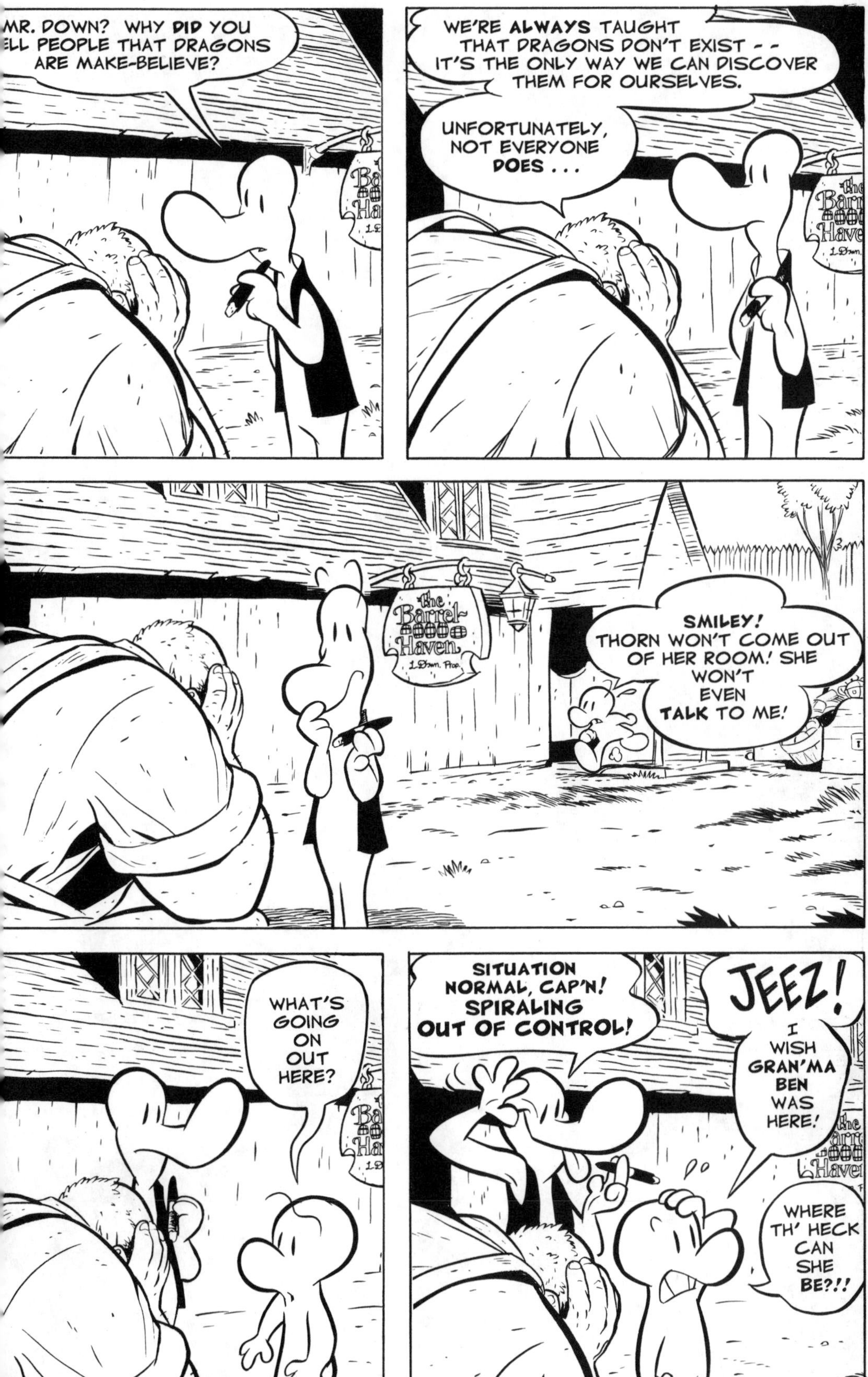
MR. DOWN? WHY DID YOU
ELL PEOPLE THAT DRAGONS
ARE MAKE-BELIEVE?
WE'RE ALWAYS TAUGHT THAT DRAGONS DON'T EXIST -- IT'S THE ONLY WAY WE CAN DISCOVER THEM FOR OURSELVES.
UNFORTUNATELY, NOT EVERYONE DOES . . .
The Barrel Haven
SMILEY! THORN WON'T COME OUT OF HER ROOM! SHE WON'T EVEN TALK TO ME!
The Barrel Haven 1. Down. Prop.
WHAT'S GOING ON OUT HERE?
SITUATION NORMAL, CAP'N! SPIRALING OUT OF CONTROL!
JEEZ! I WISH GRAN'MA BEN WAS HERE!
WHERE TH' HECK CAN SHE BE?!!

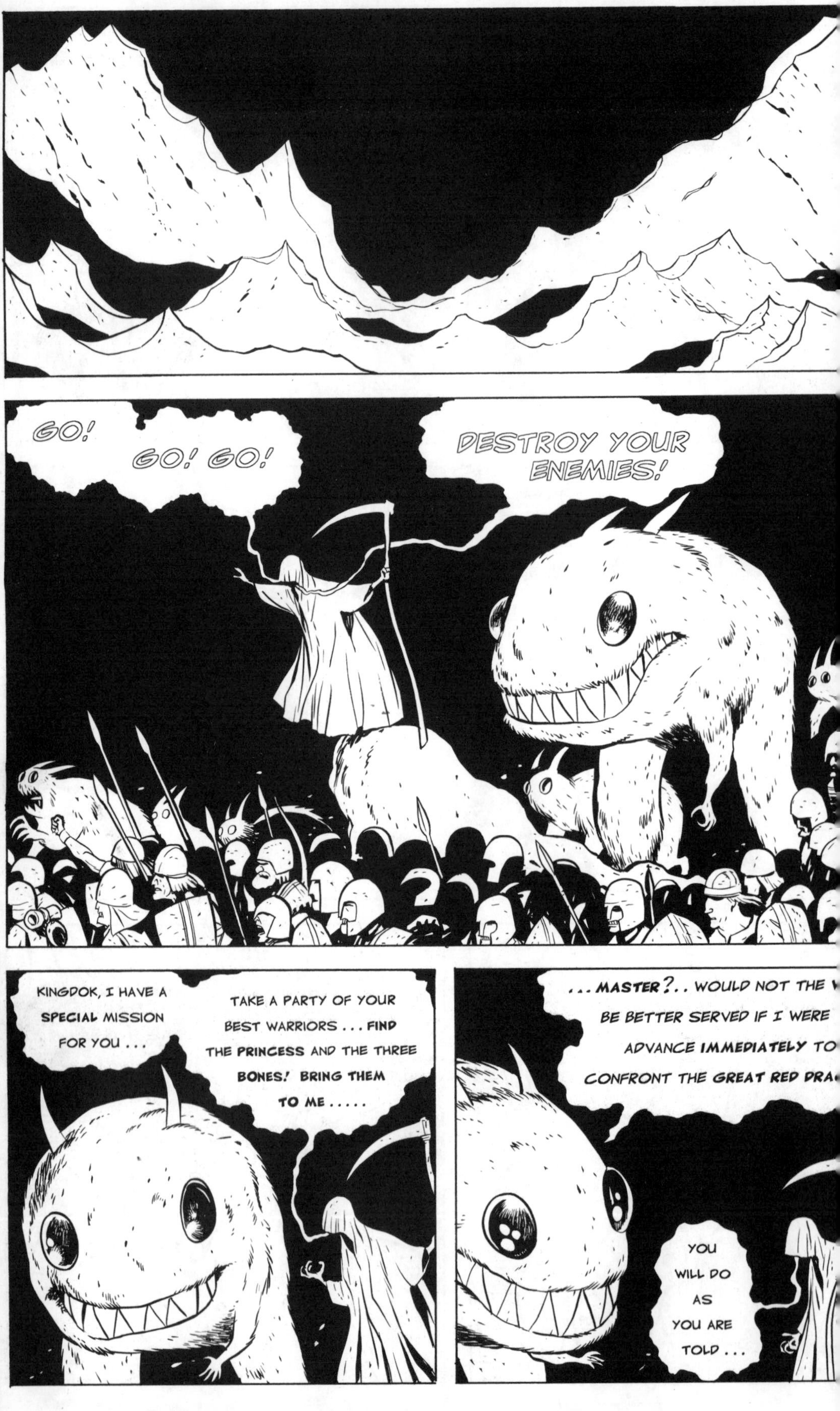
GO! GO! GO!
DESTROY YOUR ENEMIES!
KINGDOK, I HAVE A SPECIAL MISSION FOR YOU . . .
TAKE A PARTY OF YOUR BEST WARRIORS . . . FIND THE PRINCESS AND THE THREE BONES! BRING THEM TO ME . . . . .
. . . MASTER? . . WOULD NOT THE
BE BETTER SERVED IF I WERE
ADVANCE IMMEDIATELY TO
CONFRONT THE GREAT RED DRA
YOU WILL DO AS YOU ARE TOLD . . .

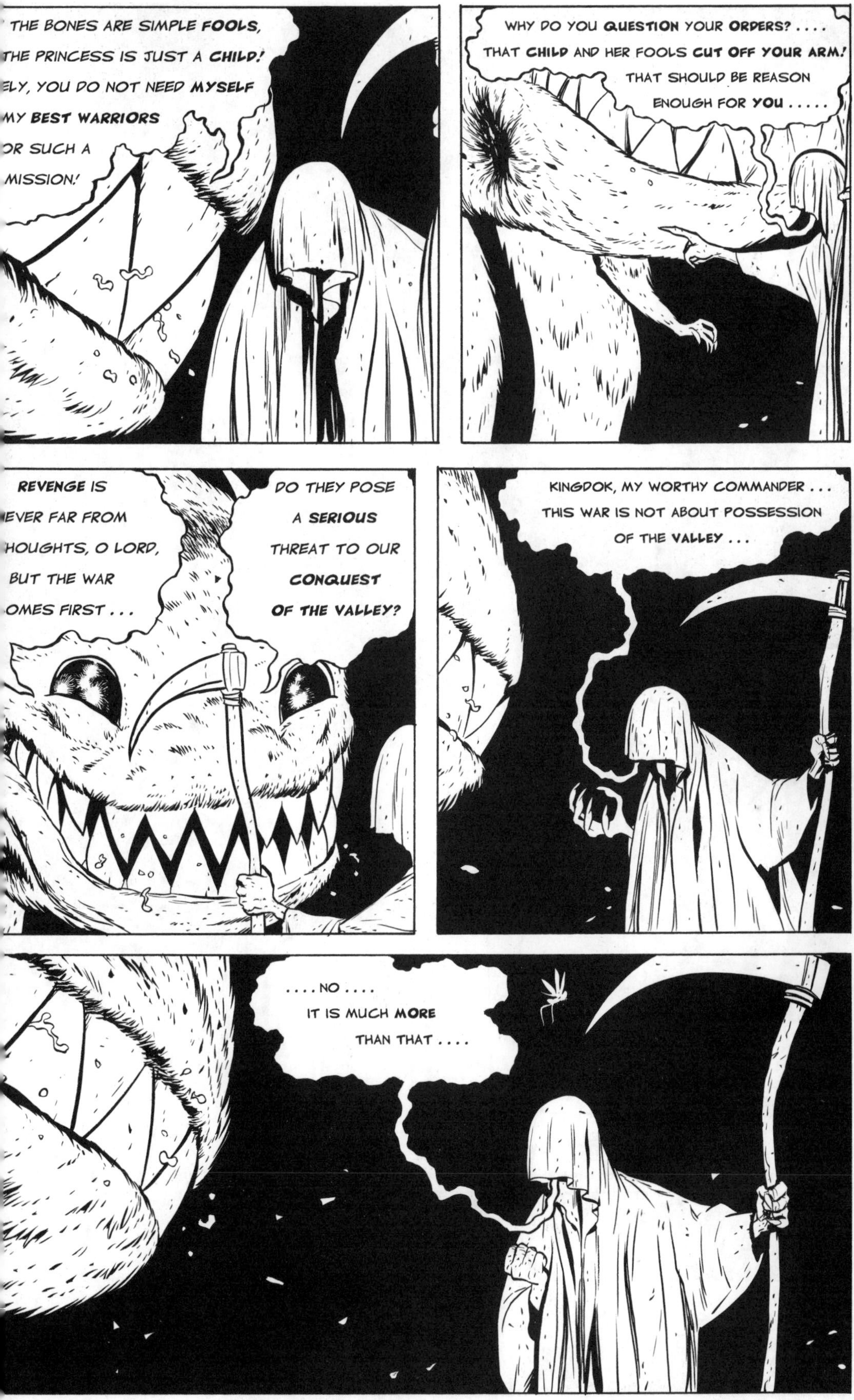
THE BONES ARE SIMPLE FOOLS, THE PRINCESS IS JUST A CHILD! ELY, YOU DO NOT NEED MYSELF MY BEST WARRIORS OR SUCH A MISSION!
WHY DO YOU QUESTION YOUR ORDERS? . . . . THAT CHILD AND HER FOOLS CUT OFF YOUR ARM! THAT SHOULD BE REASON ENOUGH FOR YOU . . . . .
REVENGE IS EVER FAR FROM HOUGHTS, O LORD, BUT THE WAR OMES FIRST . . .
DO THEY POSE A SERIOUS THREAT TO OUR CONQUEST OF THE VALLEY?
KINGDOK, MY WORTHY COMMANDER . . . THIS WAR IS NOT ABOUT POSSESSION OF THE VALLEY . . .
. . . . NO . . . . IT IS MUCH MORE THAN THAT . . . .

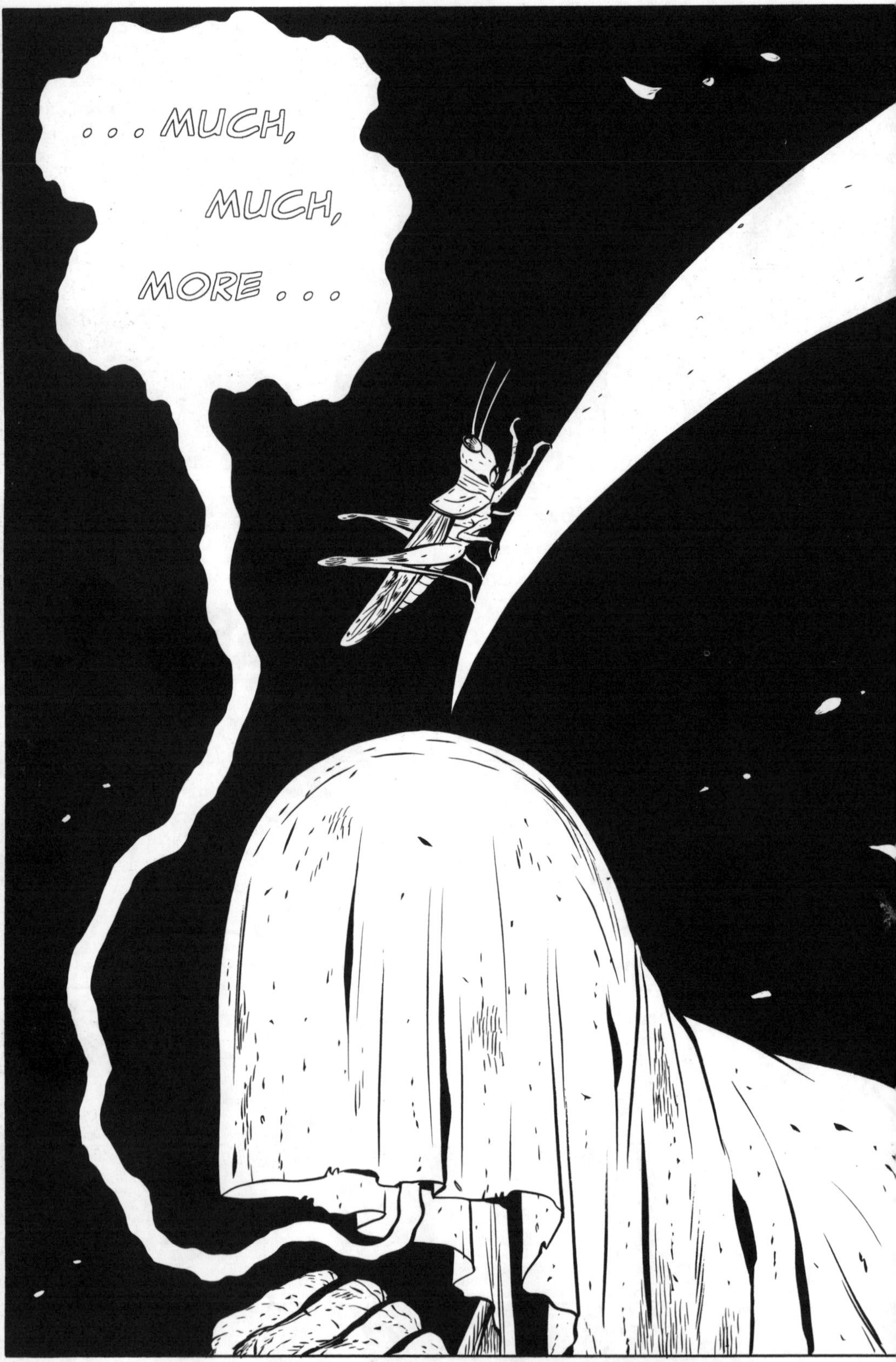
. . . MUCH,
MUCH,
MORE . . .

NEXT: THE TURNING

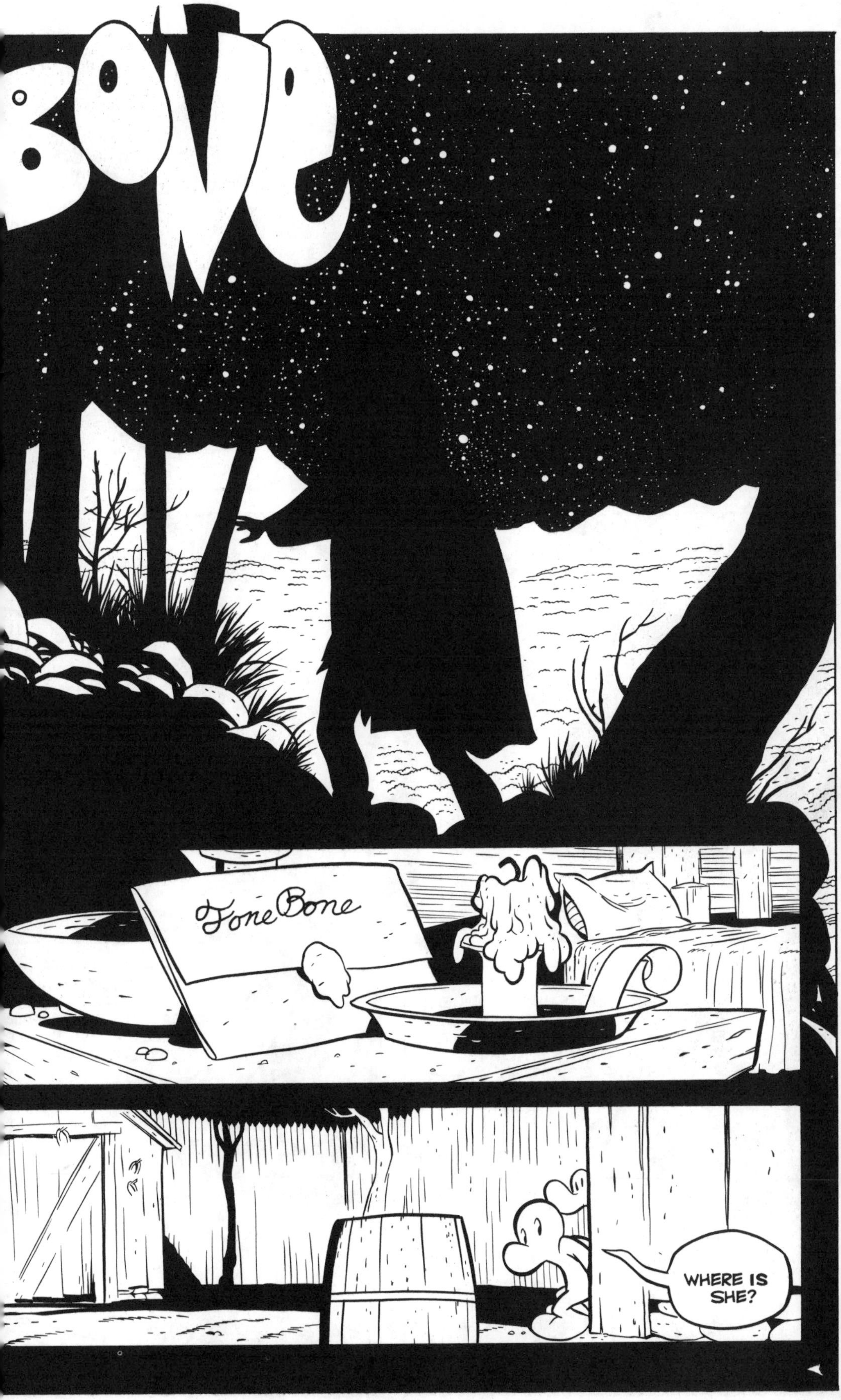
BONE
Fone Bone
WHERE IS SHE?

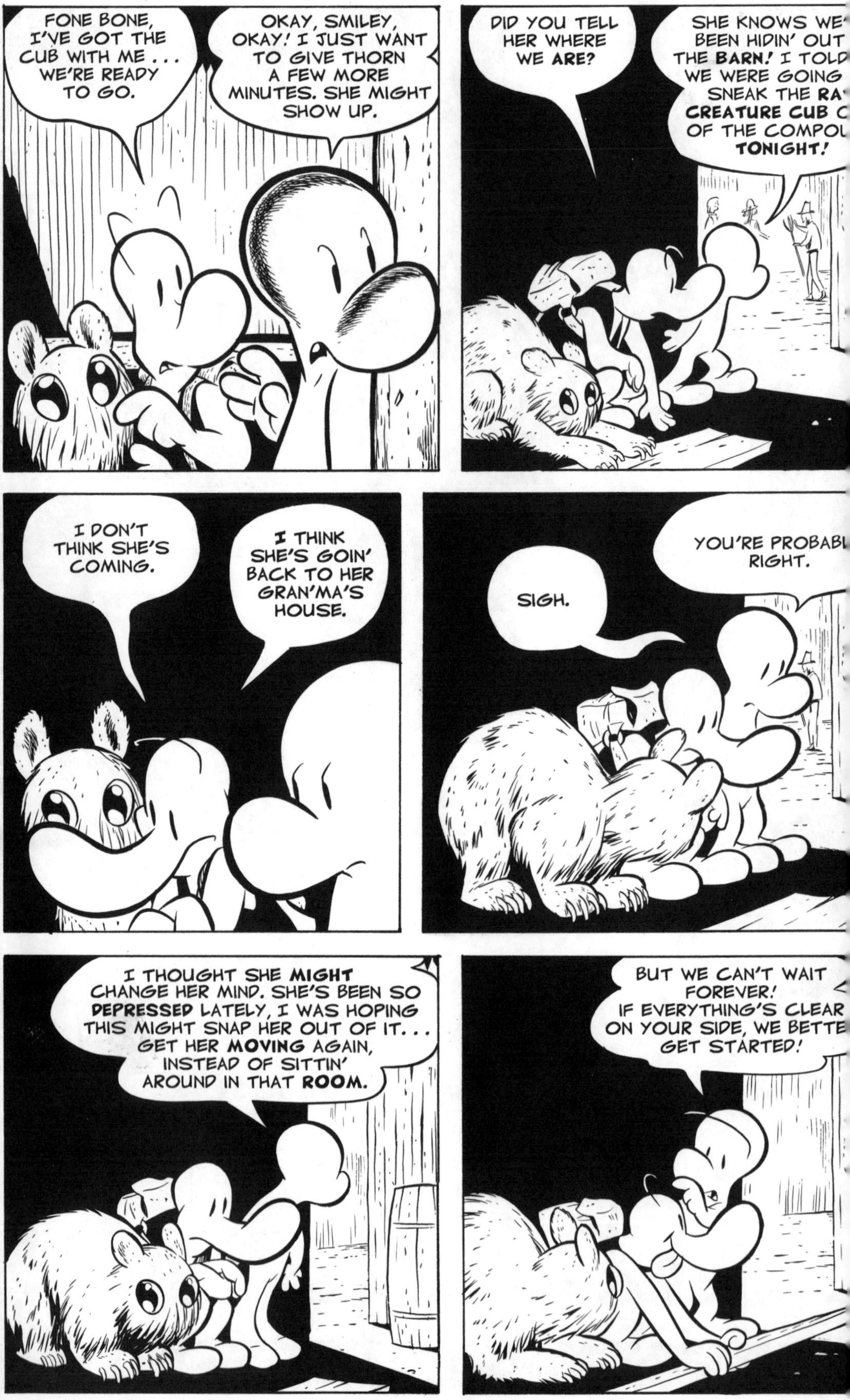
FONE BONE, I'VE GOT THE CUB WITH ME . . . WE'RE READY TO GO.
OKAY, SMILEY, OKAY! I JUST WANT TO GIVE THORN A FEW MORE MINUTES. SHE MIGHT SHOW UP.
DID YOU TELL HER WHERE WE ARE?
SHE KNOWS WE BEEN HIDIN' OUT THE BARN! I TOLD WE WERE GOING SNEAK THE RA CREATURE CUB OF THE COMPOU TONIGHT!
I DON'T THINK SHE'S COMING.
I THINK SHE'S GOIN' BACK TO HER GRAN'MA'S HOUSE.
SIGH.
YOU'RE PROBABL RIGHT.
I THOUGHT SHE MIGHT CHANGE HER MIND. SHE'S BEEN SO DEPRESSED LATELY, I WAS HOPING THIS MIGHT SNAP HER OUT OF IT. . . GET HER MOVING AGAIN, INSTEAD OF SITTIN' AROUND IN THAT ROOM.
BUT WE CAN'T WAIT FOREVER! IF EVERYTHING'S CLEAR ON YOUR SIDE, WE BETTE GET STARTED!

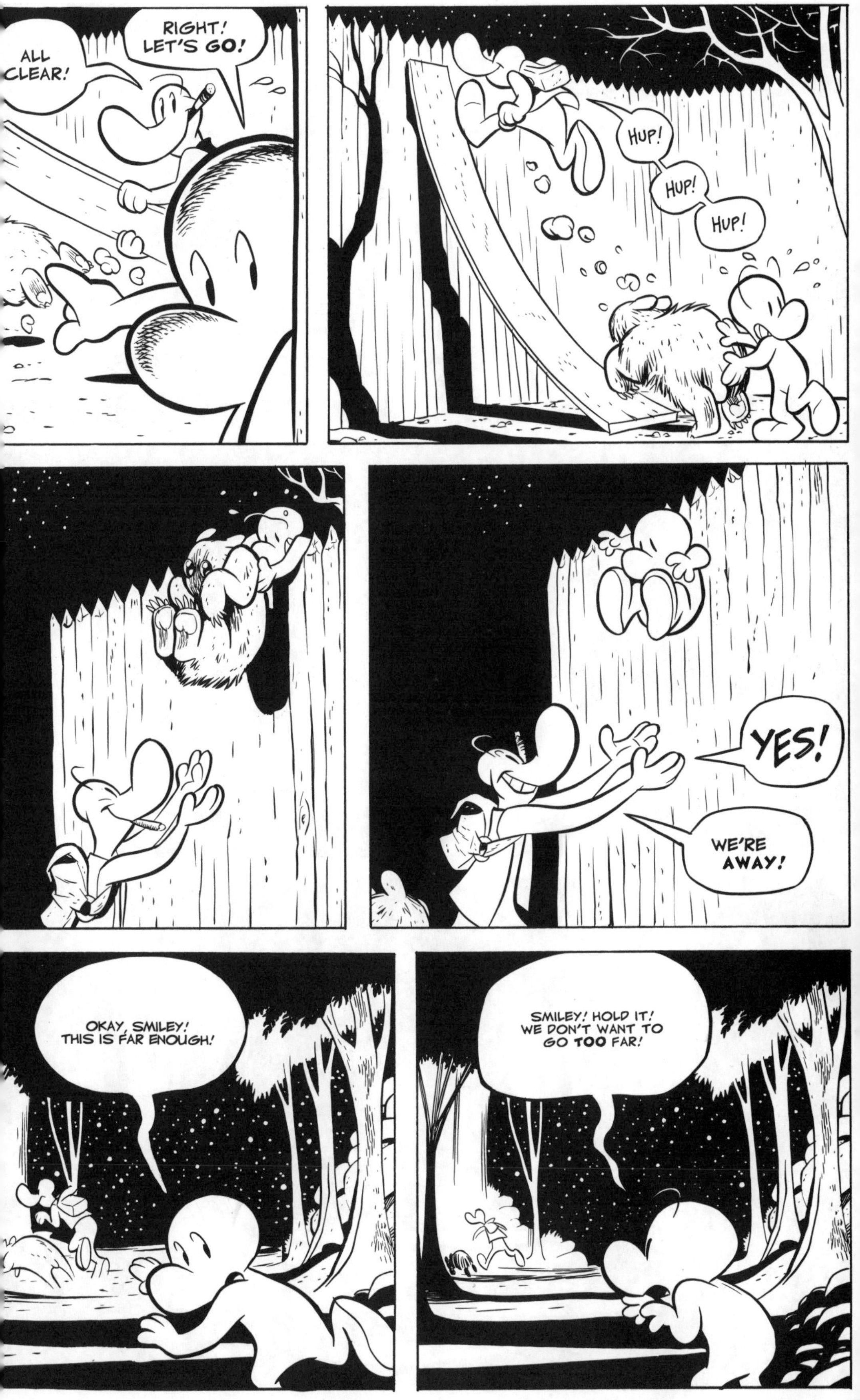
ALL CLEAR!
RIGHT! LET'S GO!
HUP!
HUP!
HUP!
YES!
WE'RE AWAY!
OKAY, SMILEY! THIS IS FAR ENOUGH!
SMILEY! HOLD IT! WE DON'T WANT TO GO TOO FAR!

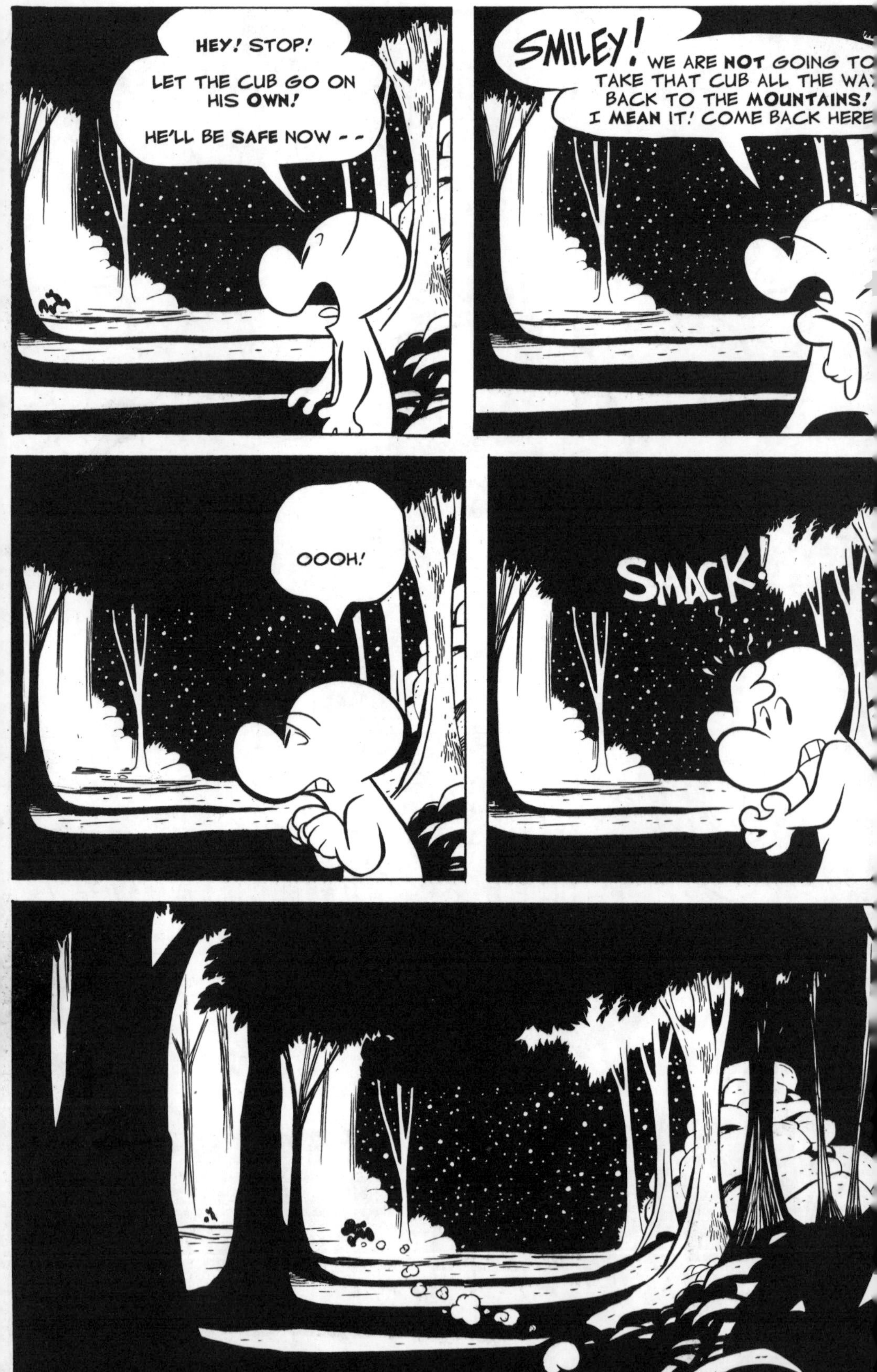
HEY! STOP!
LET THE CUB GO ON HIS OWN!
HE'LL BE SAFE NOW - -
SMILEY! WE ARE NOT GOING TO TAKE THAT CUB ALL THE WAY BACK TO THE MOUNTAINS! I MEAN IT! COME BACK HERE
OOOH!
SMACK!

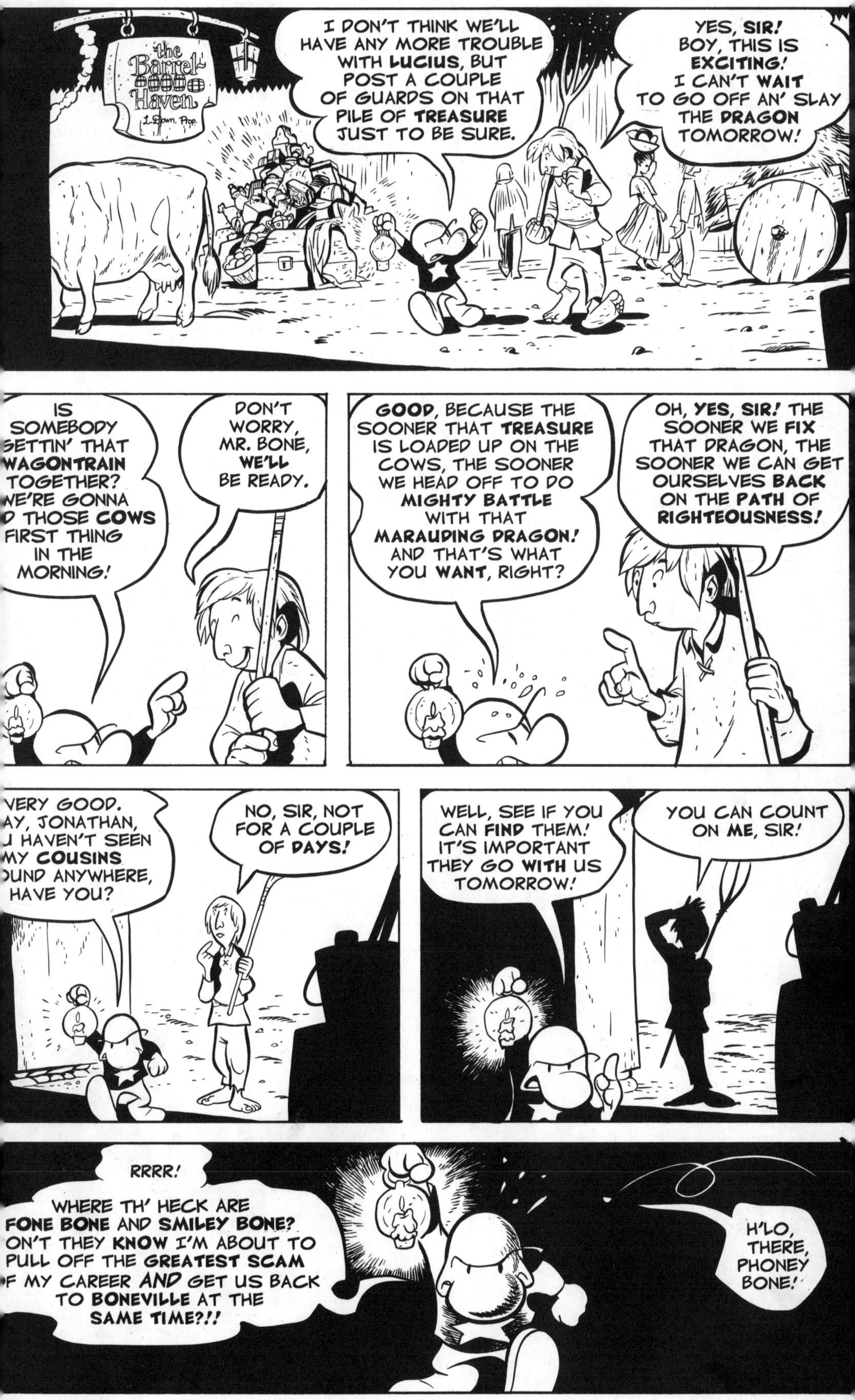
the Barrel Haven
L. Down, Prop.
I DON'T THINK WE'LL HAVE ANY MORE TROUBLE WITH LUCIUS, BUT POST A COUPLE OF GUARDS ON THAT PILE OF TREASURE JUST TO BE SURE.
YES, SIR! BOY, THIS IS EXCITING! I CAN'T WAIT TO GO OFF AN' SLAY THE DRAGON TOMORROW!
IS SOMEBODY ETTIN' THAT WAGONTRAIN TOGETHER? E'RE GONNA D THOSE COWS FIRST THING IN THE MORNING!
DON'T WORRY, MR. BONE, WE'LL BE READY.
GOOD, BECAUSE THE SOONER THAT TREASURE IS LOADED UP ON THE COWS, THE SOONER WE HEAD OFF TO DO MIGHTY BATTLE WITH THAT MARAUDING DRAGON! AND THAT'S WHAT YOU WANT, RIGHT?
OH, YES, SIR! THE SOONER WE FIX THAT DRAGON, THE SOONER WE CAN GET OURSELVES BACK ON THE PATH OF RIGHTEOUSNESS!
VERY GOOD. AY, JONATHAN, U HAVEN'T SEEN MY COUSINS OUND ANYWHERE, HAVE YOU?
NO, SIR, NOT FOR A COUPLE OF DAYS!
WELL, SEE IF YOU CAN FIND THEM! IT'S IMPORTANT THEY GO WITH US TOMORROW!
YOU CAN COUNT ON ME, SIR!
RRRR!
WHERE TH' HECK ARE FONE BONE AND SMILEY BONE? ON'T THEY KNOW I'M ABOUT TO PULL OFF THE GREATEST SCAM F MY CAREER AND GET US BACK TO BONEVILLE AT THE SAME TIME?!!
H'LO, THERE, PHONEY BONE!

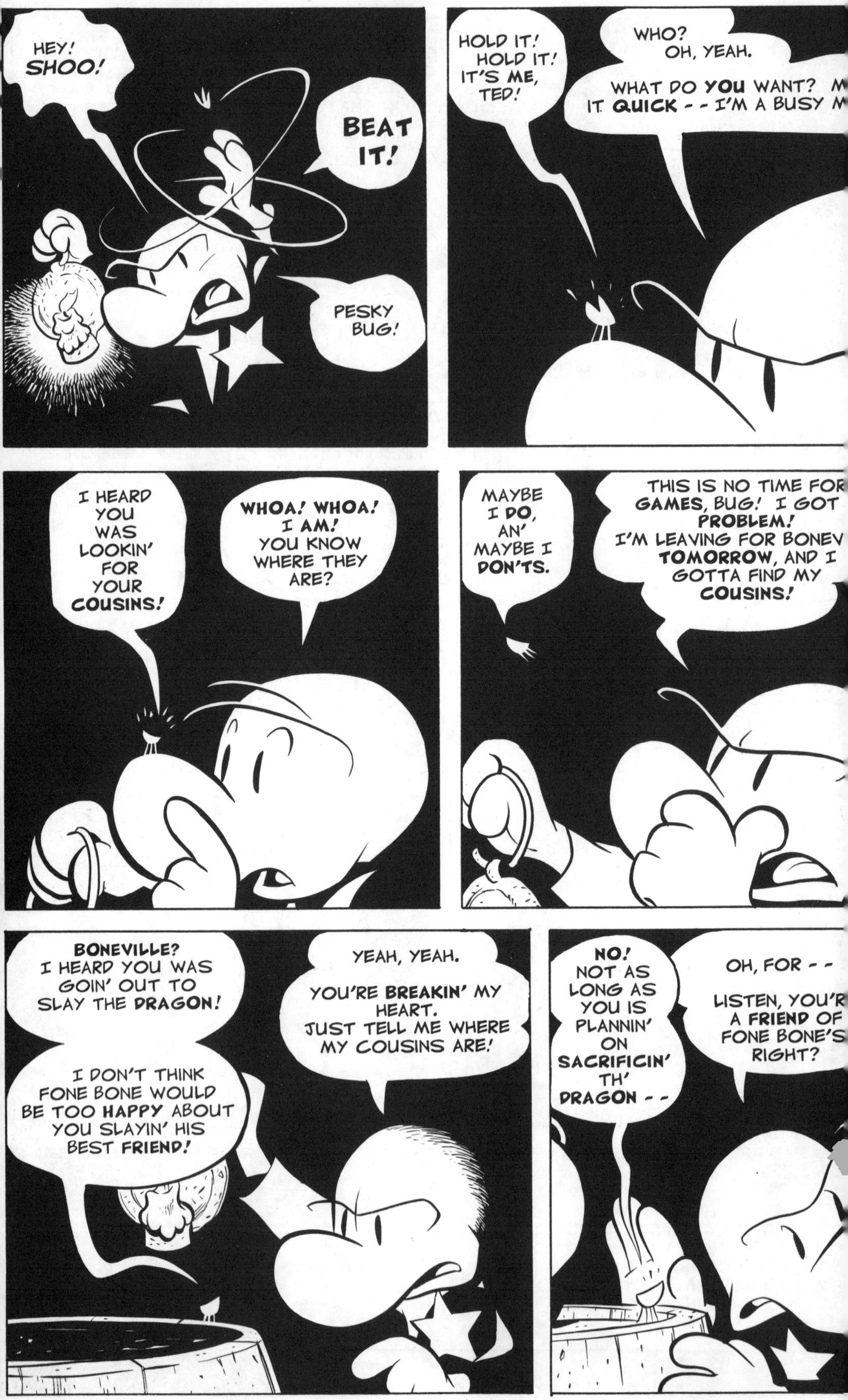
HEY! SHOO!
BEAT IT!
PESKY BUG!
HOLD IT! HOLD IT! IT'S ME, TED!
WHO? OH, YEAH.
WHAT DO YOU WANT? M
IT QUICK - - I'M A BUSY M
I HEARD YOU WAS LOOKIN' FOR YOUR COUSINS!
WHOA! WHOA! I AM! YOU KNOW WHERE THEY ARE?
MAYBE I DO, AN' MAYBE I DON'TS.
THIS IS NO TIME FOR
GAMES, BUG! I GOT
PROBLEM!
I'M LEAVING FOR BONEV
TOMORROW, AND I
GOTTA FIND MY
COUSINS!
BONEVILLE? I HEARD YOU WAS GOIN' OUT TO SLAY THE DRAGON!
I DON'T THINK FONE BONE WOULD BE TOO HAPPY ABOUT YOU SLAYIN' HIS BEST FRIEND!
YEAH, YEAH.
YOU'RE BREAKIN' MY HEART. JUST TELL ME WHERE MY COUSINS ARE!
NO! NOT AS LONG AS YOU IS PLANNIN' ON SACRIFICIN' TH' DRAGON - -
OH, FOR - -
LISTEN, YOU'R
A FRIEND OF
FONE BONE'S
RIGHT?

WHAT IF I TOLD YOU THERE WASN'T GONNA **BE** ANY SACRIFICE? WOULD YOU TELL ME WHERE FONE BONE IS **THEN**?

...AT 'RE UP O, NEY ME?

WHAT'RE YOU TALKIN' ABOUT?

I'M JUST TRYIN' TO GET THE TOWNSFOLK TO **ESCORT** ME OUT OF THE VALLEY WITH A **WAGONTRAIN** FULL OF **TREASURE**! NO ONE'S GONNA GET HURT! **TRUST ME**!

EXACTLY! THE TOWNSFOLK **THINK** WE'RE GOIN' INTO THE MOUNTAINS TOMORROW TO **CATCH A DRAGON**, BUT **REALLY**, MY COUSINS AND I ARE GONNA GIVE 'EM TH' SLIP AND RETURN TO **BONEVILLE IN TRIUMPH!**

TA N!

HOW YOU GONNA GIVE 'EM TH' **SLIP**? AIN'T THEY GONNA **NOTICE** YOU GOT TH' **TREASURE**?

THAT'S THE **BEST PART!** EVERYBODY **KNOWS** DRAGONS LOVE **TREASURE**, RIGHT? WELL, **THESE** YOKELS THINK WE NEED THE TREASURE FOR **BAIT**- - SO WHEN WE GO TO SET THE **TRAP**, WE CAN JUST **SLIP OFF** INTO TH' **DARKNESS!**

DES E BONE OW OUT HIS TLE HEME?

NO! THAT'S THE **PROBLEM!** HE DOESN'T KNOW **ANYTHING** ABOUT IT! IF I CAN'T FIND FONE BONE AND SMILEY **TONIGHT**, THEY'LL NEVER GET BACK TO **BONEVILLE!**

WELL ... I SEEN 'EM HANGIN' AROUN' THE **BARN** A LOT LATELY. MAYBE YOU SHOULD LOOK **THERE**.

THANKS, BUG!

NOW REMEMBER! DON'T **TELL** ANYBODY OR YOU'LL RUIN FONE BONE'S CHANCE TO GET HOME!

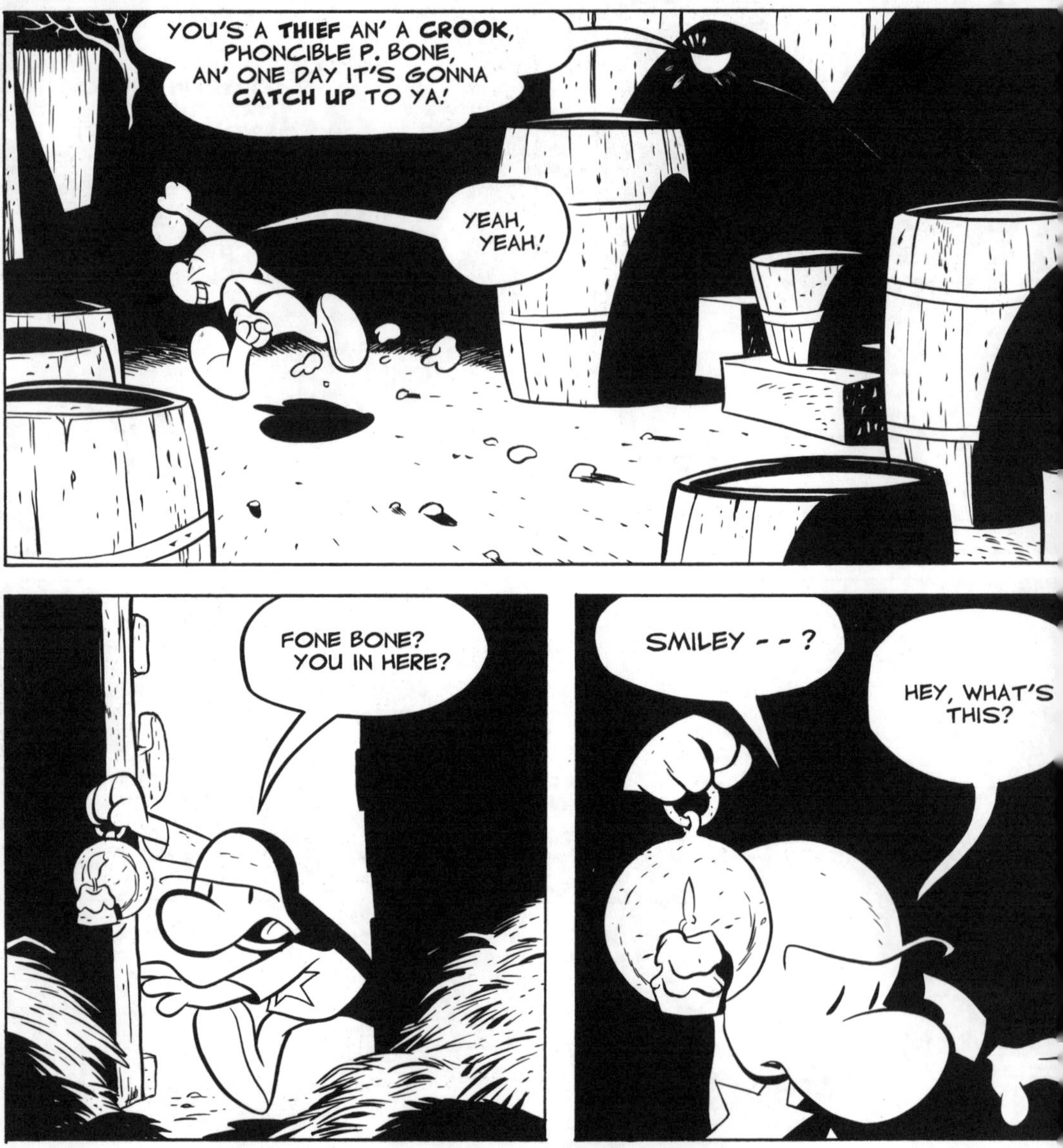
YOU'S A THIEF AN' A CROOK, PHONCIBLE P. BONE, AN' ONE DAY IT'S GONNA CATCH UP TO YA!
YEAH, YEAH!
FONE BONE? YOU IN HERE?
SMILEY - - ?
HEY, WHAT'S THIS?
CREAK!
FONE BONE? IS THAT YOU?

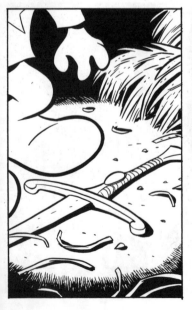

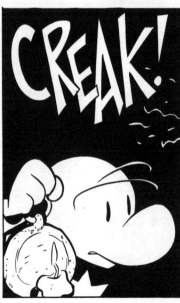

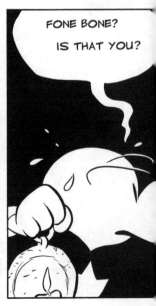

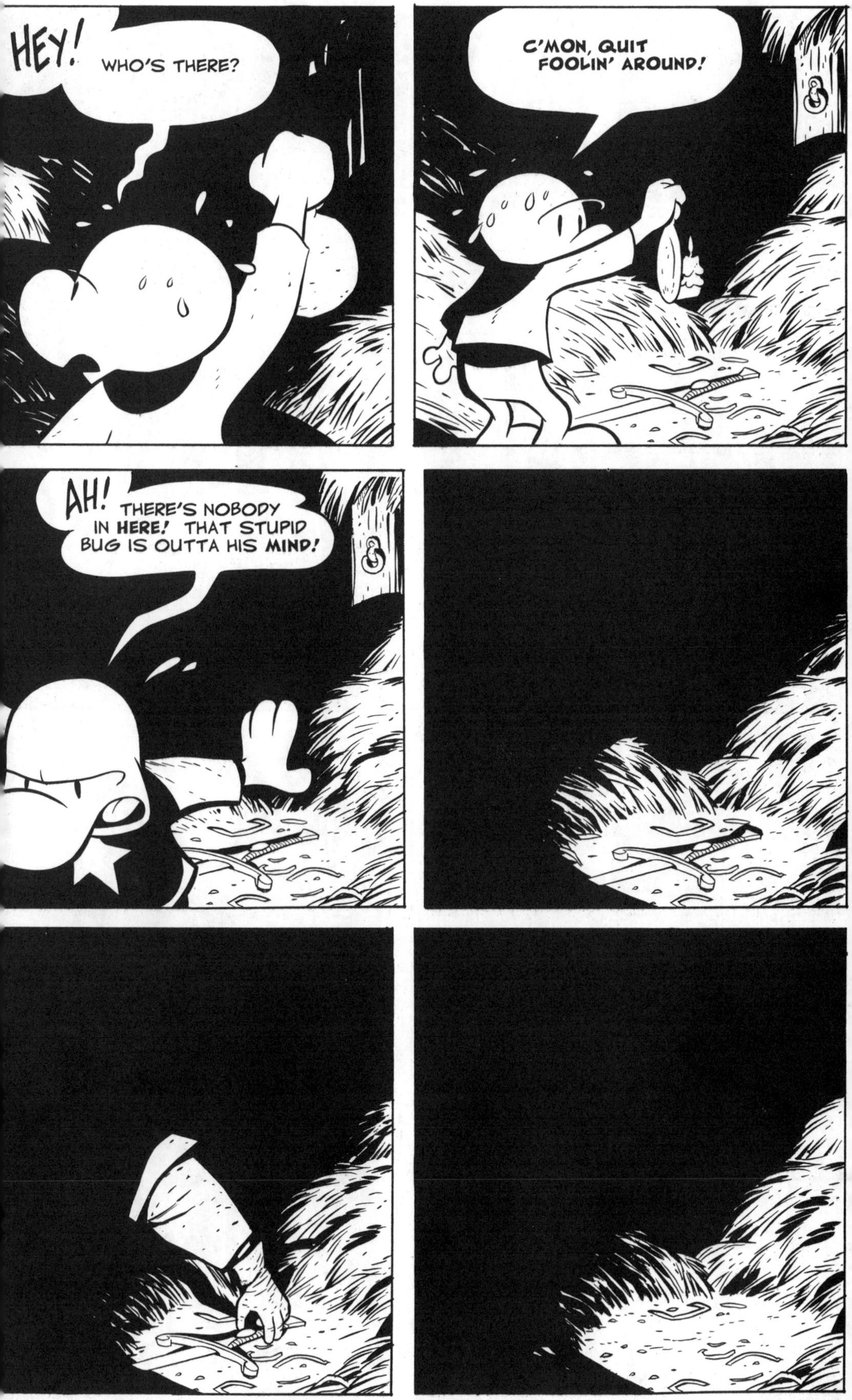

HEY! WHO'S THERE?
C'MON, QUIT FOOLIN' AROUND!
AH! THERE'S NOBODY IN HERE! THAT STUPID BUG IS OUTTA HIS MIND!

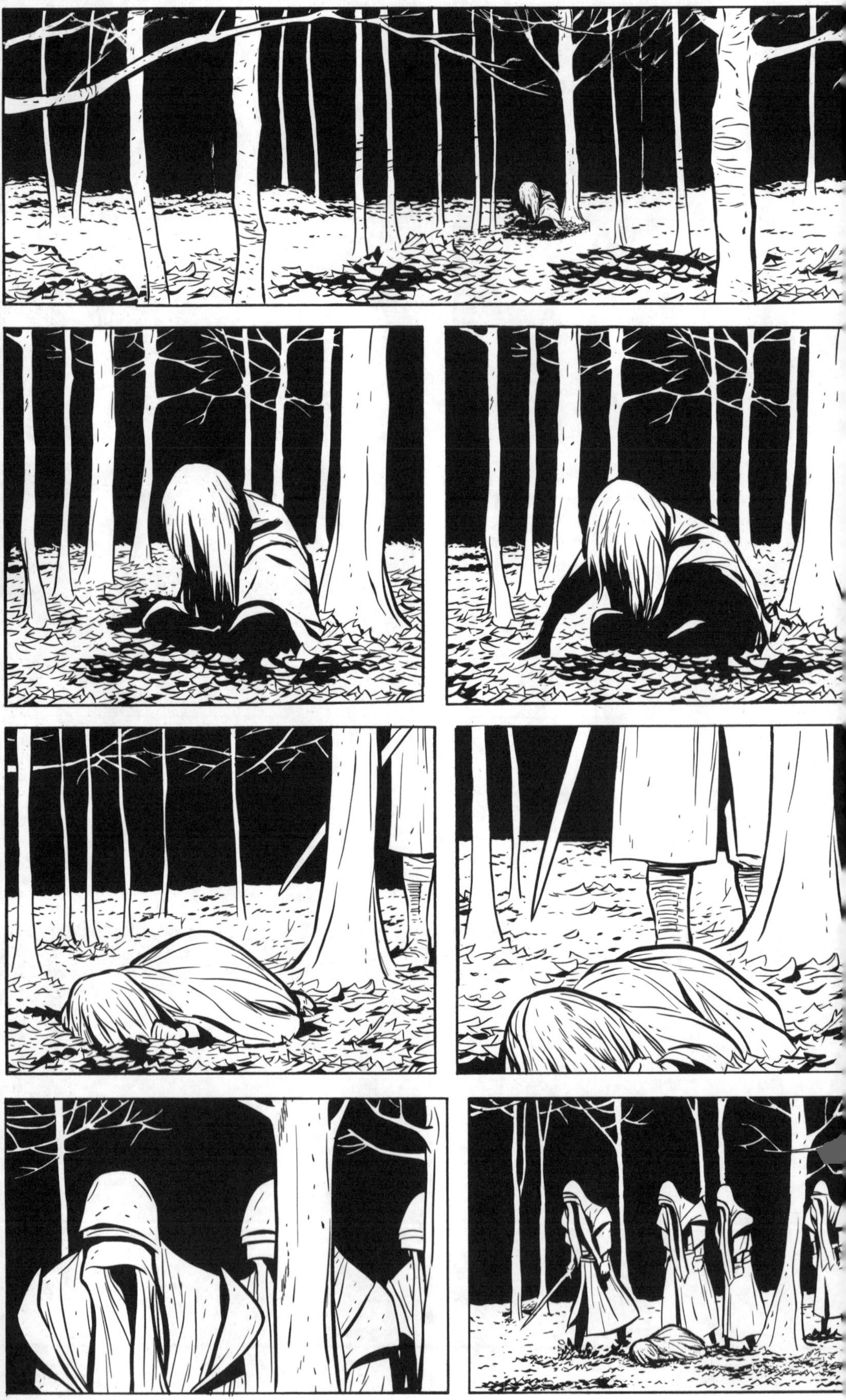

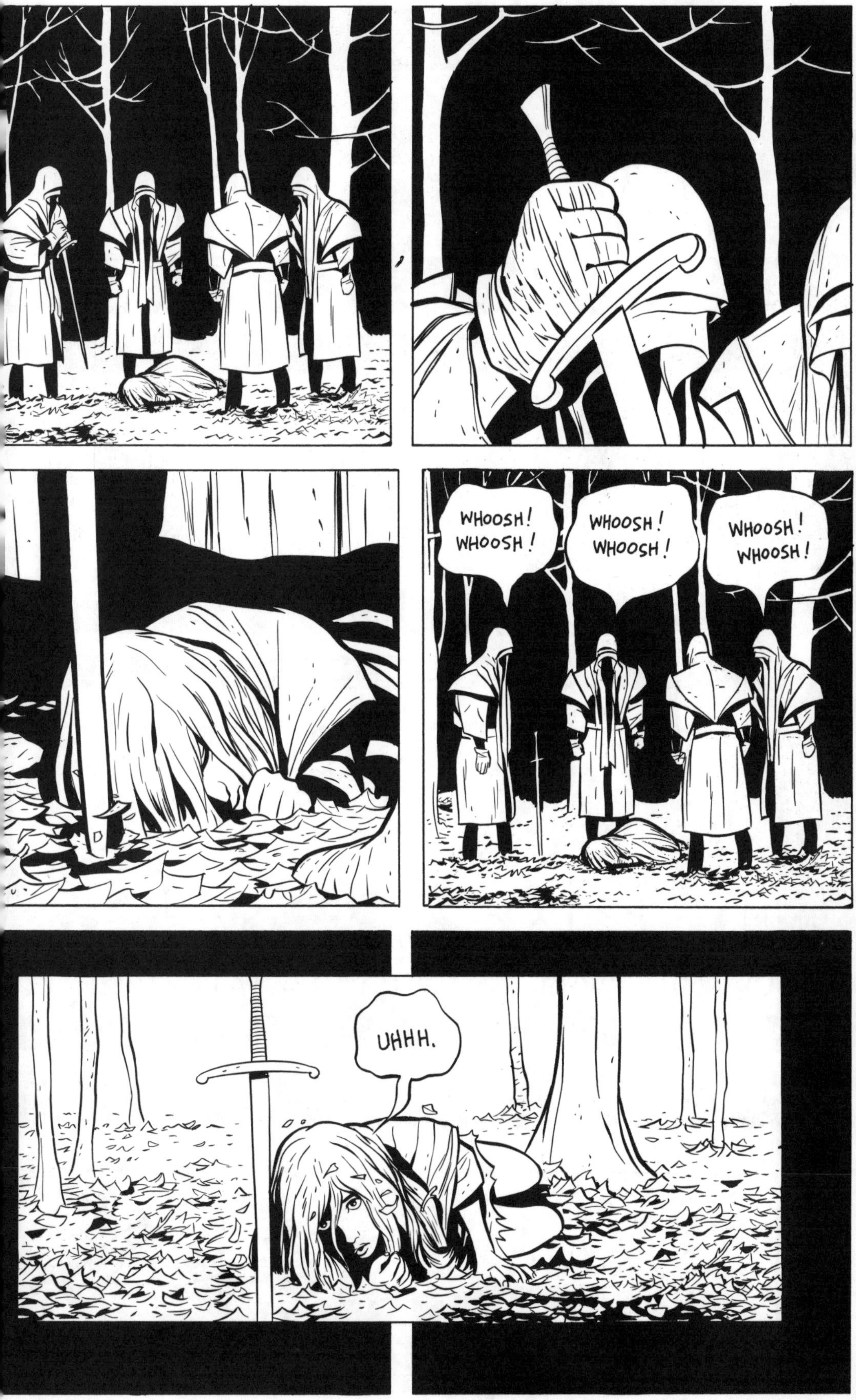
WHOOSH! WHOOSH!
WHOOSH! WHOOSH!
WHOOSH! WHOOSH!
UHHH.

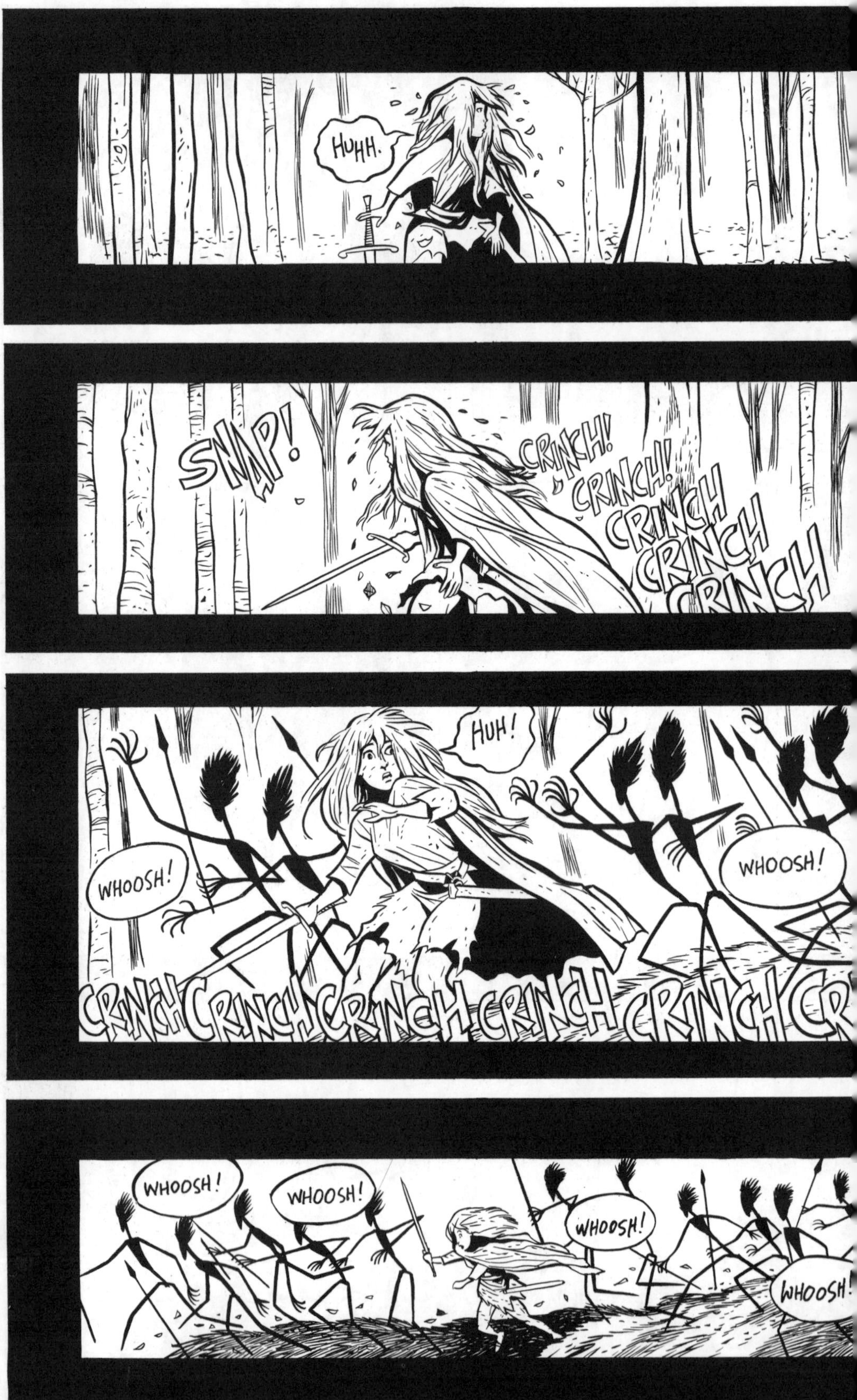
HUHH.
SNAP!
CRINCH!
CRINCH!
CRINCH
CRINCH
CRINCH
HUH!
WHOOSH!
WHOOSH!
CRINCH CRINCH CRINCH CRINCH CRINCH CR
WHOOSH!
WHOOSH!
WHOOSH!
WHOOSH!

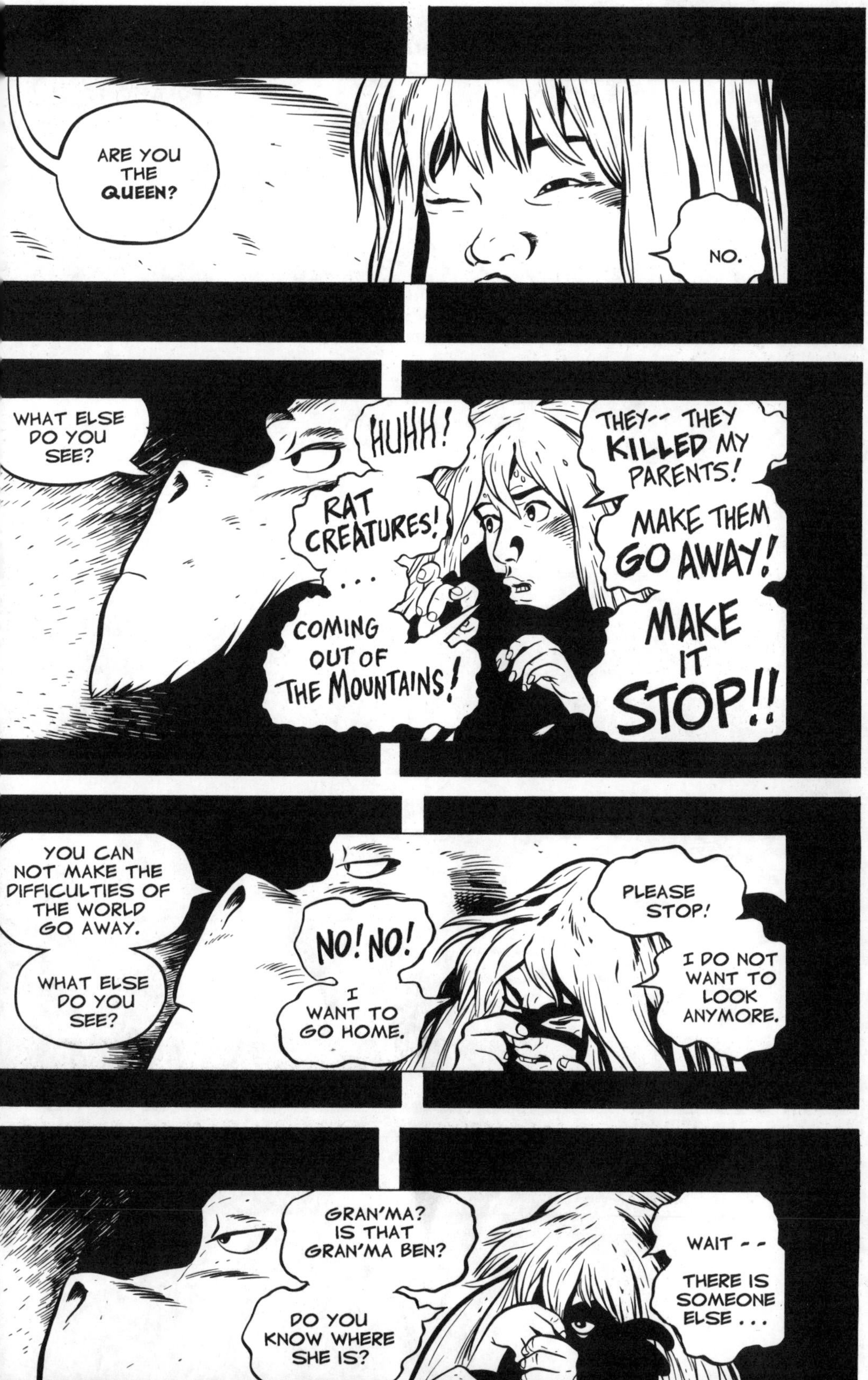
ARE YOU THE QUEEN?
NO.
WHAT ELSE DO YOU SEE?
HUHH!
RAT CREATURES!
. . .
COMING OUT OF THE MOUNTAINS!
THEY-- THEY KILLED MY PARENTS!
MAKE THEM GO AWAY!
MAKE IT STOP!!
YOU CAN NOT MAKE THE DIFFICULTIES OF THE WORLD GO AWAY.
WHAT ELSE DO YOU SEE?
NO! NO!
I WANT TO GO HOME.
PLEASE STOP!
I DO NOT WANT TO LOOK ANYMORE.
GRAN'MA? IS THAT GRAN'MA BEN?
DO YOU KNOW WHERE SHE IS?
WAIT - -
THERE IS SOMEONE ELSE . . .

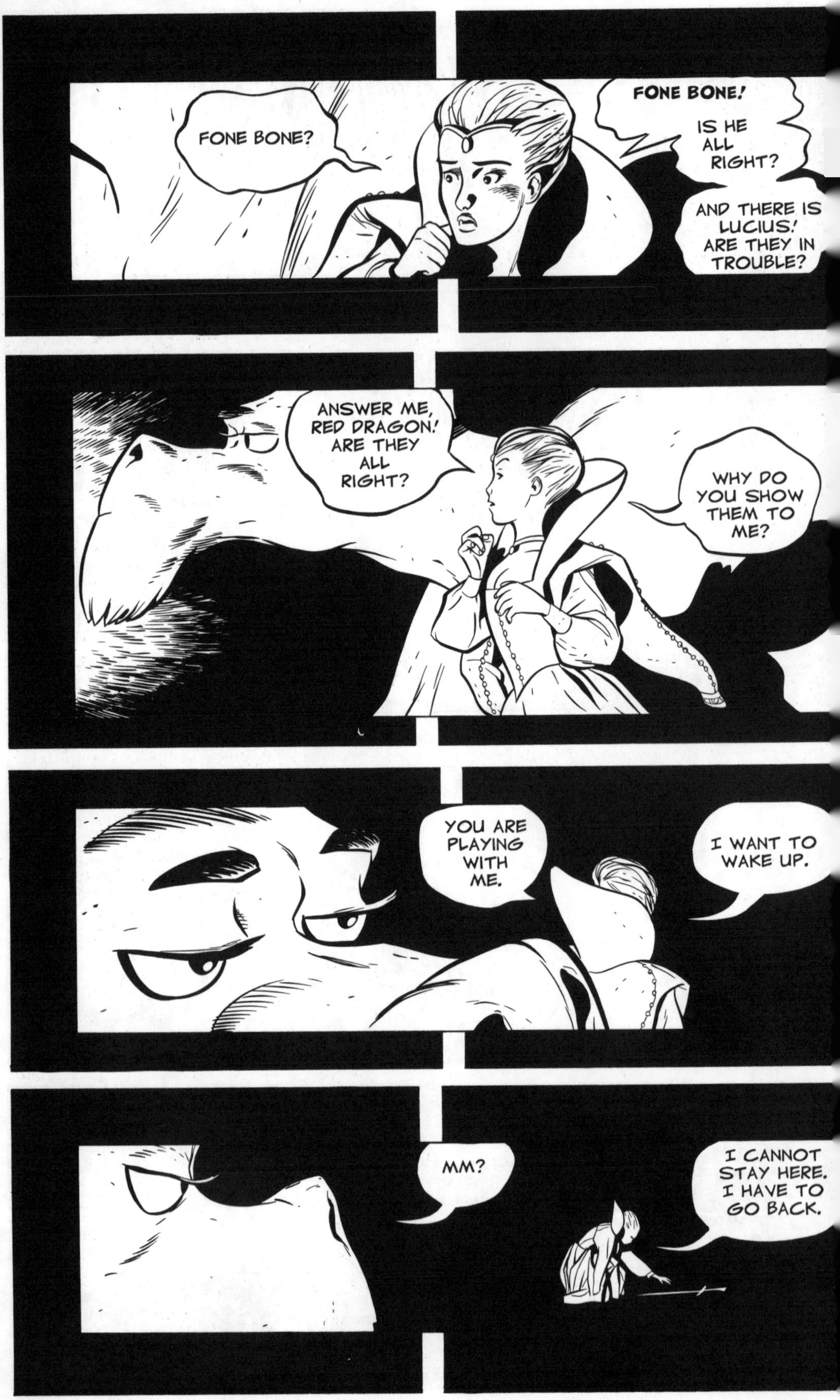
FONE BONE?
FONE BONE!
IS HE ALL RIGHT?
AND THERE IS LUCIUS! ARE THEY IN TROUBLE?
ANSWER ME, RED DRAGON! ARE THEY ALL RIGHT?
WHY DO YOU SHOW THEM TO ME?
YOU ARE PLAYING WITH ME.
I WANT TO WAKE UP.
MM?
I CANNOT STAY HERE. I HAVE TO GO BACK.

VERY WELL. IF IT IS YOUR DESIRE, I WILL TAKE YOU HOME TO THE FARMHOUSE.
NO. I WILL GO BACK TO MY FRIENDS.
I NO LONGER WISH TO GIVE UP.
WELL, WELL . . .
IT SEEMS TO ME THAT YOU ARE ALREADY AWAKE!

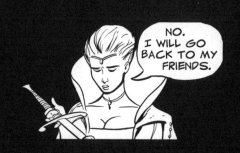

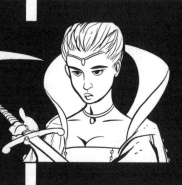

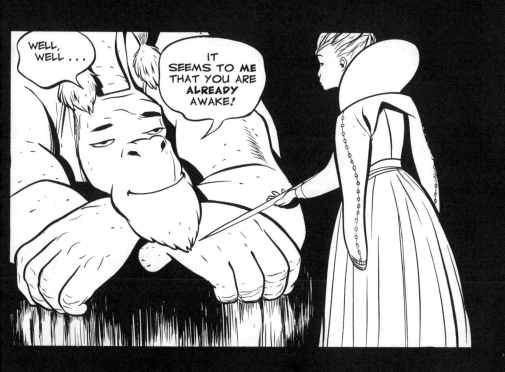

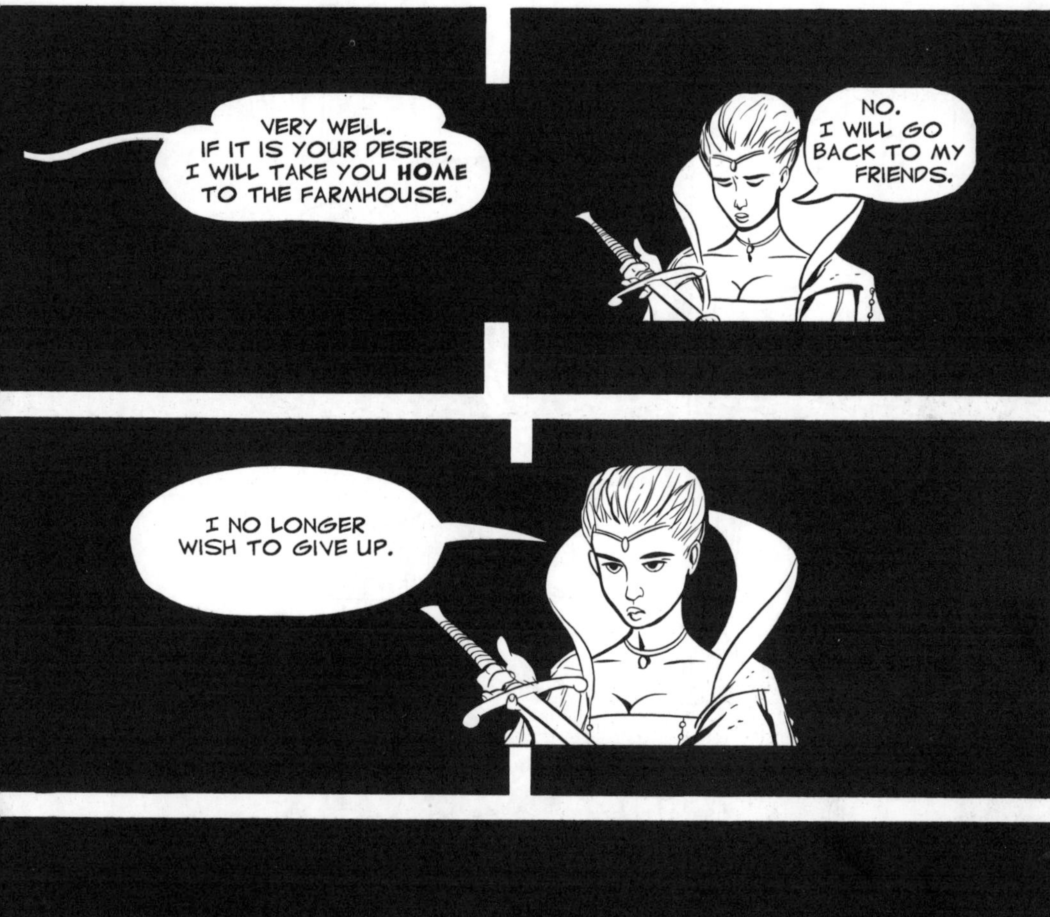

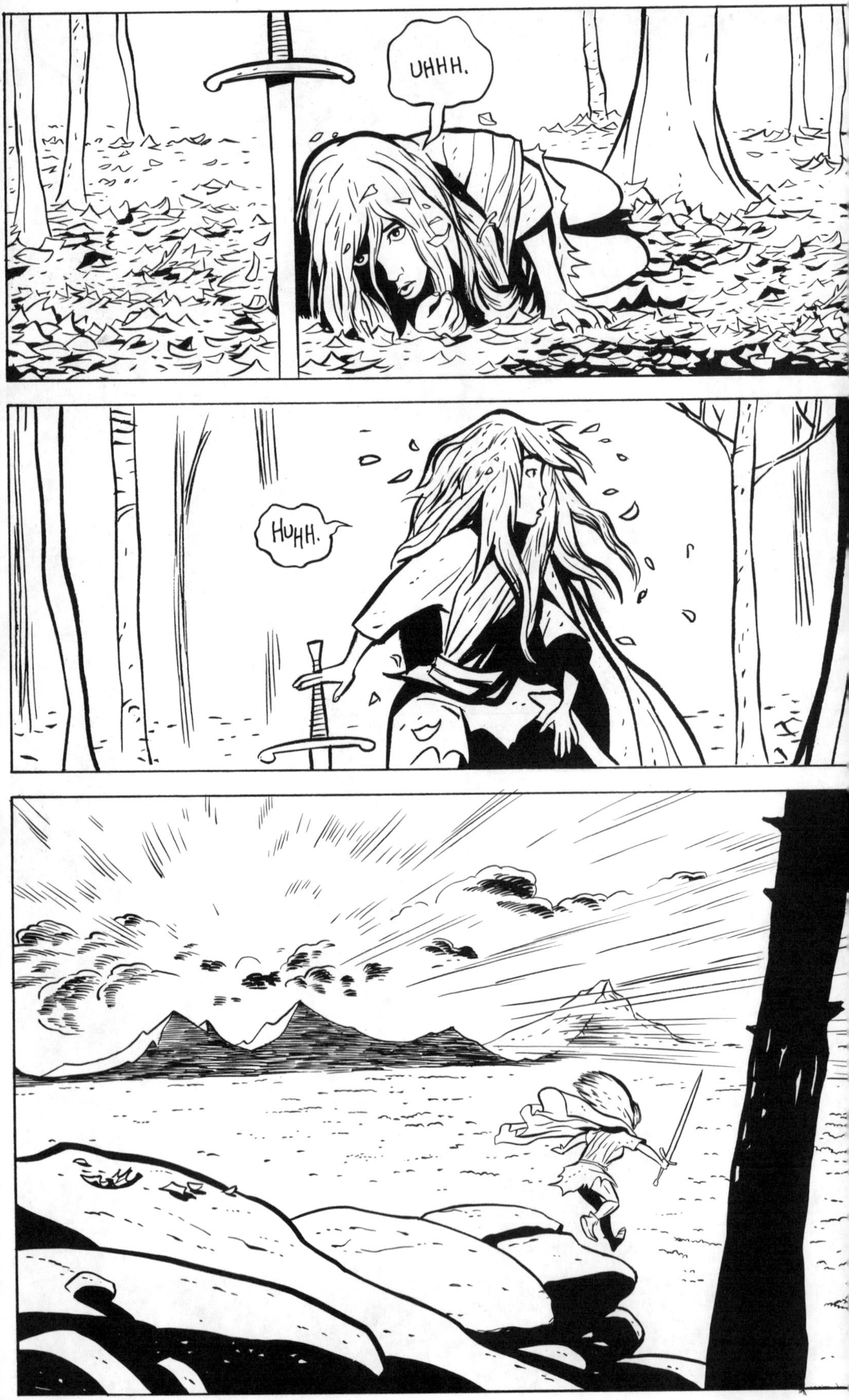
UHHH.
HUHH.

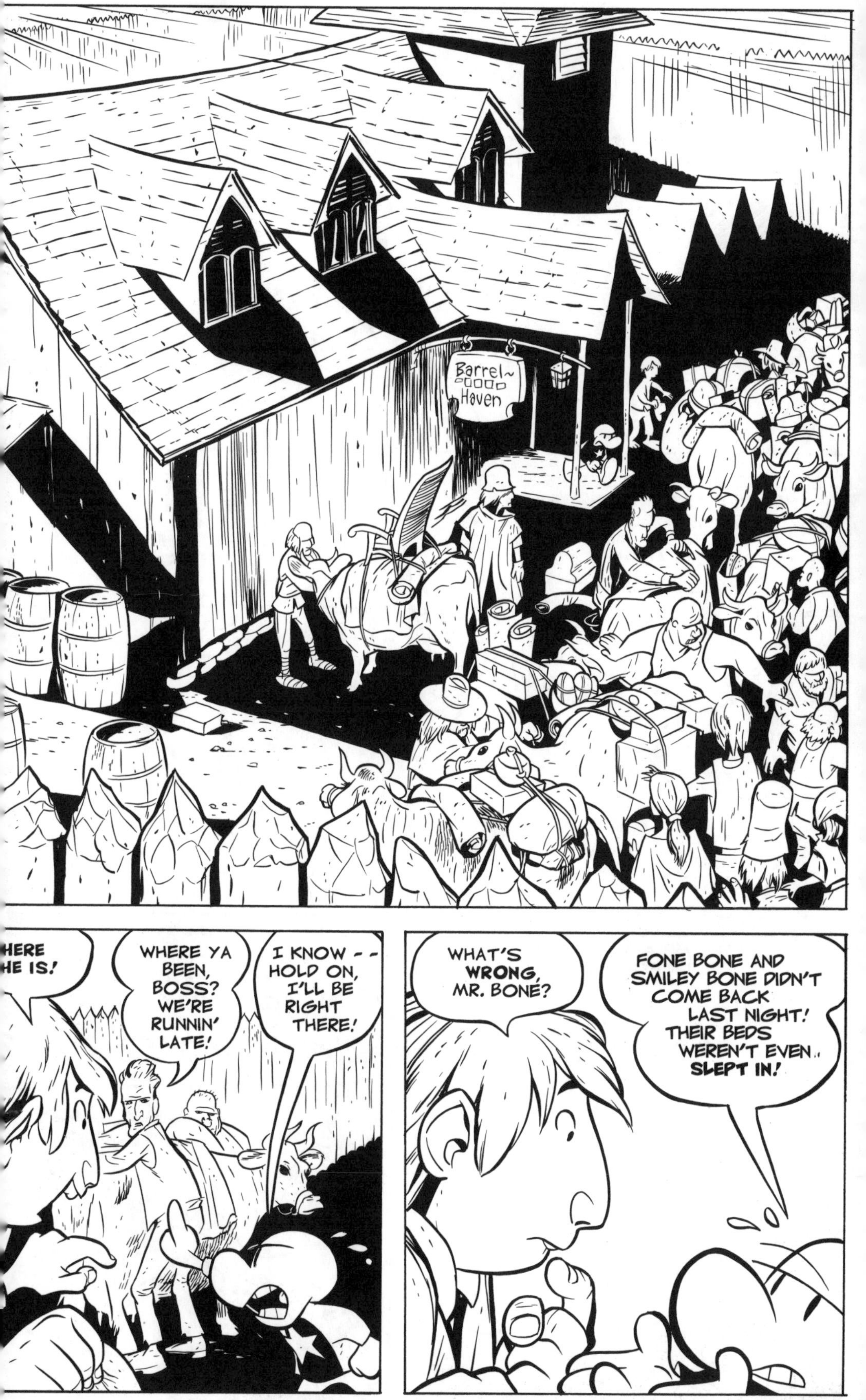

Barrel Haven
HERE HE IS!
WHERE YA BEEN, BOSS? WE'RE RUNNIN' LATE!
I KNOW -- HOLD ON, I'LL BE RIGHT THERE!
WHAT'S WRONG, MR. BONE?
FONE BONE AND SMILEY BONE DIDN'T COME BACK LAST NIGHT! THEIR BEDS WEREN'T EVEN.. SLEPT IN!

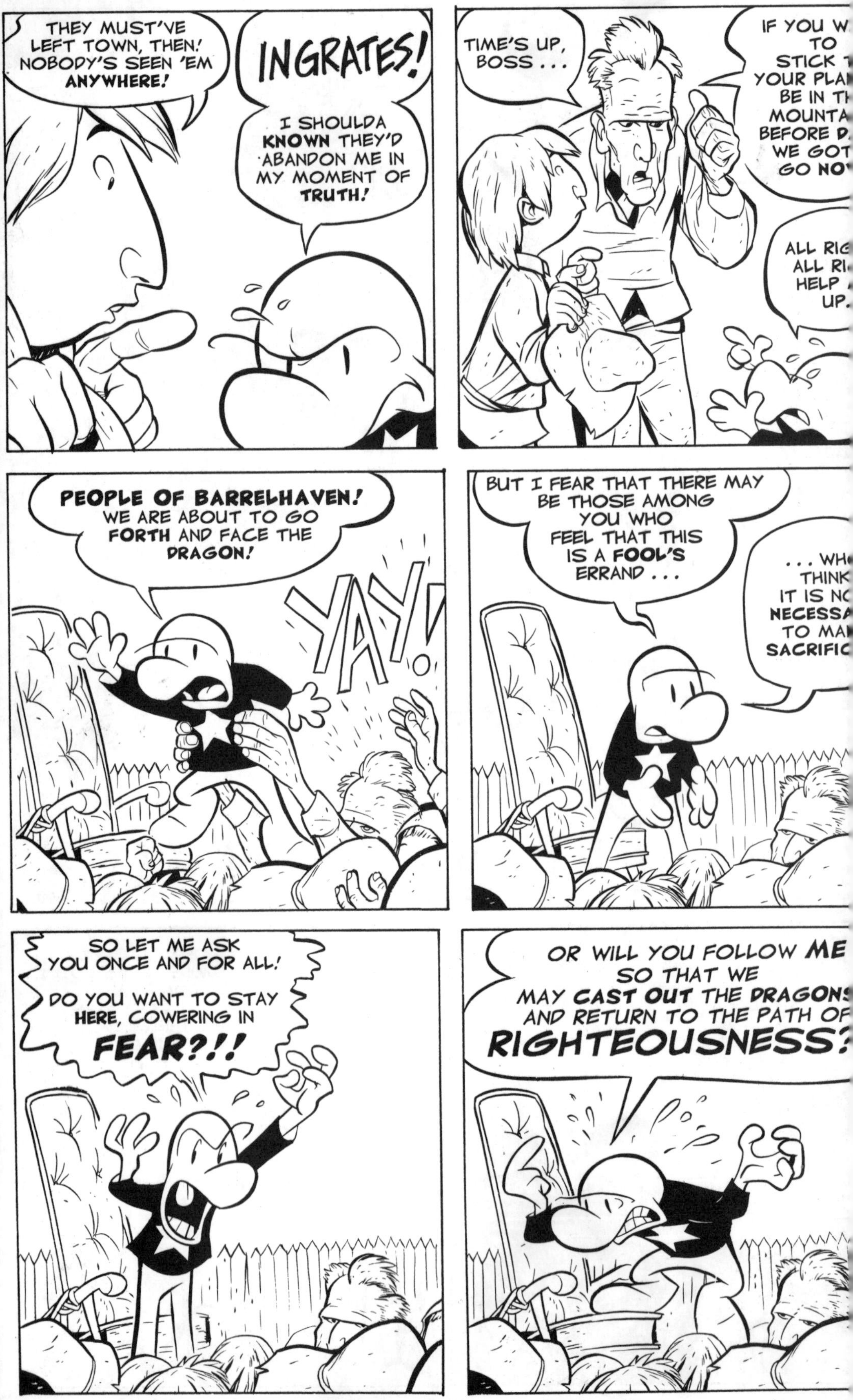
THEY MUST'VE LEFT TOWN, THEN! NOBODY'S SEEN 'EM ANYWHERE!
INGRATES!
I SHOULDA KNOWN THEY'D ABANDON ME IN MY MOMENT OF TRUTH!
TIME'S UP, BOSS . . .
IF YOU W TO STICK YOUR PLA BE IN T MOUNTA BEFORE D WE GOT GO NO
ALL RIG ALL RI HELP UP.
PEOPLE OF BARRELHAVEN! WE ARE ABOUT TO GO FORTH AND FACE THE DRAGON!
YAY!
BUT I FEAR THAT THERE MAY BE THOSE AMONG YOU WHO FEEL THAT THIS IS A FOOL'S ERRAND . . .
. . . WH THINK IT IS NO NECESSA TO MA SACRIFIC
SO LET ME ASK YOU ONCE AND FOR ALL! DO YOU WANT TO STAY HERE, COWERING IN FEAR?!!
OR WILL YOU FOLLOW ME SO THAT WE MAY CAST OUT THE DRAGONS AND RETURN TO THE PATH OF RIGHTEOUSNESS?

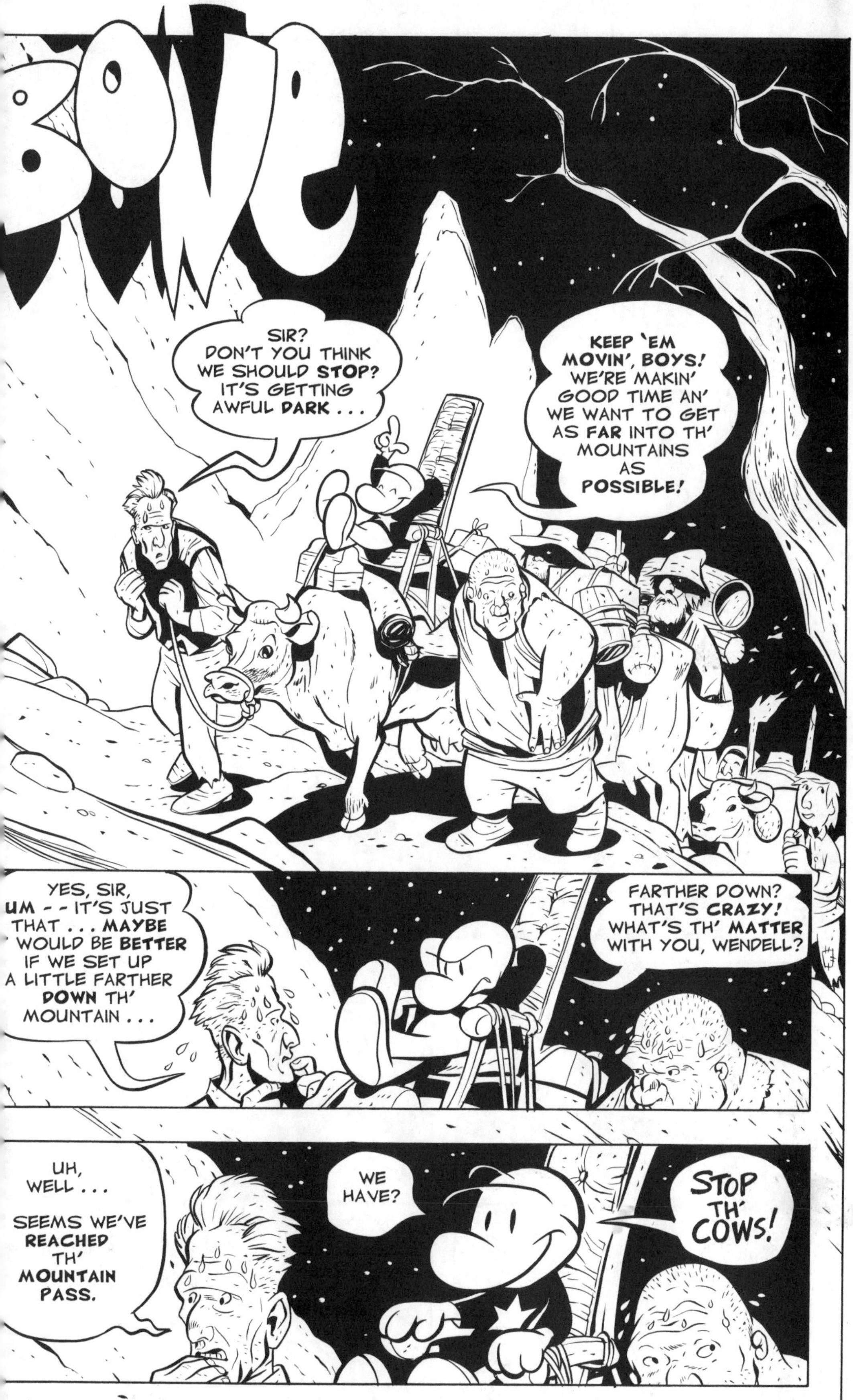
BONE
SIR? DON'T YOU THINK WE SHOULD STOP? IT'S GETTING AWFUL DARK . . .
KEEP 'EM MOVIN', BOYS! WE'RE MAKIN' GOOD TIME AN' WE WANT TO GET AS FAR INTO TH' MOUNTAINS AS POSSIBLE!
YES, SIR, UM - - IT'S JUST THAT . . . MAYBE WOULD BE BETTER IF WE SET UP A LITTLE FARTHER DOWN TH' MOUNTAIN . . .
FARTHER DOWN? THAT'S CRAZY! WHAT'S TH' MATTER WITH YOU, WENDELL?
UH, WELL . . .
SEEMS WE'VE REACHED TH' MOUNTAIN PASS.
WE HAVE?
STOP TH' COWS!

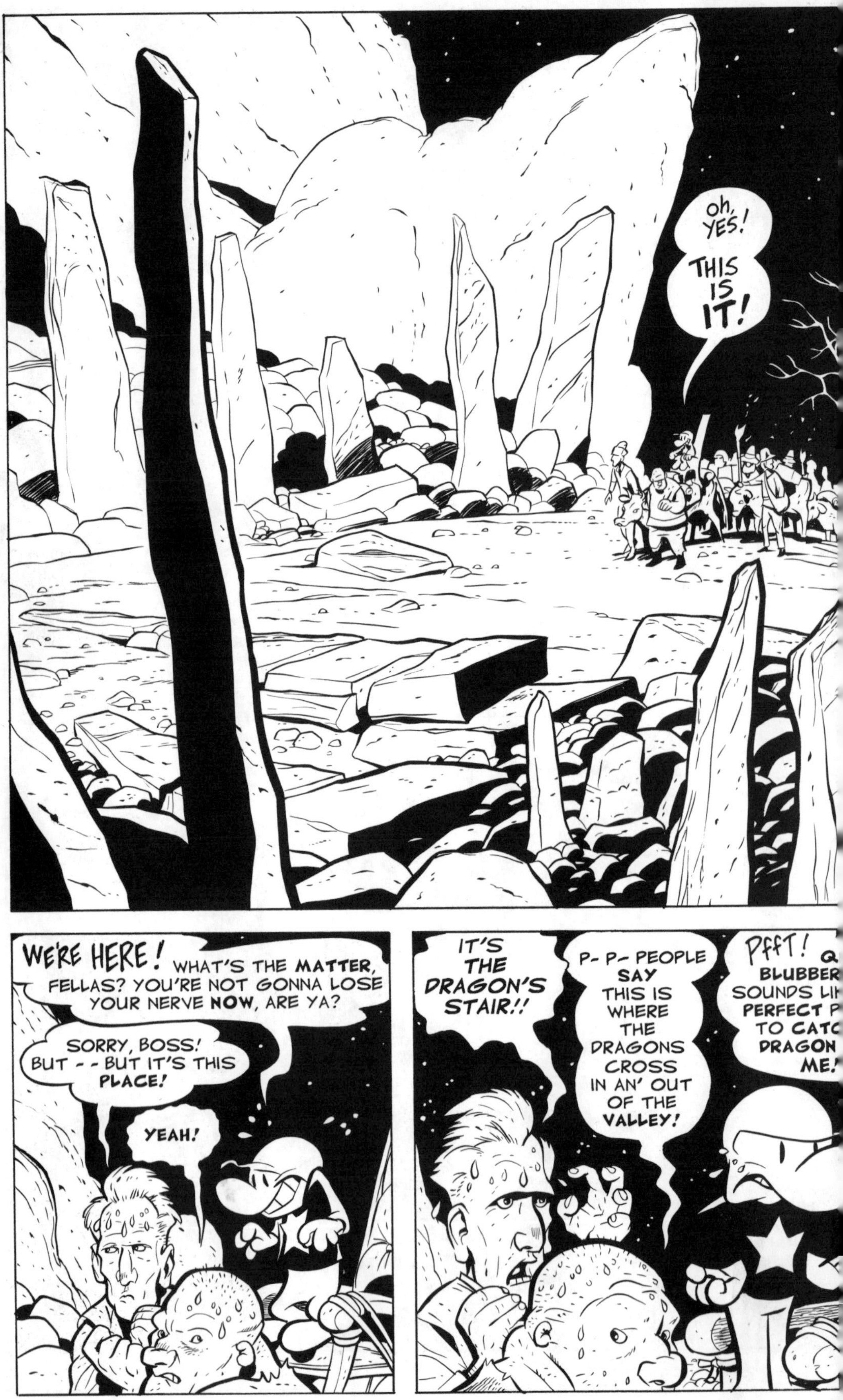

OH, YES! THIS IS IT!
WE'RE HERE! WHAT'S THE MATTER, FELLAS? YOU'RE NOT GONNA LOSE YOUR NERVE NOW, ARE YA?
SORRY, BOSS! BUT - - BUT IT'S THIS PLACE!
YEAH!
IT'S THE DRAGON'S STAIR!!
P- P- PEOPLE SAY THIS IS WHERE THE DRAGONS CROSS IN AN' OUT OF THE VALLEY!
PFFT! Q BLUBBER SOUNDS LI PERFECT P TO CATC DRAGON ME!

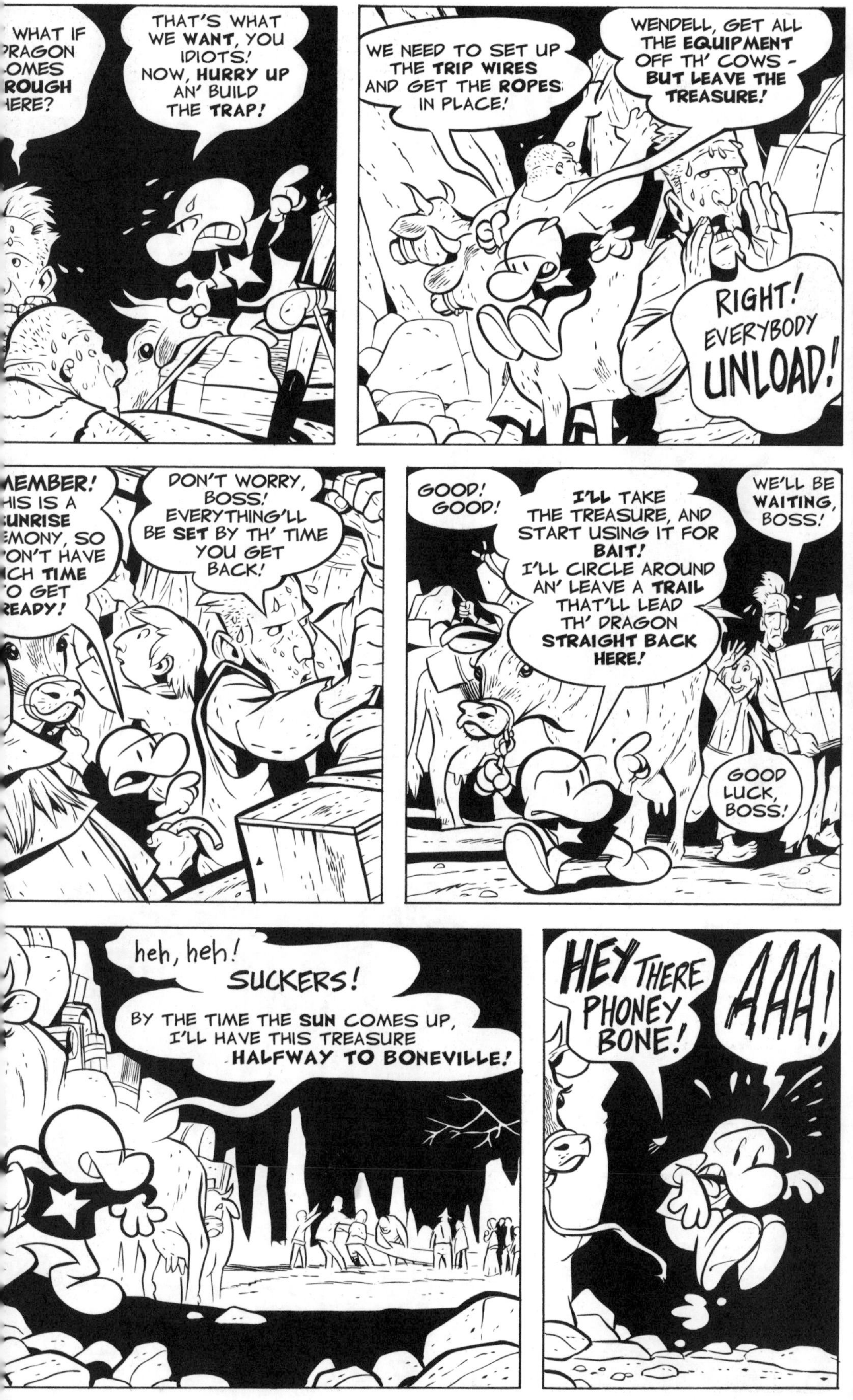
WHAT IF RAGON OMES ROUGH HERE?
THAT'S WHAT WE WANT, YOU IDIOTS! NOW, HURRY UP AN' BUILD THE TRAP!
WE NEED TO SET UP THE TRIP WIRES AND GET THE ROPES IN PLACE!
WENDELL, GET ALL THE EQUIPMENT OFF TH' COWS - BUT LEAVE THE TREASURE!
RIGHT! EVERYBODY UNLOAD!
EMBER! HIS IS A UNRISE EMONY, SO ON'T HAVE CH TIME O GET READY!
DON'T WORRY, BOSS! EVERYTHING'LL BE SET BY TH' TIME YOU GET BACK!
GOOD! GOOD!
I'LL TAKE THE TREASURE, AND START USING IT FOR BAIT! I'LL CIRCLE AROUND AN' LEAVE A TRAIL THAT'LL LEAD TH' DRAGON STRAIGHT BACK HERE!
WE'LL BE WAITING, BOSS!
GOOD LUCK, BOSS!
heh, heh! SUCKERS!
BY THE TIME THE SUN COMES UP, I'LL HAVE THIS TREASURE HALFWAY TO BONEVILLE!
HEY THERE PHONEY BONE!
AAA!

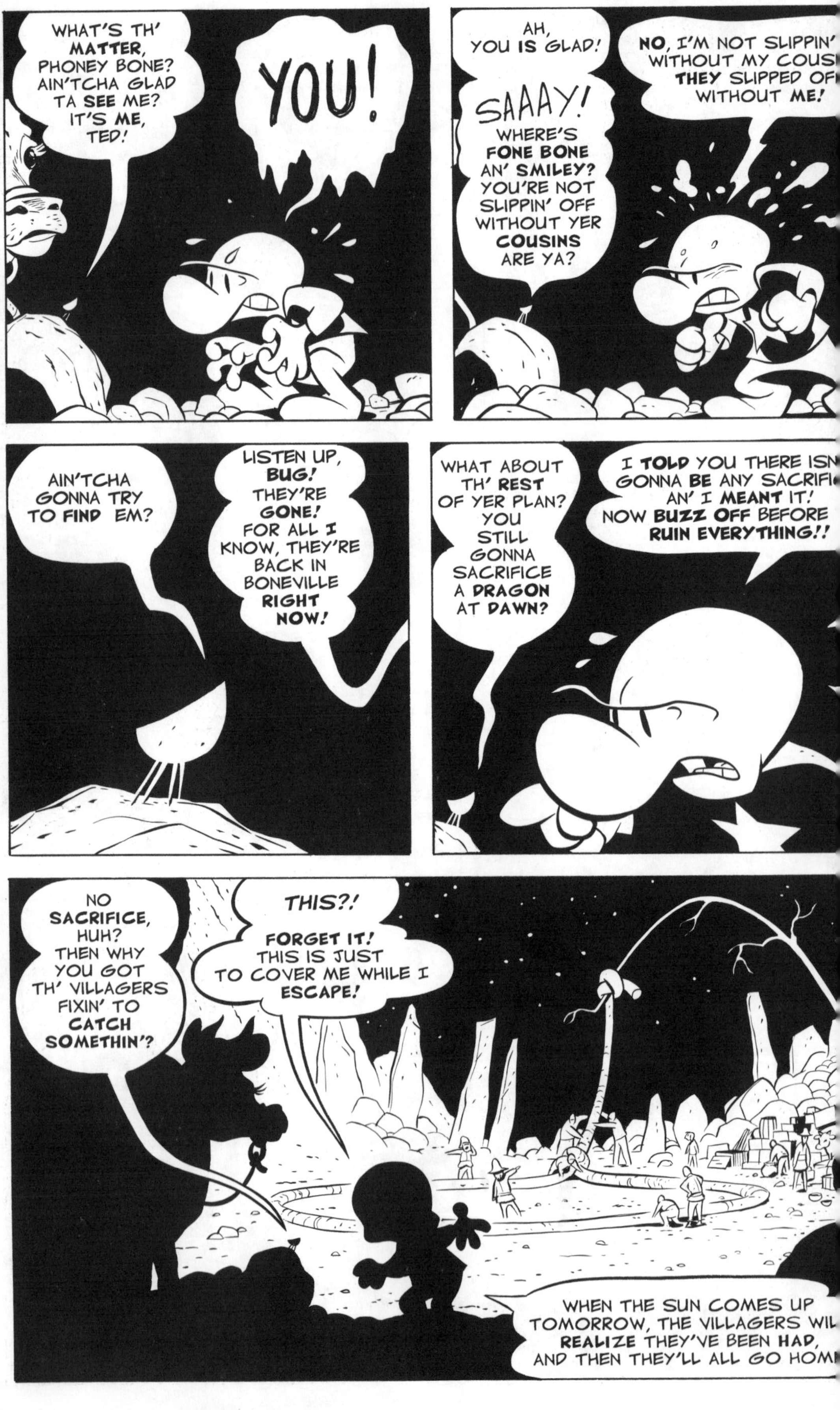
WHAT'S TH' MATTER, PHONEY BONE? AIN'TCHA GLAD TA SEE ME? IT'S ME, TED!
YOU!
AH, YOU IS GLAD!
SAAAY! WHERE'S FONE BONE AN' SMILEY? YOU'RE NOT SLIPPIN' OFF WITHOUT YER COUSINS ARE YA?
NO, I'M NOT SLIPPIN' WITHOUT MY COUS THEY SLIPPED OF WITHOUT ME!
AIN'TCHA GONNA TRY TO FIND EM?
LISTEN UP, BUG! THEY'RE GONE! FOR ALL I KNOW, THEY'RE BACK IN BONEVILLE RIGHT NOW!
WHAT ABOUT TH' REST OF YER PLAN? YOU STILL GONNA SACRIFICE A DRAGON AT DAWN?
I TOLD YOU THERE ISN GONNA BE ANY SACRIFI AN' I MEANT IT! NOW BUZZ OFF BEFORE RUIN EVERYTHING!!
NO SACRIFICE, HUH? THEN WHY YOU GOT TH' VILLAGERS FIXIN' TO CATCH SOMETHIN'?
THIS?!
FORGET IT! THIS IS JUST TO COVER ME WHILE I ESCAPE!
WHEN THE SUN COMES UP TOMORROW, THE VILLAGERS WIL REALIZE THEY'VE BEEN HAD, AND THEN THEY'LL ALL GO HOM

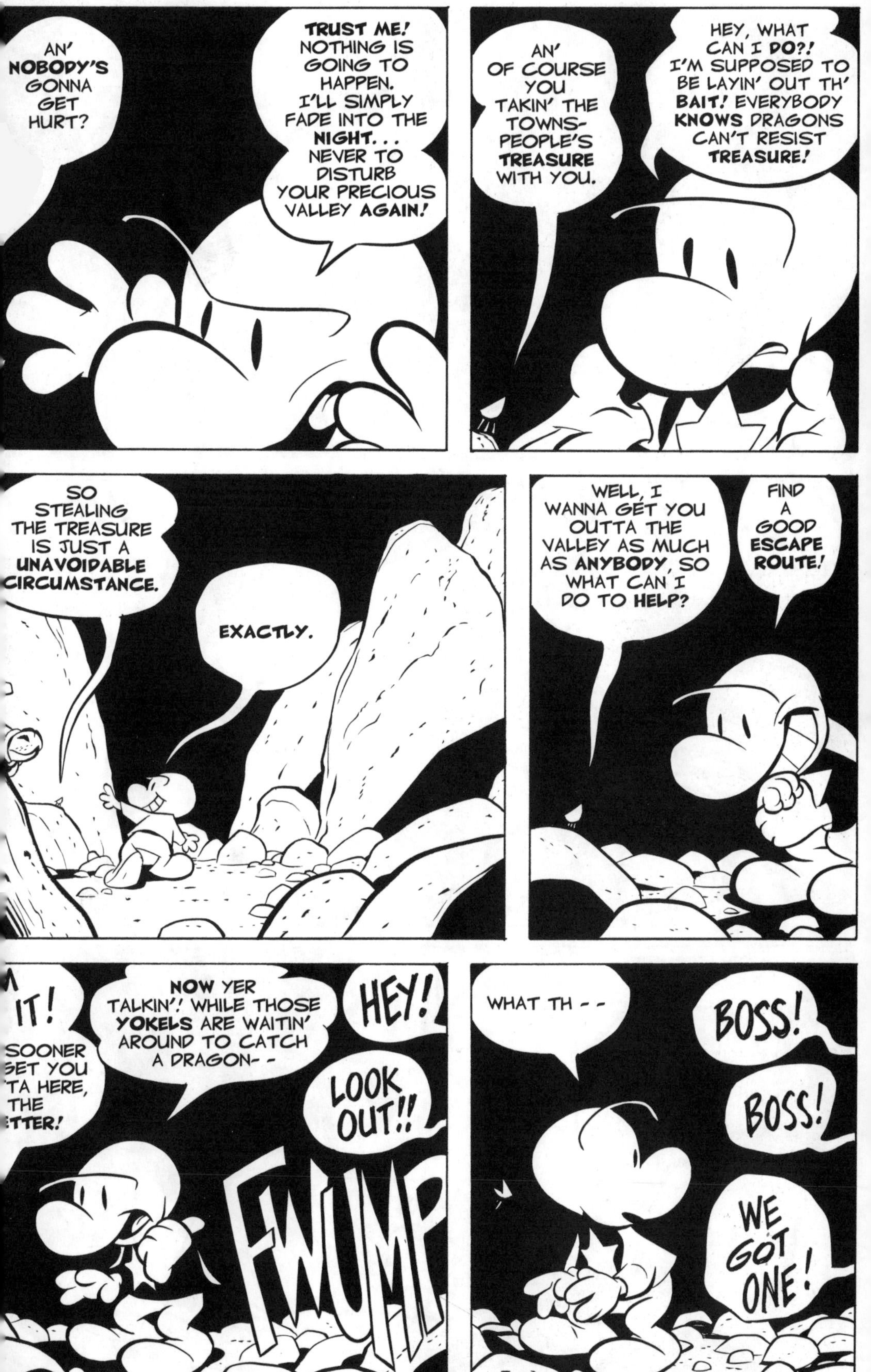
AN' NOBODY'S GONNA GET HURT?
TRUST ME! NOTHING IS GOING TO HAPPEN. I'LL SIMPLY FADE INTO THE NIGHT... NEVER TO DISTURB YOUR PRECIOUS VALLEY AGAIN!
AN' OF COURSE YOU TAKIN' THE TOWNS-PEOPLE'S TREASURE WITH YOU.
HEY, WHAT CAN I DO?! I'M SUPPOSED TO BE LAYIN' OUT TH' BAIT! EVERYBODY KNOWS DRAGONS CAN'T RESIST TREASURE!
SO STEALING THE TREASURE IS JUST A UNAVOIDABLE CIRCUMSTANCE.
EXACTLY.
WELL, I WANNA GET YOU OUTTA THE VALLEY AS MUCH AS ANYBODY, SO WHAT CAN I DO TO HELP?
FIND A GOOD ESCAPE ROUTE!
IT!
SOONER GET YOU 'TA HERE, THE ETTER!
NOW YER TALKIN'! WHILE THOSE YOKELS ARE WAITIN' AROUND TO CATCH A DRAGON--
HEY!
LOOK OUT!!
FWUMP
WHAT TH --
BOSS!
BOSS!
WE GOT ONE!

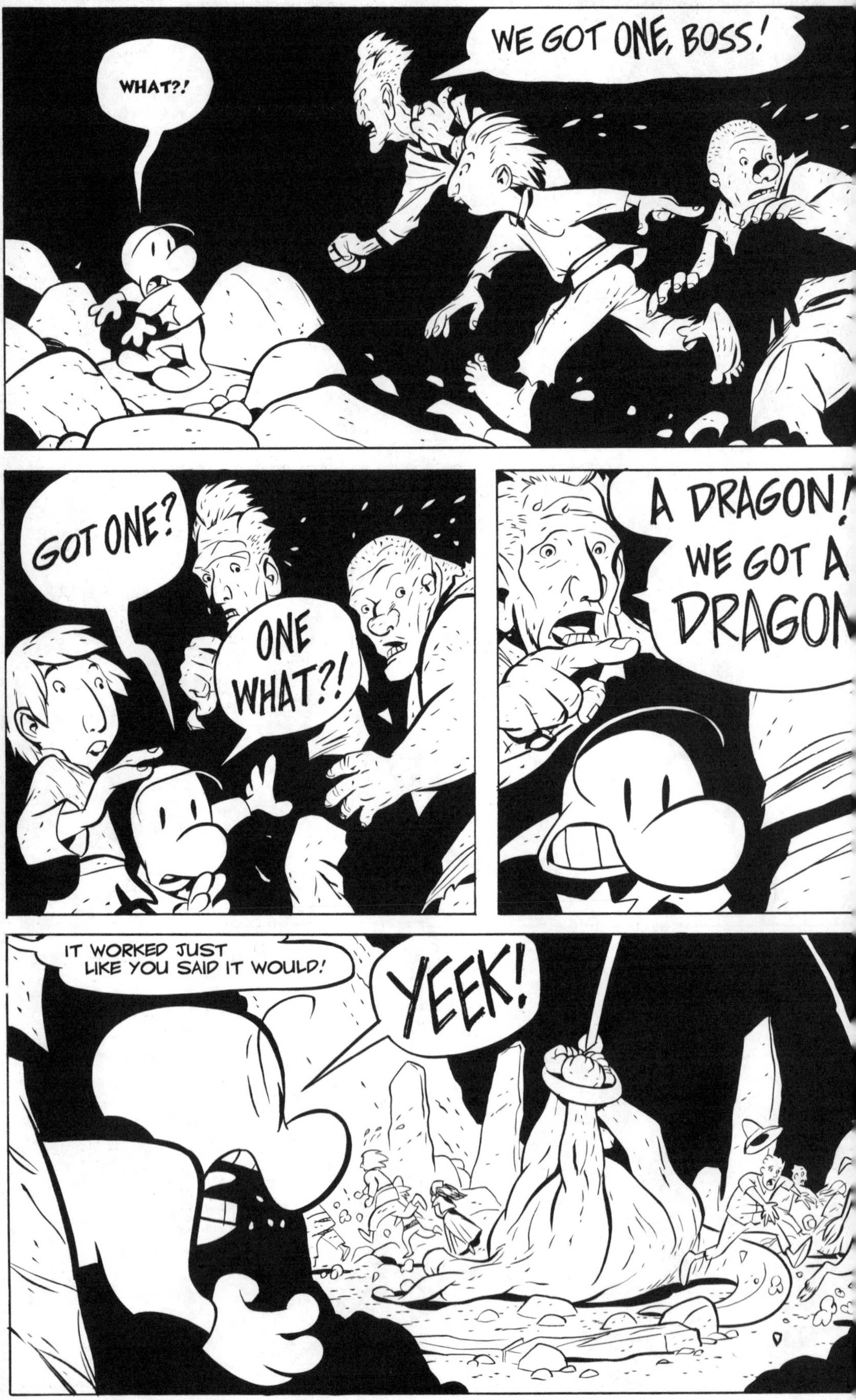
WHAT?!
WE GOT ONE, BOSS!
GOT ONE?
ONE WHAT?!
A DRAGON! WE GOT A DRAGON
IT WORKED JUST LIKE YOU SAID IT WOULD!
YEEK!

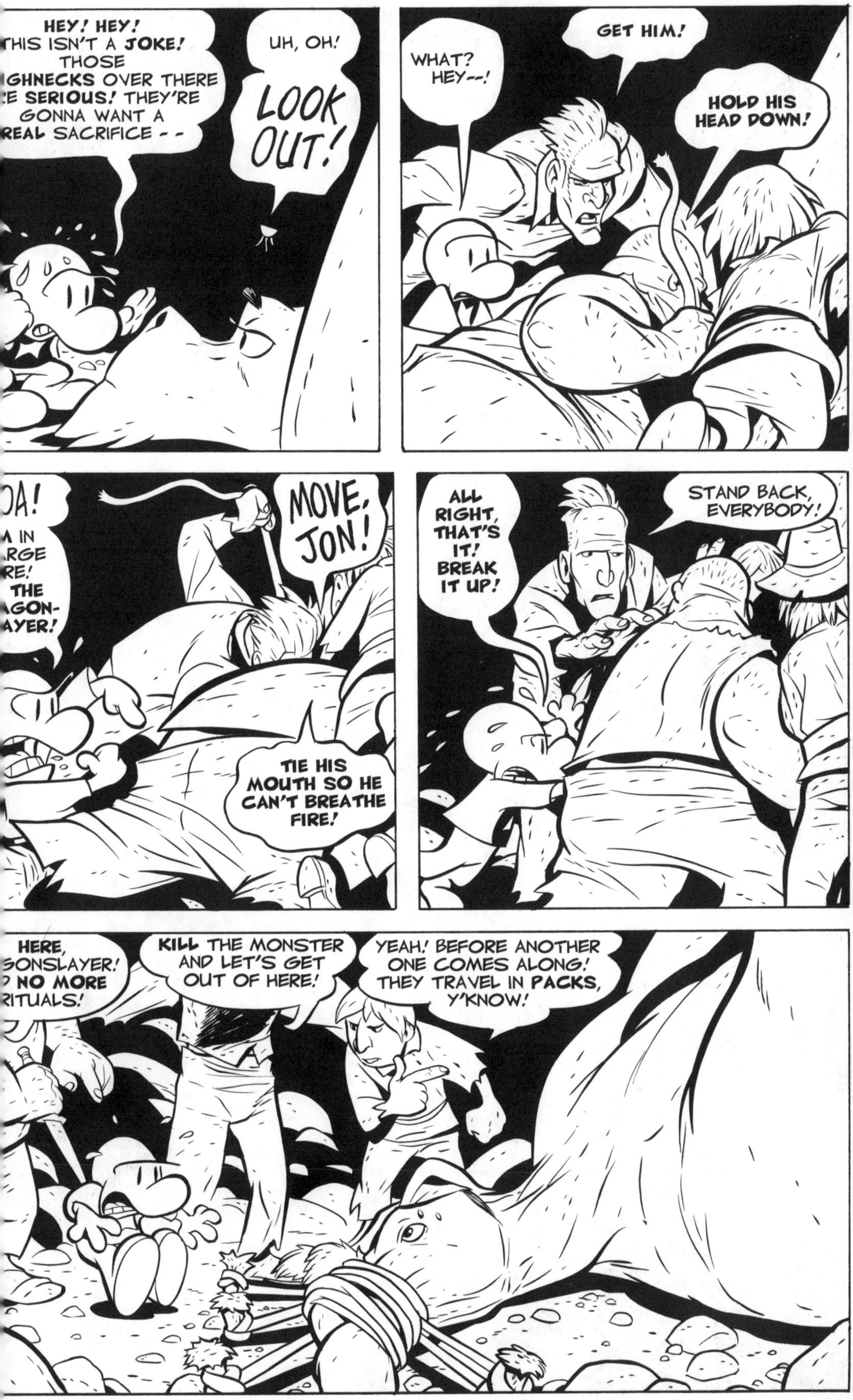
HEY! HEY! THIS ISN'T A JOKE! THOSE IGHNECKS OVER THERE E SERIOUS! THEY'RE GONNA WANT A REAL SACRIFICE - -
UH, OH!
LOOK OUT!
WHAT? HEY--!
GET HIM!
HOLD HIS HEAD DOWN!
OA! A IN ARGE RE! THE AGON-AYER!
MOVE, JON!
TIE HIS MOUTH SO HE CAN'T BREATHE FIRE!
ALL RIGHT, THAT'S IT! BREAK IT UP!
STAND BACK, EVERYBODY!
HERE, GONSLAYER! NO MORE RITUALS!
KILL THE MONSTER AND LET'S GET OUT OF HERE!
YEAH! BEFORE ANOTHER ONE COMES ALONG! THEY TRAVEL IN PACKS, Y'KNOW!

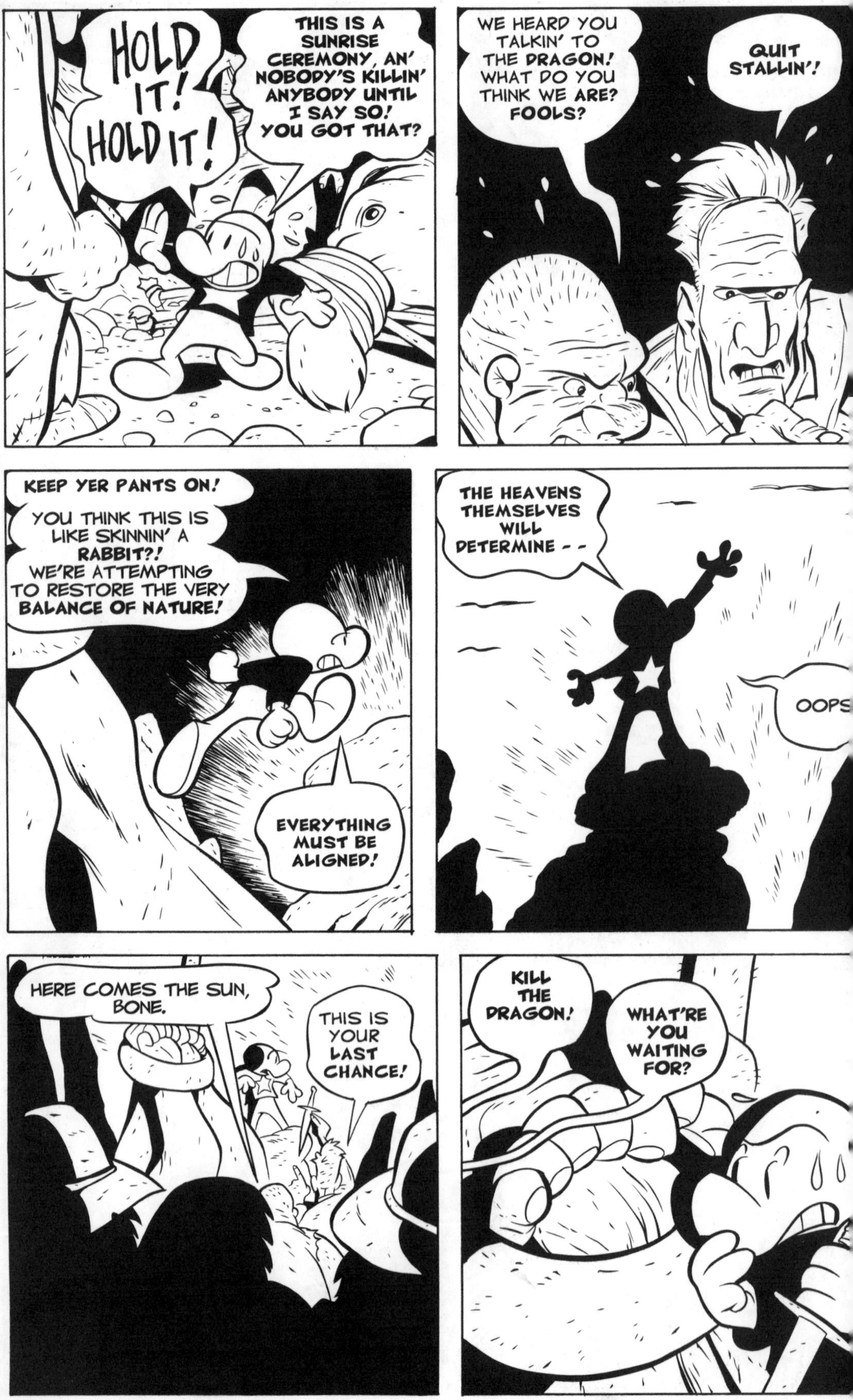
HOLD IT! HOLD IT!
THIS IS A SUNRISE CEREMONY, AN' NOBODY'S KILLIN' ANYBODY UNTIL I SAY SO! YOU GOT THAT?
WE HEARD YOU TALKIN' TO THE DRAGON! WHAT DO YOU THINK WE ARE? FOOLS?
QUIT STALLIN'!
KEEP YER PANTS ON!
YOU THINK THIS IS LIKE SKINNIN' A RABBIT?! WE'RE ATTEMPTING TO RESTORE THE VERY BALANCE OF NATURE!
EVERYTHING MUST BE ALIGNED!
THE HEAVENS THEMSELVES WILL DETERMINE --
OOPS
HERE COMES THE SUN, BONE.
THIS IS YOUR LAST CHANCE!
KILL THE DRAGON!
WHAT'RE YOU WAITING FOR?

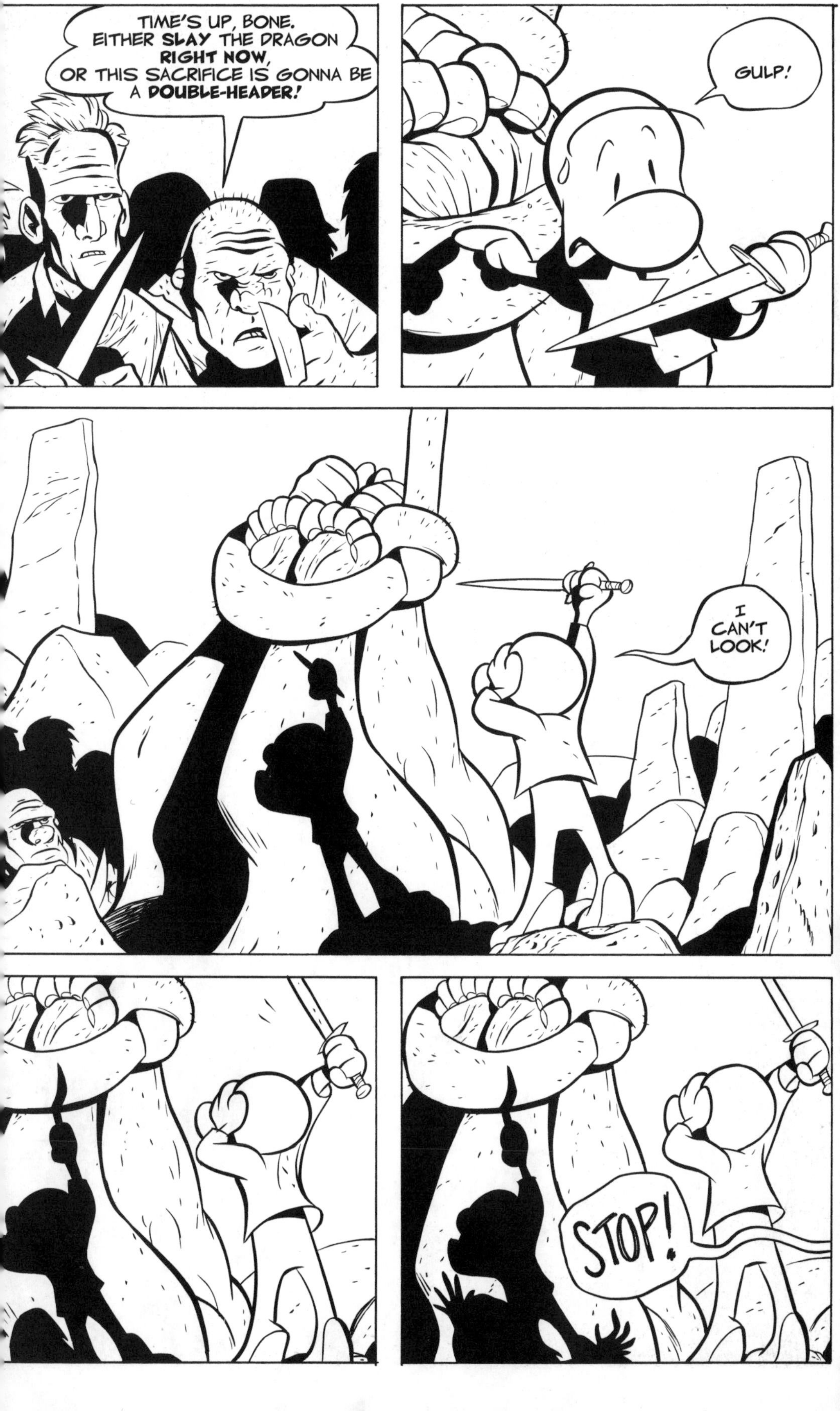

TIME'S UP, BONE. EITHER **SLAY** THE DRAGON **RIGHT NOW**, OR THIS SACRIFICE IS GONNA BE A **DOUBLE-HEADER!**
GULP!
I CAN'T LOOK!
STOP!

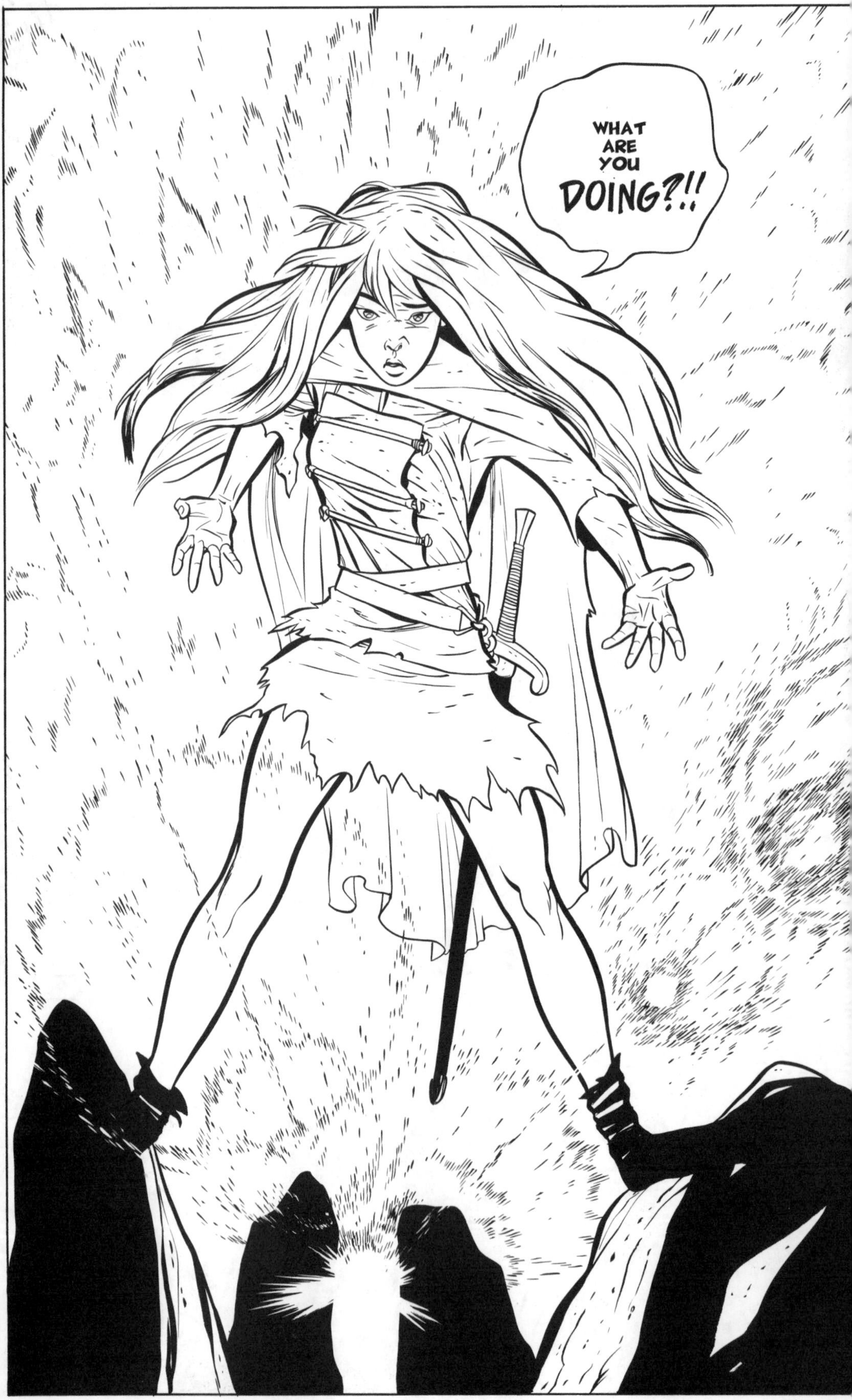
WHAT ARE YOU DOING?!!

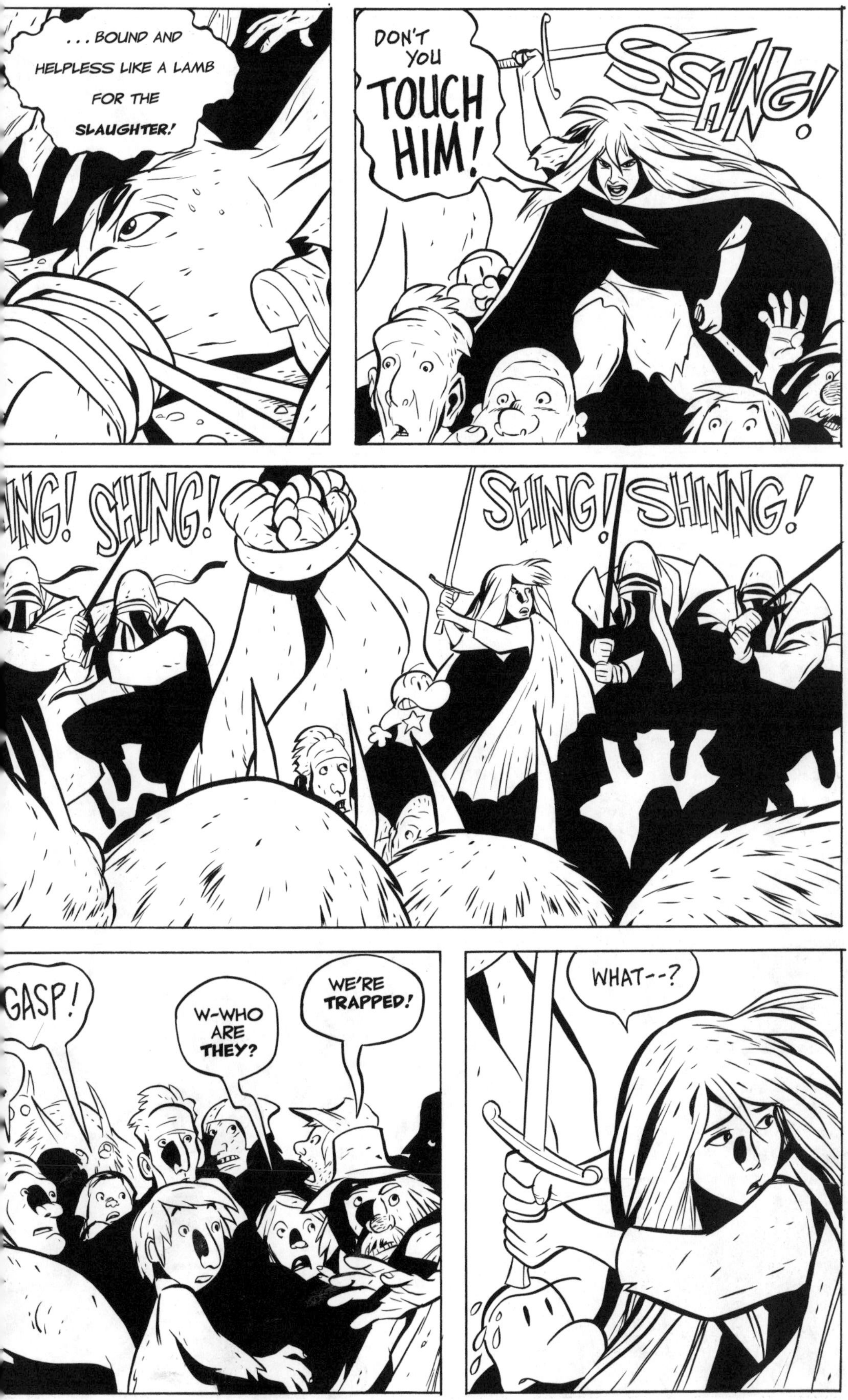

. . . BOUND AND HELPLESS LIKE A LAMB FOR THE SLAUGHTER!
DON'T YOU TOUCH HIM!
SSHING!
NG! SHING!
SHING! SHINNG!
GASP!
W-WHO ARE THEY?
WE'RE TRAPPED!
WHAT--?

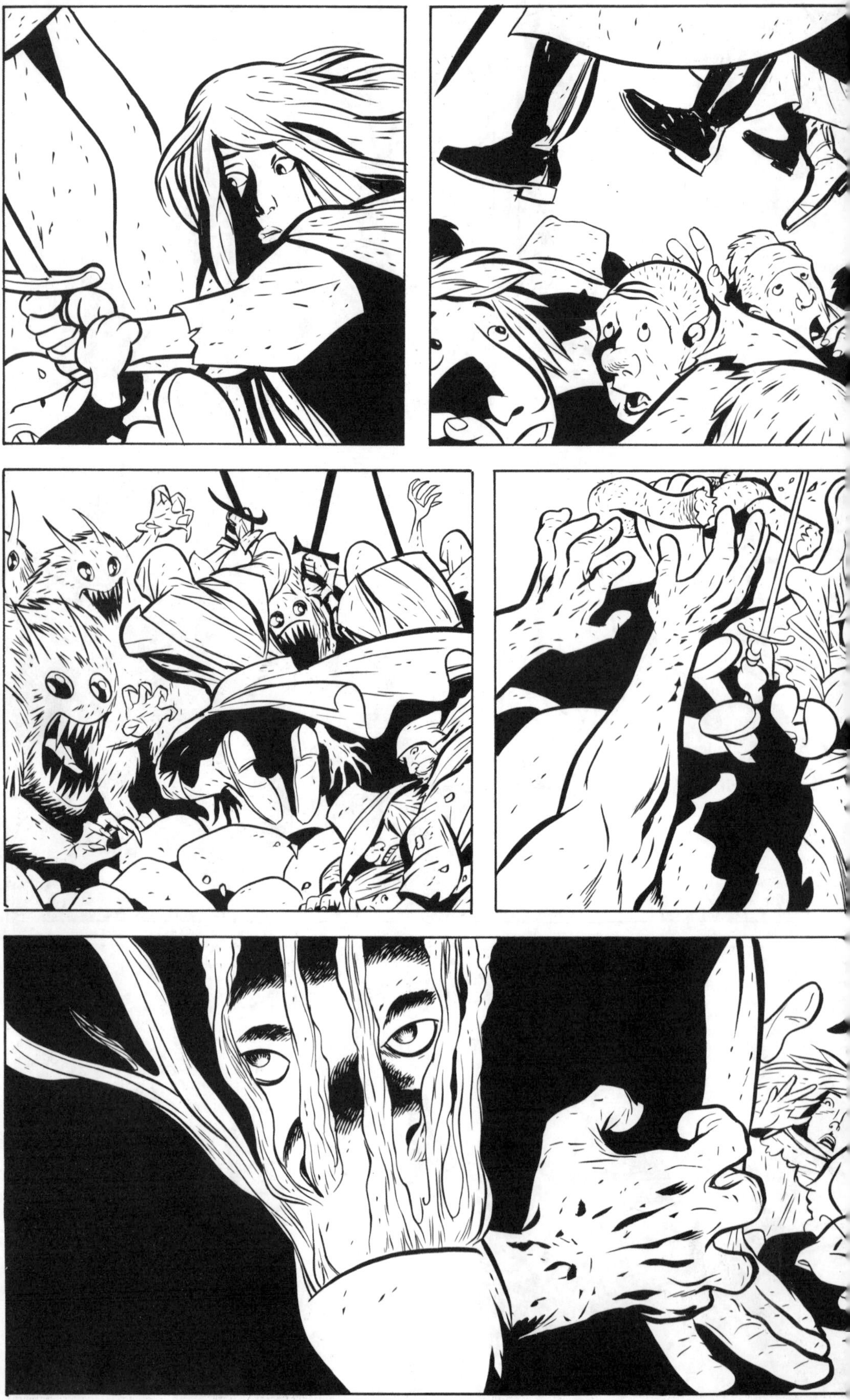

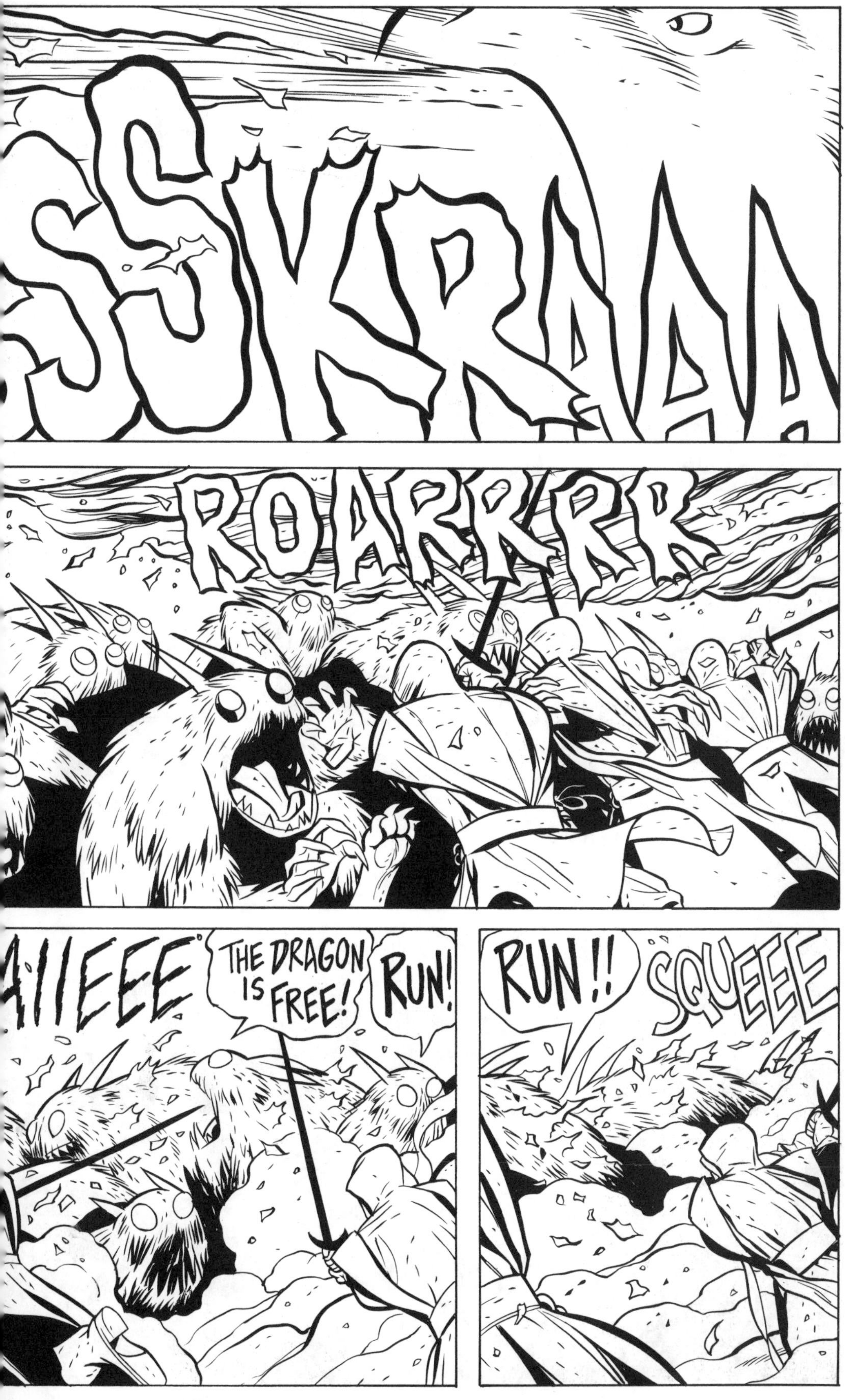
SSKRAAA
ROARRRR
AIIEEE
THE DRAGON IS FREE!
RUN!
RUN!!
SQUEEE

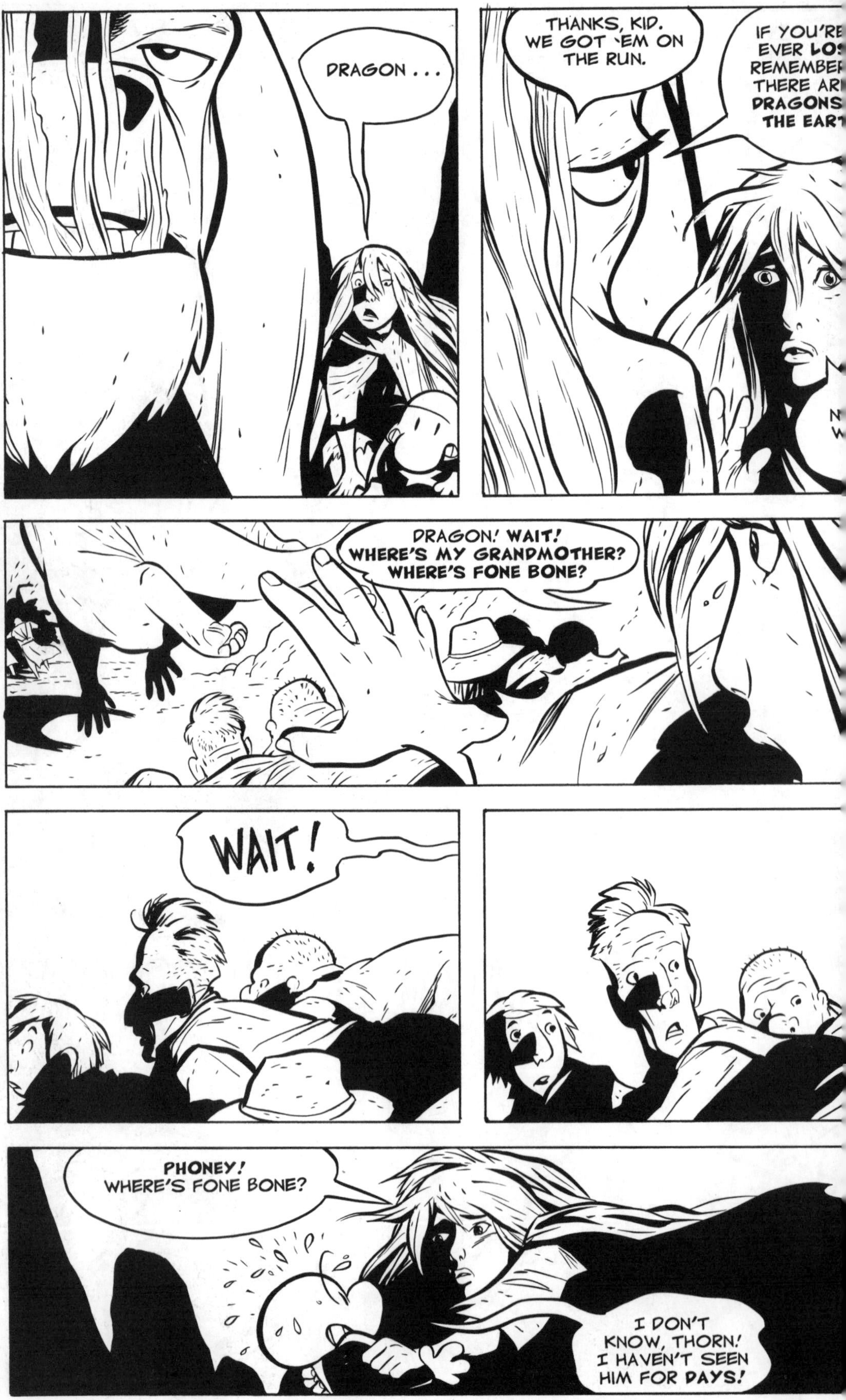
DRAGON . . .
THANKS, KID. WE GOT 'EM ON THE RUN.
IF YOU'RE EVER LOS REMEMBER THERE AR DRAGONS THE EART
DRAGON! WAIT! WHERE'S MY GRANDMOTHER? WHERE'S FONE BONE?
WAIT!
PHONEY! WHERE'S FONE BONE?
I DON'T KNOW, THORN! I HAVEN'T SEEN HIM FOR DAYS!

OTHER BOOKS BY JEFF SMITH

THE FIRST TRILOGY

BONE VOLUME ONE: OUT FROM BONEVILLE

BONE VOLUME TWO: THE GREAT COW RACE

BONE VOLUME THREE: EYES OF THE STORM

THE SECOND TRILOGY

BONE VOLUME FOUR: THE DRAGONSLAYER

BONE VOLUME FIVE: ROCKJAW, MASTER OF THE EASTERN BORDER

BONE VOLUME SIX: OLD MAN'S CAVE

THE THIRD TRILOGY

BONE VOLUME SEVEN: GHOST CIRCLES

BONE VOLUME EIGHT: TREASURE HUNTERS

PREQUELS

STUPID, STUPID RAT TAILS: THE ADVENTURES OF BIG JOHNSON BONE,
FRONTIER HERO
(WRITTEN BY TOM SNIEGOSKI, DRAWN BY JEFF SMITH)

ROSE
(WRITTEN BY JEFF SMITH, PAINTED BY CHARLES VESS)

Available in fine bookstores and comic shops everywhere
For more information or to order online visit us at
www.boneville.com